A
DICTIONARY OF
CIVIL SOCIETY,
PHILANTHROPY
AND
THE NON-PROFIT SECTOR

A
DICTIONARY OF
CIVIL SOCIETY,
PHILANTHROPY
AND
THE NON-PROFIT SECTOR

Helmut K. Anheier and Regina A. List

FIRST EDITION

 Routledge
Taylor & Francis Group

LONDON AND NEW YORK

First Edition 2005

Routledge
Haines House, 21 John Street, London WC1N 2BP
(A member of the Taylor & Francis Group)

Reprinted 2006

© Helmut K. Anheier 2005

ISBN 1 85743 166 9

Development Editor: Cathy Hartley
Copy Editor and Proof-reader: Vera Browne

Typeset in Times New Roman 10.5/13.5

Typeset by AJS Solutions, Huddersfield and Dundee
Printed in the UK by MPG Books, Bodmin, Cornwall

FOREWORD

The purpose of this dictionary is to introduce greater conceptual clarity to an increasingly unsettled terminology that has been developing in the field of philanthropy and non-profit organizations over time. Confusion about the meaning of volunteering, association, civil society, non-profit organization, foundation and charity has handicapped communication and understanding, particularly in inter-disciplinary and international contexts. In the past, the terminological tangles so characteristic of this field may well have mattered less, yet as this set of institutions has achieved greater social, economic and policy relevance, the need for greater clarity now seems more urgent. Indeed, the lack of a multi-disciplinary dictionary dedicated to the topic of philanthropy, non-profit organizations, non-governmental organizations (NGOs), civil society, etc. has long been a major complaint among academics and students in the field, as well as among practitioners and policy-makers. The present dictionary was developed with these multiple audiences and uses in mind.

An unsettled, evolving terminology is not necessarily a chronic weakness of a research agenda, curriculum or policy field—it can also be a sign of a fertile, developing intellectual field, as we hope is the case in the area of philanthropy and non-profit and non-governmental organizations. In the context of this evolving intellectual field, our primary aim was to make an inventory of the conceptual landscape, and to take stock; it was not to set some standards—however defined—or to privilege one definition over another. None the less this meant that we had to come to terms with the diversity and richness of organizations located between the market and the state—a task complicated by the great profusion of terms: 'non-profit sector', 'charities', 'third sector', 'independent sector', 'voluntary sector', 'NGOs', 'philanthropy', and, in the European context, 'social economy' and 'social enterprise', among others.

Behind these many terms lie, of course, different purposes and also often intellectual, juridical and political traditions. Definitions are neither true nor false, and they are ultimately judged by their usefulness in describing a part of reality which is of interest to us. Specifically, a definition must be simpler than the reality it seeks to describe. In the social sciences, we typically try to come up with definitions that facilitate communication, generate insights, and lead to better understanding. If we have achieved even some small measure of this objective, the efforts that flowed into writing the dictionary have been worthwhile.

January 2005

ACKNOWLEDGMENTS

This dictionary would not have been possible without the contributions of many colleagues and friends around the world. But most importantly, it would not have been possible without the encouragement and the now legendary patience of Cathy Hartley, our editor at Europa Publications, now part of Routledge of Taylor & Francis. We would like to thank Marcus Lam who has been a terrific and tireless researcher for the project. He conducted numerous background researches, and skilfully helped manage the process of compiling the 600 or so entries that make up this dictionary. Laurie Spivak, the manager of the Center for Civil Society at the University of California, Los Angeles, deserves special thanks, as do Andrea Ozdy and Sabina Dewan who served as research assistants.

Some of our most sincere thanks are reserved for the **Editorial Committee**:

Volker Then (Germany)
James A. Smith (USA)
Avner BenNer (USA)
Nicholas Deakin (UK)

as well as for the **International Advisory Committee**:

Edith Archambault	France
Christoph Badelt	Austria
Gian Paolo Barbetta	Italy
Masa Deguchi	Japan
Paul Dekker	Netherlands
Richard Fries	UK
Ben Gidron	Israel
Stanley Katz	USA
Eva Kuti	Hungary
Hakon Lorentzen	Norway
Mark Lyons	Australia
Kumi Naidoo	South Africa

Alejandro Natal	Mexico
Joseph Rodriguez	Spain
John Simon	USA
Rupert Strachwitz	Germany
Raj Tandon	India
Andres Thompson	Argentina
Stefan Toepler	USA
Burton Weisbrod	USA
Filip Wijkström	Sweden
Julian Wolpert	USA
Annette Zimmer	Germany

The advice of these committees and their generous intellectual support are gratefully acknowledged.

The dictionary project was able to link up with the International Network on Strategic Philanthropy (INSP), and some of the terms relating to philanthropy were drafted specifically for this network. We thank Dirk Eilinghoff of the Bertelsmann Foundation for making this arrangement possible, and for the financial support received. We would also like to thank the members of the **special INSP working group on the dictionary**:

Christine Castille (Belgium)
Richard Fries (UK)
Mario Gioannini (Italy)
Tobias Henkel (Germany)
Diana Leat (UK)
James A. Smith (USA)
Danielle Walker (UK)

Finally, the dictionary benefited from the contribution of a number of scholars from different countries who volunteered to draft entries and thereby relieved the authors of some of the more difficult tasks in defining terms that are culturally specific or highly technical. **Contributors** are:

Frank Adolff, Centre for European and North American Studies, University of Göttingen, Germany: state–society relations

Chris Ankersen, London School of Economics, UK: Canadian International Development Agency (CIDA), Freemasons, Stockholm International Peace Research Institute (SIPRI)

Edith Archambault, University of Paris-Sorbonne, Paris, France: Abbé Pierre, Association Française contre les myopathies (AFM), ATTAC, François Bloch-Lainé, Catholic Committee Against Hunger (CCFD), centralization, Coluche, co-operatives, Alexis de Tocqueville, Émile Durkheim, Fondation de France, Bernard Kouchner, law of 1901, market failure, Médecins sans Frontières, mutuality, Mancur Olson, social economy, solidarity, UNIOPSS

Giuseppe Caruso, University of London, UK: World Social Forum

Masayuki Deguchi, The Graduate University for Advanced Studies, Osaka, Japan: community foundation, corporate foundation, corporate giving, corporate sponsorship, Japan Foundation Center, Inamori Foundation, *kōeki hōjin*, Nippon Foundation, Sasakawa Peace Foundation, Toyota Foundation

Paul Dekker, Social and Cultural Planning Office and University of Tilburg, the Netherlands: *verzuiling*

Freda Donoghue, Centre for Non-profit Management, School of Business Studies, Trinity College Dublin, Ireland: Charles Feeney, partnerships, Mary Redmond, Mary Robinson

Ben Gidron, Israeli Center for Third Sector Research (ICTR), Ben Gurion University of the Negev, Israel: self-help groups, zedaka

Mario Gioannini, Compagnia di San Paolo, Italy: assets, banking foundations, cost disease theory, cost benefit analysis, evaluation, impact evaluation, public charities, public foundations

Marlies Glasius, London School of Economics, UK: human rights, rule of law

Paola Grenier, London School of Economics, UK: social entrepreneurship, Michael Young

Hagai Katz, Center for Civil Society, University of California, Los Angeles, USA: Antonio Gramsci, sunk costs

Eva Kuti, Budapest College of Management, Hungary: István Bibó, György (George) Konrád, Adam Michnik, one percent provision, public benefit companies, public law foundations, Solidarność, George Soros

Marcus Lam, Center for Civil Society, University of California, Los Angeles, USA

Myles McGregor-Lowndes, Centre of Philanthropy and Non-profit Studies, Queensland, University of Technology, Brisbane, Australia: charity law

Jennifer E. Mosley, Center for Civil Society, University of California, Los Angeles, USA: free-rider problem, lobbying, outdoor relief, political action committee, poor laws, social justice, workhouses

Ebenezer Obadare, London School of Economics, UK: Adam Ferguson, Ernest Gellner, uncivil society

Philipp Schwertmann, Maecenata Institut, Berlin, Germany: Körber Foundation, Robert-Bosch-Stiftung

Marek Skovajsa, The Institute of Sociology of the Academy of Sciences of the Czech Republic, Prague, Czech Republic: Charter 77 Foundation, Czech Donors' Forum, European Voluntary Service (EVS), Foundation Investment Fund (FIF), Armand Hammer, Václav Havel, Josef Hlávka, Hlávka Foundation, Jan Hus Educational Foundation, People in Need Foundation, Petr Pithart, Přemysl Pitter

Rainer Sprengel, Maecenata Institut, Berlin, Germany: donor, fundraising foundations, individual giving, political foundations, strategic philanthropy

Stefan Toepler, George Mason University, USA: section 501(c)(3), cross-subsidization, crowding out, mandatory pay-out requirement, merger, operating foundations, private voluntary organizations, public sector payments, resource-dependency theory, service provider organizations, supporting organizations, warm glow

Of course, final responsibility for the dictionary, its strengths and weaknesses, are ours alone. As an initial effort, we are well aware that this dictionary may show the flaws characteristic of such first editions; yet we hope that it also shows some of the promise on which others and we ourselves could build in the future.

CONTENTS

THE AUTHORS

Helmut K. Anheier has been a professor at the School of Public Affairs of the University of California, Los Angeles (UCLA), since 2001, where he directs the UCLA Center for Civil Society and the UCLA Center for Globalization and Policy Research. He is also Centennial Professor of Social Policy at the London School of Economics and Political Science, where he founded and directed the Centre for Civil Society (1998–2002). After graduating from Yale (Ph.D. 1986), he held appointments at Rutgers University and Johns Hopkins University, and worked as social affairs officer for the United Nations. His main interests are in the field of philanthropy, globalization, comparative methodology, and organizational studies. He is author of over 250 publications in several languages, including the *Global Civil Society Yearbook*, and a textbook, *Nonprofit Organizations: Approaches, Management, Policy* (Routledge, 2005). He is the founding editor of *Voluntas* (1990–98) and of the new *Journal of Civil Society* (Routledge, 2005).

Regina A. List was Research Projects Manager at the Johns Hopkins Center for Civil Society Studies and Co-ordinator for Developing Countries for the Johns Hopkins Comparative Nonprofit Sector Project, as well as overall Project Manager. She is a co-author of *Global Civil Society: Dimensions of the Nonprofit Sector, Volume One* and *Cross-border Philanthropy*, among other works. After completing an M.A. in International Development at the American University (Washington, DC), she served as Program Co-ordinator and Executive Director of the Esquel Group Foundation. She is currently an independent writer and editor living in Hamburg, Germany.

THE DICTIONARY AND HOW TO USE IT

Definitions do not exist in the abstract. They serve specific purposes and objectives. Because social scientists, practitioners and policy-makers are likely to have different objectives in mind, the complex terminology in the field should not surprise us, in particular in an international perspective. Selecting the entries for this dictionary was therefore a complex process that involved many difficult choices. A basic premise was that given the unsettled nature of the field, the dictionary should not only cover terms and concepts but also include entries on internationally relevant organizations and personalities in the field of civil society, philanthropy and the non-profit sector. Another premise was that the dictionary should be international and incorporate entries on and from different parts of the world, thereby acknowledging the diversity of the field from a cross-national perspective.

The field of philanthropy, civil society, non-profit organizations and NGOs is far from unified. It is a conglomerate of separate intellectual approaches and traditions, and, as some analysts have remarked, terminological chasms seem to exist among them. In compiling this dictionary, we have tried to be aware of these different strands, which include:

- a tradition of philanthropic studies, largely US-based and focused on the role of foundations and philanthropy in American society;
- an emphasis on non-profit organizations in economics;
- the rich intellectual approaches to voluntary associations, voluntarism and social capital in sociology;
- the study of interest associations and political associations in political science;
- the burgeoning literature on NGOs in developmental studies and international relations;

- the study of the social economy and its institutions in Europe; and
- the significant interest in civil society across the social science and policy fields.

In trying to address these different approaches and traditions, we used a stepwise approach whereby we developed an initial list of concepts, organizations and personalities to be covered. For concepts, we did so by taking four 'soundings' that roughly correspond to the intellectual and policy divisions in the field, although much overlap exists among them: philanthropy, civil society, non-profit organizations and social economy, and NGOs. In each of these four 'streams', policy fields, traditions and literatures, we tried to identify key concepts, i.e. terms that are indispensable and necessary for basic conceptual coverage; major concepts, i.e. more general terms that are significant elements of the knowledge base; and technical concepts, i.e. terms that are more specific and technical in nature. Table 1 offers an illustration of our approach.

Table 1: Developing a list of concepts

	PHILANTHROPY	CIVIL SOCIETY	NON-PROFIT ORGANIZATIONS	NON-GOVERNMENTAL ORGANIZATIONS
Key concepts	e.g. Foundation	e.g. Social capital	e.g. Non-profit management	e.g. Social entrepreneurship
Major concepts	e.g. Operating foundation	e.g. Human rights	e.g. Public goods	e.g. Solidarity
Technical concepts	e.g. Pay-out rate	e.g. Global Compact	e.g. Unrelated business income	e.g. Overseas development assistance

We submitted this initial list to the Editorial Committee and the International Advisory Committee for comments and, in particular, encouraged each member to suggest additions and modifications. As for organizations and personalities, we proceeded in a similar fashion. After several iterations, including a final one after all entries had been drafted, we arrived at a list that forms the basis of the dictionary.

This dictionary covers some 600 terms: around 348 conceptual terms, 160 organizations and 100 personalities from the field of civil society, philanthropy and the non-profit sector.

Entries are arranged in alphabetical order from A to Z, and cross-references from one entry to another are in bold.

We have generally not included bibliographic references but offer a brief bibliography of relevant English-language titles at the end of the dictionary, which can guide the reader to additional literature.

CIVIL SOCIETY, PHILANTHROPY AND THE NON-PROFIT SECTOR: AN INTRODUCTION

For a long time, social scientists and policy-makers paid little attention to concepts like philanthropy, voluntarism, social capital, civil society or non-profit organizations, and perhaps even less to the question of what these different forms and activities might have in common. The focus of much social science thinking and policymaking was elsewhere, i.e. with markets and governments. Compared with the world of government and business, analysing the complex and varied landscape of non-profit and civil society institutions seemed less important, and perhaps also too daunting a task relative to its theoretical importance for understanding society and its policy relevance in such fields as employment, welfare, health, education or international development. This attitude, however, began to change over the course of the last two decades of the 20th century.

Today, the non-profit sector has become a major economic and social force. Parallel to the increase in economic importance is the greater policy recognition non-profit organizations enjoy at local, national and international levels. Prompted in part by growing doubts about the capacity of the state to cope with its own welfare, developmental, and environmental problems, political analysts across the political spectrum have come to see non-profits as strategic components of a middle way between policies that put primacy on 'the market' and those that advocate greater reliance on the state. Some governments see in non-profit and community organizations an alternative to welfare services provided by the public sector. This is seen most clearly in the USA in the so-called 'faith-based initiative' in providing services and relief to the poor, or the school voucher programme for both private and public schools. At the international level, institutions—such as the World Bank, the United Nations and the European Union—and many developing countries are searching for a balance between state-led and market-led approaches to development, and are allocating more responsibility to non-governmental organizations, commonly referred to as NGOs.

Like the term NGO or non-profit sector, civil society is a contested concept. There is little agreement on its precise meaning, though much overlap exists among core conceptual components. In a generic sense, civil society refers to the set of institutions, organizations and behaviours situated between the state, the business world and the family. This would include voluntary organizations of many different kinds, philanthropic institutions, social, cultural and political movements and dimensions of the public sphere, forms of social capital, political participation and social engagement, and the values and behavioural patterns associated with them. In its transnational dimension, the term goes beyond the notion of both nation state and national society, and allows us to examine critical aspects of globalization and the emergence of a new social, cultural and political sphere.

Civil society cuts across disciplinary boundaries and brings into focus some of the long-standing and nagging questions about the relationship between economy, polity and society. Indeed, civil society may well emerge as the most significant conceptual innovation of the social sciences at the turn of the century. The concept signals the beginning of an intellectual shift away from disciplinary specialization on 'the' state and 'the' market to more general debate about key aspects of the human condition. This shift, and the growing importance of the term 'civil society' in virtually all social sciences may well be indicative of a potential paradigmatic change among the major social sciences more generally.

A Growing Phenomenon

At the *local* level, civil society institutions and non-profit organizations have become part of community-building and empowerment strategies. Numerous examples from around the world show how policy-makers and rural and urban planners use non-profit and community organizations for local development and regeneration. These range from community development organizations in Los Angeles or Milan to organizations among slum dwellers in Cairo or Mumbai, and from neighbourhood improvement schemes in London or Berlin to local councils in Rio de Janeiro, where representatives of local non-profit groups sit next to political party leaders, business persons and local politicians.

At the *national* level, non-profit organizations are increasingly involved in welfare, health care, education reform and public–private partnerships. Prominent cases include the expansion of non-profit service providers for the elderly in the USA, the establishment of hospital foundations as a means to modernize the National Health Service in the UK, the transformation of state-held cultural assets into non-profit museums in former East Germany, and the privatization of day-care centres and social service agencies in former state-socialist countries more generally. In a number of countries, the greater role of non-profit organizations in welfare reform is aided by laws that facilitate their establishment and operations, with Japan and the NPO Law passed in 1998, initial reforms in the People's Republic of China, and policy innovations in Hungary as the most notable examples. Since the mid-1990s, most developed market economies in Europe, North America and the Asia-Pacific region have seen a general increase in the economic importance of non-profit organizations as providers of health, social, educational and cultural services of many kinds. On average, the non-profit sector accounts for about 6% of total employment in Organisation for Economic Co-operation and Development (OECD) countries, or nearly 10% with volunteer work factored in.

At the *international* level, we observe the rise of international non-governmental organizations (INGOs) and an expanded role in the international system of governance. The number of known INGOs increased from about 13,000 in 1981 to more than 47,000 by 2001. The number of INGOs reported in 1981 would make up just under 28% of the stock of INGOs 20 years later. What is more, formal organizational links between NGOs and international organizations like the United Nations Development Programme (UNDP), the World Health Organization (WHO) or the World Bank increased by 46% between 1990 and 2000.

At the *global* level, recent decades have witnessed the emergence of a global civil society and transnational non-profit organizations of significant size and with complex organizational structures that increasingly span many countries and continents. Examples include Amnesty International with more than one million members, subscribers and regular donors in more than 140 countries and territories. The Friends of the Earth Federation comprises about 5,000 local groups and one million members. The Coalition against Child Soldiers has established partners and national coalitions engaged in advocacy, campaigns and public education in nearly 40 countries. Care International is an international NGO with over 10,000 professional staff. Its US headquarters alone has an income of around US $450m. The International Union for the Conservation of Nature brings together 735 NGOs, 35 affiliates, 78 states, 112 government agencies, and some 10,000 scientists and experts from 181 countries in a unique world-wide partnership.

All these developments suggest that non-profit organizations are part of the transformation of societies from industrial to post-industrial, and from a world of nation-states to one of transnational, even globalizing economies and societies, where the local level none the less achieves greater relevance and independence. The full recognition of the immensely elevated position and role of non-profit organizations at the beginning of the 21st century is the main difference to the latter part of the previous century, when non-profits were '(re)discovered' as providers of human services in a welfare state context.

Non-profit organizations are now seen as a part of the wider civil society and welfare systems of modern societies. Next to the institutional complexes of the state or public sector on the one hand, and the market or the world of business on the other, non-profit organizations form a third set of institutions that are private, voluntary and for public benefit. They thus combine a key feature of the public sector, i.e. serving public benefit, with an essential characteristic of the for-profit sector, i.e. its private and voluntary nature.

Even though they have been recognized as a distinct group or sector only in recent decades, non-profit organizations have long been integral parts of the social, economic and political developments in many countries, both in the developed market economies of North America, Europe and Japan, and also in the transition economies of Central and Eastern Europe, and in the developing countries of Africa, Asia and Latin America. What is more, this set of institutions has become more central to policy debates in most parts of the world, in particular since the end of the cold war and attempts to reform welfare systems, government budget priorities and labour markets. This involves four main aspects that inform the selection of terms of this dictionary:

1. The non-profit sector is now a *major economic and social force* at local, national and international levels. Its expansion is fuelled by, among other factors, greater demands for human services of all kinds, welfare reform and privatization policies, the spread of democracy, and advances in information and communications technology with subsequent reductions in the cost of organizing.

2. Even though the *research agenda has expanded significantly* over the last decade, our understanding of the role of these institutions is still limited, and data coverage frequently remains patchy. Whereas theories of

non-profit institutions developed largely in the field of economics and organizational theory, social capital and civil society approaches have expanded the research agenda on non-profits in important ways, and invited contributions by sociology and political science.

3. Whereas in the past the non-profit sector frequently constituted something close to the 'terra incognita' of policy-making, it has now become the *focus of major policy initiatives*. These policy debates will undoubtedly have major implications for the future of non-profits around the world: they could, in the end, amount to a highly contradictory set of expectations that push and pull these institutions in very different directions.

4. Likewise, whereas in the past the *management of non-profit organizations* was seen as esoteric and irrelevant, and their organizational structures as trivial, there is now much greater interest in understanding how private institutions operating in the public interest ought to be managed and organized—not only bringing more attention to aspects of management models and styles appropriate to non-profits, but also to questions of governance, accountability and impact.

When the foundations of non-profit sector research were laid just over two decades ago, it would have been difficult to anticipate the significant growth not only in the social, economic and political importance of the non-profit sector, but also in the advancement of research in the area. Indeed, until then, social scientists did not pay much attention to the non-profit sector and related topics. This has changed, and a highly active research agenda has emerged since the early 1980s, in particular after a group of social scientists loosely connected to the Program on NonProfit Organizations (PONPO) at Yale University, among others, began to address the role of non-profit organizations in market economies in a systematic way.

Generally, however, a 'two sector worldview' dominated, i.e. the 'market v. state model' of industrial society. It was an 'either/or' perspective that was challenged only in the 1980s: the crisis of the welfare state, the limits of state action in dealing with social problems, the political challenge of neo-liberalism and the end of the cold war. Specifically, the greater interest in non-profits and the non-profit sector can be attributed to:

- The rise in its economic importance in social services, health care, education and culture, and the emergence of non-profit organizations that increasingly operate beyond local levels, even across national borders, combined with a withdrawal of the state in providing welfare and related services.

- An opening of political opportunities outside and beyond conventional party politics at the national level, and internationally, due to an end of the cold war and a superpower—the US—being in favour of a minimalist, liberal state; the rise of a 'New Policy Agenda' that emphasizes the role of NGOs as part of an emerging system of global governance.
- Major reductions in the cost of communication, in particular for telecommunication and Internet access, which increases information-sharing while reducing co-ordination costs overall. The development of communications technologies has decreased the costs of organizing locally and nationally, as well as internationally.
- Generally favourable economic conditions in major world economies since the late 1940s and a considerable expansion of populations living in relative prosperity.
- A value change over the last 25 years in most industrialized countries that emphasizes individual opportunities and responsibilities over state involvement and control.
- A major expansion of democracy across most parts of the world, with freedom of expression and associations granted in most countries. The development of domestic and international rule of law since the 1970s has greatly facilitated the growth of civil society organizations.

For economists, a basic argument for a greater non-profit role in both developing and developed countries is based on public administration, which suggests that non-profits or NGOs are efficient and effective providers of social and other services that governments may find costlier and more ineffectual to offer themselves. As a result, co-operative relations between governments and non-profits in welfare provision have become a prominent feature in countries such as the USA, Germany, France and the UK.

Research suggests that the presence of an effective partnership between the state and non-profit organizations is one of the best predictors for the scale and scope of non-profit activities in a country. Where such partnerships exist, e.g. in the USA, the Netherlands, Israel or Australia, the scale of the non-profit sector is larger than in countries where no such working relationship is in place in the delivery of welfare, health and education. The latter is the case in most developing countries as well as in Central and Eastern Europe.

By contrast, sociologists and political scientists emphasize the social integrative function and indirect contributions of non-profit organizations. Norms of reciprocity, citizenship and trust are embodied in networks of civic associations.

The non-profit or voluntary sector forms the social infrastructure of civil society. Non-profits create as well as facilitate a sense of trust and social inclusion that is seen as essential for the functioning of modern societies. Thus, civil society is not only a bulwark against a state that could become too powerful, or a mechanism that creates social cohesion, it is much more than that: a general principle of societal constitution based on individualism and communal responsibility as well as self-organization.

Institutionalization

Although the study of philanthropy, voluntary association and the social economy has a longer history in Europe, the modern field of non-profit studies began in the USA, and then quickly expanded and took roots in other countries. The Commission on Private Philanthropy and Public Needs (1973–1975), better known as the 'Filer Commission' after its chairman, John H. Filer, produced the most far-reaching and detailed report of American philanthropy ever undertaken until then, and it became the stepping stone for further developments. The scholarship produced by the Filer Commission also generated the intellectual interest that led to the establishment of the PONPO at Yale University in 1978. The Program was founded to foster interdisciplinary research on issues relevant to understanding non-profit organizations and the contexts in which they function. Since then, research and teaching programmes have expanded greatly in the USA and elsewhere, and have led to an enormous expansion in dedicated centres in the USA, Canada, Europe, Japan, Australia and elsewhere. At present over 200 teaching programmes exist in the USA, Europe and other countries, with thousands of students and a growing number of alumni.

The field of civil society and non-profit studies has emerged as a fundamentally interdisciplinary field; even though the initial theoretical thrust in the 1980s came predominantly from economics and other social sciences, intellectual bridges were quickly built. While much has been achieved in recent years both conceptually and empirically, as the following entries will demonstrate, there remain major challenges that relate to the future role of non-profit organizations in welfare reform, their relations with the state, increased competition and substitutability with for-profit corporations, and globalization, to name a few. What is more, as mentioned above, the field is far from unified and includes separate intellectual approaches with different terminologies and traditions. In compiling this dictionary, we have tried to acknowledge them to the furthest extent possible.

ABBREVIATIONS

Benelux	Belgium, Netherlands and Luxembourg
DC	District of Columbia
eV	eingetragener Verein
GDP	Gross Domestic Product
i.e.	id est (that is to say)
Jr	Junior
m.	million
NGO	Non-governmental organization
OECD	Organisation for Economic Co-operation and Development
Ph.D.	Doctor of Philosophy
Sr	Senior
UK	United Kingdom
UN	United Nations
US(A)	United States (of America)
v.	versus

A

Abbe, Ernst (1840–1905)

A mathematics and physics professor at Germany's University of Jena, Ernst Abbe became Carl Zeiss's business partner in the development of optical glass technology. Following Zeiss's death, Abbe formed the Carl-Zeiss-Stiftung (Carl Zeiss Foundation) to protect both the Zeiss firm and the Schott Glassworks from individual owner interests. In 1891, he transferred his shares of both companies to the Stiftung (as later did Zeiss's heir and the founder of Schott Glassworks). The firms' profits go to the foundation which, after making **grants** for scientific research and cultural activities, distributes the funds back to the firms to finance growth and employee benefits programmes. Many of these, including paid holidays, profit-sharing and a retirement plan, were introduced by Abbe himself.

Accountability

Accountability in a general sense refers to having to answer for one's behaviour. Within a **non-profit organization**, accountability refers to reporting relationships between the **board of directors** and **stakeholders**; within the board, between the treasurer or chairperson to the board as a whole; and between the executive officer and staff and the board.

Because of the multiple stakeholders and constituencies to which non-profit organizations are accountable, they have to meet different forms or requirements of accountability. Among them are: performance accountability covering **mission**–activity fit, the performance of the chief executive and the staff, financial aspects (**budget**, **audits**, contracts, funds), and programme oversight; legal and fiscal accountability in terms of laws and regulations; and public accountability, i.e. to the public at large as well as to representative **organizations** and regulatory agencies.

As non-profit organizations have become more incorporated into social services and health-care provision in particular, and as competitive bidding and contracting have become more frequent, accountability has likewise achieved greater prominence for **non-profit management** and boards.

ActionAid

Established in the UK in 1972 by Cecil Jackson Cole, ActionAid is a registered charity dedicated to eradicating poverty by working with poor and marginalized people to overcome the injustice and inequity that cause poverty. ActionAid works in over 30 countries in Africa, Asia, Latin America, and the Caribbean with poor local communities, national governments, and international organizations on programmes to improve access to food, water, education, health care and shelter. ActionAid UK, along with its sister organizations in Europe and elsewhere, recently created ActionAid International with a secretariat in South Africa, an international **board of trustees**, and national associate **organizations** around the world.

Website: www.actionaid.org

Active Citizenship

The term 'active citizenship' was introduced in the British (and later European) social policy debate in the 1990s, and emphasizes communal and societal responsibilities and obligations of individual citizens. This focus was to complement citizens' rights and entitlements. The concept, though eminently political in motivation, was favoured across the political spectrum as a way to push for welfare reform and greater social inclusion of the unemployed, disadvantaged youths and the elderly in deprived urban and suburban areas. Active citizenship became a key social policy concept of Britain's New Labour government in the late 1990s and a cornerstone of domestic policies that encouraged **volunteering** and social participation as well as responsibilities. Programmes to foster active citizenship in the UK frequently involved **voluntary associations** and community groups. (See also **Citizenship**.)

Addams, Jane (1860–1935)

Following the interruption of her medical studies, Illinois-born Jane Addams visited Europe in 1888 and encountered the Toynbee Hall Settlement House for the poor in London's East End, which inspired her to become a co-founder of a similar settlement in Chicago. Hull House opened in 1889, becoming a model for social settlements around the world, and eventually expanded from its initial child-care focus, diversifying to include education, art, music and recreation for all ages. Addams was an advocate of child-labour laws, juvenile protection programmes and women's suffrage, and received the Nobel Peace Prize in 1931 for leading the Women's International League for Peace and Freedom.

Konrad-Adenauer-Stiftung
Konrad Adenauer Foundation

The Konrad Adenauer Foundation, named after the first Chancellor of the Federal Republic of Germany, is a **political foundation**, established in 1964 out of the Society for Christian Democratic Education. The Foundation is active throughout Germany and in some 120 countries, conducting political education and research, granting scholarships, researching the history of Christian Democracy, and advocating for European unification, international understanding and development policy co-operation. Its current focal points are **social economy**, the future of the European order and the ethical foundations for modern **civil society**.

Website: www.kas.de

Adhocracy

Adhocracy is a management structure in which all members of the organization have some broad level of authority to make decisions and take actions affecting the implementation of tasks and operations. Because of its flexibility, it is believed that there is no structure better suited to solving complex, ill-structured problems like those often tackled by **non-profit organizations**. Adhocracy is the opposite of **bureaucracy**, in which everyone has a defined and permanent role.

Advocacy

In legal terms, advocacy is the active espousal of a political or policy position, a point of view, or a course of action. It covers a variety of actions that range from highly regulated and formalized **lobbying** by interest associations (exemplified by political campaign activity) to attempts to shape public opinion, demonstrations and boycotts, as well as litigation and the use of the legal system to influence public policy.

Advocacy is often considered one of the distinctive roles of **non-profit organizations**, and it is closely linked to the notion of non-profits as value guardians. In the political process that determines the design and contours of policies, the needs of groups in danger of being underrepresented or discriminated against are not always taken into account by the standard electoral process of competitive democracies. Non-profit organizations are said thus to fill in to give voice to the minority and particularistic interests and values they represent and to serve as critics and watch-dogs of government with the aim of effecting change or improvements in social and other policies. Non-profits are thus the primary mechanism by which particularistic values are promoted and guarded. The resulting expressive diversity in society in turn is said to contribute to pluralism and democratization.

Many non-profits combine advocacy with service delivery, or form special advocacy **organizations** in case tax law prohibits certain types of lobbying. Advocacy has experienced significant growth, which some analysts attribute to greater diversity of modern society and to the decline of traditional political party systems. Non-profit advocacy organizations account for only 2% of total non-profit expenditure in over 20 countries included in the Johns Hopkins Comparative Non-profit Sector Study, although actual advocacy activities are likely to command a higher share due to **product bundling**.

Affiliates

'Affiliate' and 'affiliated **organization**' are somewhat imprecise terms that cover a variety of inter-organizational relations: a local chapter, franchises, an auxiliary group, or a branch office of a (usually) national parent organization. It usually signals some inter-organizational status short of **membership**, and a looser relation that refers to either a network of like-minded organizations that pool resources and efforts around a common cause, or local or regional entities that are part of a larger, central organization. Whereas the former describes some horizontal organizational arrangement among equals, the latter tends to involve power differences and delegation of authority. In some instances, affiliated entities are part of a joint group for purposes of **tax exemption**; in other cases, organizations join to create service organizations to achieve greater **economies of scale**.

Affinity Cards

Affinity cards are a financial **marketing** and **fundraising** tool used by **non-profit organizations**. In most cases, they are credit or charge cards issued to members of a specific group, (e.g. alumni of a university), or to the general public for support of specific causes, such as the environment or the arts. Commercial firms carry out the financial operations involved in issuing, using and billing, and the non-profit organizations receive a percentage of the profits generated. The tax law in most countries treats such profit-sharing and transfer activities as taxable, **unrelated business income**.

Aga Khan Foundation

Founded in 1967 by His Highness Prince Karim Aga Khan, the Aga Khan Foundation (AKF) is a private, non-profit **foundation** established under Swiss law dedicated to promoting creative solutions to problems that impede social development, primarily in Asia and East Africa. It has branches and independent affiliates in 12 countries. The AKF makes **grants** in the areas of health, education, rural development and **NGO** enhancement, primarily to grassroots **organizations**. It is a modern vehicle for facilitating **philanthropy** and **volunteering** in the Ismaili Muslim community, with basic funding provided by the Aga Khan and additional programme funds provided by government, foundation and business-sector partners. The AKF is part of the Aga Khan Development Network, a group of eight development organizations dedicated to improving living conditions and opportunities for the poor.

Website: www.akdn.org

Agence Canadienne de Développement International (ACDI) – *see* Canadian International Development Agency (CIDA)

Allavida (Alliances for Voluntary Initiatives and Development)

Allavida was established in the UK in 2001 through the **merger** of Charity Know How and *Alliance* magazine, both of which were formerly part of the **Charities Aid Foundation (CAF)**. Allavida's goal is to provide the resources (i.e. the funding, skills and information) that people and **organizations** working for the development of their communities need in order to achieve their own objectives. Allavida takes a holistic approach to development in the regions in which it operates, encompassing training and **capacity-building**, small **grants**, support for networks and emerging **civil society** resource organizations, including local grant-making bodies, and information gathering and dissemination.

Website: www.allavida.org

Allocative Efficiency

Allocative efficiency, also referred to as Pareto efficiency or Pareto optimality, is a term used in welfare economics and game theory to describe the allocation of scarce resources in such a way that no reallocation could make any individual better off without making at least one other individual worse off. For example, a Pareto-efficient supply of health-care services under the condition of scarce resources would imply better health-care provision for all while leaving no consumer worse off. **Non-profit organizations** contribute to allocative efficiency to the extent to which all resources they command are allocated to the most highly valued uses.

Alms

Alms are clothing, food, money, or other material items given to the poor. Alms-giving is a central element of many major religious creeds, including **Christianity** (see **charity**), **Islam** (see **Zakat**) and Judaism (see **Zedaka**).

Altruism

Introduced by French sociologist and philosopher Auguste Comte in the mid-19th century, the term 'altruism' was to establish the opposite reference point to the self-gratifying, utility-maximizing 'economic man' of economic theory. Based on the Latin phrase *alteri huic*—which literally translates as 'to this other'—, altruism refers to a specific kind of behaviour intended to benefit another being in a selfless way, even if such altruistic actions and their possible outcomes might involve risks for the actor and sacrifices in welfare or well-being, including one's own life.

The literature has identified a number of critical aspects of altruism relative to non-altruistic behaviour: it is expressed through action rather than intention alone; altruistic action is goal-directed but can be based on diffuse value patterns; the goal of altruistic action is to benefit the welfare of others in direct and intended ways; altruistic motivations and actions constitute altruisms, not outcomes and results; altruism involves the reduction of one's own welfare; by contract, if both the intended altruist and the intended recipient obtain welfare benefits, collective welfare rather than altruism is involved; and altruism sets no conditions and is carried out without anticipation of reward. If these elements apply, we speak of pure altruism; if some are present but others are not, such actions are called either particularistic altruism, which is often the case in relation to actions in families, ethnic and national groups or **religions**, or quasi-altruism, which involves some form of benefit to the actor. Some see altruistic behaviour along a continuum, with pure self-interest and pure altruism as the two poles, and modal or normal behaviour, including particularistic altruism, in between these extremes. Others use altruism interchangeably with quasi-altruistic behaviour such as giving, sharing, co-operating, helping, and different forms of other-directed or pro-social behaviour.

There are four major approaches to understanding altruism: sociological explanations emphasize individual characteristics and value patterns associated with altruism, e.g. religion, socio-economic status, or political preferences; economic theories treat altruism as part of a **cost–benefit** calculus and point to intangible, psychological rewards; evolutionary biology stresses kin or group selection, whereby select members 'step aside' to promote the survival of the species; and psychological approaches explore the role of altruism in socialization and identity formation.

Amato, Giuliano (1938–)

A lawyer by training, Giuliano Amato served twice as Italy's Prime Minister (1992–1993 and 2000–2001). While in office as Treasury Minister in 1988, Amato drafted the law which, after being signed by the new Treasury Minister Guido Carli and passed by the Italian Parliament in 1990, drastically changed Italy's banking system by restructuring ownership rights. Publicly controlled savings banks were split into two separate entities: a commercial joint stock bank and a so-called **banking foundation**, thus increasing the number and **assets** of Italian foundations literally overnight. In 2001, European Union leaders appointed Amato Vice-Chairman of the Convention charged with drafting the European Constitutional Treaty. He was Full Professor of Italian and Comparative Constitutional Law at the University of Rome from 1975 to 1997 and is currently professor at the European University Institute in Fiesole (Florence).

Amnesty International

Formed in 1961, Amnesty International (AI) is a democratic, self-governing movement dedicated to research and action focused on preventing and ending **human rights** abuses. As of 2004, AI's extensive network included more than 1.5m. members, supporters and subscribers in over 150 countries and territories in the world and over 7,500 volunteer groups world-wide. Its international secretariat is headquartered in London. AI is funded primarily through national chapters and volunteer groups and accepts no funds from governments for its work investigating and campaigning against human rights violations. In 1977, the movement received the Nobel Peace Prize.

Website: www.amnesty.org

Anarchism

Anarchism is a political theory or doctrine holding that society can and should be organized without a coercive State. Behind this theory are the following beliefs: that society is natural and people are good, but corrupted by artificial institutions; that any authority (such as the State) that hinders human development should be opposed and that the concentration of economic power in the hands of business corporations should be prevented. However, aside from this set of common beliefs, anarchist thinkers differ widely in their approaches and support a range of proposals from the most extreme individualism to complete collectivism (see **Proudhon**). Although the anarchist movement is largely defunct, the doctrine retains importance as a philosophical attitude, a political tendency, and a source of social protest, e.g. the highly visible (and sometimes destructive or violent) anti-globalization protests at international conferences which began during the late 1990s.

Andrews, Frank Emerson (1902–1978)

A pioneer in the study of **philanthropy** and **foundations** in the USA, Frank Emerson Andrews was also a renowned scholar in various other fields, including mathematics. Andrews worked with the Russell Sage Foundation in New York (see **Sage, Margaret Olivia Slocum**) from 1928 to 1956 as director of publications and director of philanthropic research; and with its support and that of the **Carnegie Corporation of New York**, he launched the **Foundation Center** and served as its first president for over a decade, from 1956-1967. His publications on foundations and philanthropy include *Corporation Giving* (1952); *Philanthropic Foundations* (1956); *Attitudes Towards Giving* (1953); and *Legal Instruments of Foundations* (1958).

Annenberg, Walter (1908–2002)

Walter Annenberg was a US media executive, publisher, diplomat and American broadcasting pioneer. In his later years, Annenberg received attention for his philanthropic activities, particularly in higher education and public television. He endowed communications programmes bearing his name at the University of Pennsylvania and at the University of Southern California. He also created a US $150m. fund administered by the US Corporation for Public Broadcasting that would provide educational programmes for college credit through television. Upon his death, he **bequeathed** his art collection, worth more than $1,000m., to the New York Metropolitan Museum of Art.

Annual Giving Programmes

Annual giving programmes (AGP) are a **fundraising** and **marketing** tool used by many **non-profit organizations** to increase giving **revenue** by recruiting new **donors** and renewing and augmenting past contributions. The system allows requesting organizations to contact current donors at regular intervals during the year, target specific donor groups for special events, and develop relationships with prospective donors as part of a year-long cycle of planned fundraising activities. AGPs capitalize on the fact that regular communication with donors increases commitment, loyalty and, ultimately, the frequency and the amount of donations. Funds raised can be for the purposes of current expenditures, special programmes or **endowment**.

Annual Reports

Annual reports serve several purposes. They may be required as a legal document to be filed with the respective competent authorities (e.g. Ministry of the Interior, Charity Commission, Internal Revenue Service, local government office) and be part of the application, reinstatement or oversight process. Other uses of annual reports are to inform members, clients and users as well as **donors** and supporters of the organization. In its most narrow meaning, the term refers to the annual financial statements of **non-profit organizations** in terms of expenditure and **revenues**, **assets** and liabilities. Increasingly, organizations post their annual reports on the Internet, and some are also moving away from the notion of issuing annual reports in print and towards web-based, regularly-updated information on **mission**, objectives, programmes and activities, as well as financial data.

Anonymous Giving

An anonymous gift is a contribution which, by specific wish of the **donor**, is not publicly attributed to him or her. The reasons behind giving anonymously can range from an effort to shield the donor from publicity to religious practice. In Judaism, for example, anonymous giving is among the highest degrees of **charity** (see **Zedaka**). Many **gift**-pooling **organizations**, such as **community foundations** and the **United Way** in the USA, as well as a number of recipient organizations, now offer funding vehicles to facilitate anonymous giving.

Anti-Slavery International

Established in the UK in 1839 as the British and Foreign Anti-Slavery Society, Anti-Slavery International works at the local, national and international levels to eradicate slavery and forced labour in all forms. The organization seeks to achieve its aims through: urging governments of countries with slavery to develop and implement anti-slavery measures; **lobbying** governments and intergovernmental agencies to make slavery a priority issue; supporting research to assess the scale of slavery; and raising public awareness about it. A precursor of the modern **international NGO**, Anti-Slavery International has consultative status with the UN Economic and Social Council and has members world-wide.

Website: www.antislavery.org

Antistatism

Antistatism refers to the fear of centralized authority and a suspicion of the State. The USA and other Anglo-American societies are characterized generally by antistatism, which is manifested in a relatively limited central government and a political life that has revolved around the local rather than the national polity. (See also **Centralization**.)

Arbeiterwohlfahrt (AWO)

Workers' Welfare

Founded in 1919, the Arbeiterwohlfahrt has historically been linked to the German Social Democratic Party. For the Social Democrats, who advocated public rather than private welfare provision, the Arbeiterwohlfahrt was created out of both political and economic necessity: political because other major parties at that time began to provide social services as a means of attracting and keeping members, and economic because public services were significantly reduced following the First World War. Today, AWO is one of the largest networks of private, non-profit social service providers in Europe and offers a wide range of social services and emergency relief.

Website: www.arbeiterwohlfahrt.de

Articles of Organization

'Articles of organization' is a legal term that refers to the document by which an organization is created. As a charter for an unincorporated organization and, according to the legal system and jurisdiction involved, there are a number of elements the articles must contain in order to address a variety of organizational 'tests', provisions and requirements. These elements would typically include: name of the organization; stated purpose; the minimum number of founding members, their names and addresses (for **membership** organizations), the officers of the organization, the members of the initial **board of directors** or **board of trustees**; the registered agent and incorporators (for corporations); the dissolution or liquidation procedure; and the legal seat. (See **Bylaws**.)

Ashoka

Ashoka was founded in 1980 as an organization to support and develop **social entrepreneurship** around the world. Ashoka provides this support through stipends and professional services to approximately 150 'Ashoka Fellows' each year, who work in the fields of learning and education, environment, health, **human rights**, civic participation and economic development. Since 1982, Ashoka has selected over 1,400 individuals in 48 countries to be Ashoka Fellows. Headquartered in Virginia, USA, Ashoka also maintains offices in Africa, Europe, Asia and Latin America.

Website: www.ashoka.org

Asia Pacific Philanthropy Consortium (APPC)

Founded in 1994, the Asia Pacific Philanthropy Consortium (APPC) is an informal network of **organizations** that facilitate the growth and development of philanthropic organizations in Asia. APPC does so by serving as catalyst, convenor and network builder, as well as providing support for research and the creation of national **philanthropy** information centres. Its activities focus on improving the regulatory, economic and legal environment for philanthropy; **capacity-building**; identifying resources within Asia and abroad; and increasing public support and awareness for philanthropy.

Website: www.asianphilanthropy.org

Asociación Española de Fundaciones
Spanish Association of Foundations

The Asociación Española de Fundaciones was created in 2003 through the **merger** of the Centro de Fundaciones (Foundation Centre) and the Confederación Española de Fundaciones (Spanish Confederation of Foundations). The Asociación's main objectives are to provide its some 600 foundation members with information about current events in the sector; training and seminars on relevant topics; legal, financial and other advice; contacts and opportunities for exchange with other foundations through affinity groups; and links with foundations outside Spain, especially in Europe and Ibero-America.

Website: www.fundaciones.org

Aspen Institute Non-Profit Sector Research Fund

The Non-profit Sector Research Fund was established in 1991 by the Aspen Institute, a Washington, DC-headquartered **non-profit organization** that supports seminars, policy programmes and leadership development initiatives. The Fund seeks to enhance the legitimacy and visibility of **non-profit sector** studies through financial support of scholars and research projects. Since its inception, the Fund has awarded approximately US $10m. for over 400 research projects in various areas of non-profit studies. The Fund focuses its research grant-making on non-profits and public policy; non-profit relations with business and government; and **foundation** policy and practice.

Website: www.nonprofitresearch.org

Asset Test

To qualify for **Section 501(c)(3)** tax-exempt status in the USA, a **non-profit organization** must demonstrate procedures that prohibit **assets** or income from being distributed to individuals as owners, managers or their equivalents, except for fair compensation for services rendered. Furthermore, the organization may not be used for the personal benefit of founders, board members, managers, staff or associates. Such stipulations are equivalent to a **non-distribution constraint** and are often referred to as the asset test.

An assets test, a technical term used by the US Internal Revenue Service, is one of the three tests, next to an **endowment** test and a support test, by which a private foundation in the USA can be considered an **operating foundation**. A private foundation will meet the assets test if 65% or more of its assets are either devoted directly to the active conduct of its exempt activity, to a functionally related business, or to a combination of the two, or consist of stock of a corporation controlled by the foundation, of which substantially all the assets are devoted to the above purposes. This test is intended to apply to libraries and museums.

Assets

The assets of a **foundation** or other **non-profit organization** are generally described as the total amount of capital or principal (e.g. cash, stocks, bonds, real estate) it controls. Assets are managed in order to maximize return from investment according to a chosen level of risk; the income resulting from asset management is used to support the organization's activities. A minimum ratio between the market value of the assets and total grant expenditures can be imposed by law. In the USA, for instance, private foundations have to meet a **mandatory pay-out requirement**: that is, the amount they spend annually for charitable purposes (i.e. **grants** and connected administrative expenses) must be approximately 5% of the average market value of their assets. The market value of the assets held by a foundation is the most commonly-used indicator of its dimension, although different approaches to valuing assets at either market or **book value** exist.

Association of Charitable Foundations (ACF)

Established in 1989, the Association of Charitable Foundations is the United Kingdom's support organization for grant-making **trusts** and **foundations** of all types. The Association aims to enhance the understanding of trusts and foundations among grant-seekers and the general public; to facilitate communication and co-operation among its members; to encourage the development of **philanthropy** and of new grant-making **organizations**; and to advocate for and influence favourable public policies. In 2002, this **grant-makers' association** had over 300 members.

Website: www.acf.org.uk

Association of Foundations in the Netherlands – *see* Vereniging van Fondsen in Nederland

Association Française contre les Myopathies (AFM)

French Muscular Dystrophy Association

Established in 1958, AFM is the most active of many **organizations** focused on supporting medical research to cure genetic diseases and on bettering the living conditions of people afflicted by these diseases. In 1987, AFM first launched its telethon **fundraising** campaign, with growing success every year (raising some €100m. in 2003) and with the involvement of temporary volunteers throughout France. AFM established Généthon, the foremost centre in France for research on genetic diseases, supporting government-employed research teams with its privately-raised funds, and thereby breaking the quasi-monopoly held by public agencies over the direction of basic research.

Website: www.afm-france.org

Association for Research on Non-Profit Organizations and Voluntary Action (ARNOVA)

The Association for Research on Non-Profit Organizations and Voluntary Action (ARNOVA) was established in 1971 as an interdisciplinary scholarly **membership** association committed to strengthening the research community in the emerging field of non-profit and philanthropic studies. As of 2004, ARNOVA had over 1,200 members including scholars, researchers and non-profit professionals, most of them USA-based. Principal activities include an annual conference, publications, electronic discussions and special interest groups. ARNOVA's official journal, the *Non-profit and Voluntary Sector Quarterly*, is a leading publication in **non-profit sector** studies.

Website: www.arnova.org

Association of Voluntary Agencies for Rural Development

Founded in 1958 and based in Delhi, the Association of Voluntary Agencies for Rural Development (AVARD) is a non-profit **association** of some 550 **voluntary** agencies engaged in rural development activities throughout India. Its main goal is to strengthen voluntary action and the long-term growth of rural development **NGO**s by promoting co-operation among NGOs, acting as a **clearing-house** for information, and providing **capacity-building**, training and research support.

Website: www.indianngos.com/avarddelhi

Associations

'Association' is a widely-used and often ill-specified term that covers any formal group of people or organizational entities joined together for a particular purpose. That purpose is usually public in nature, in the sense that members form an association for pursuing some common interest that they might not be able to achieve by themselves as individual actors. **Membership** forms the basis of associations, and members can be individuals, **organizations** or both. However, it is also used to refer to different types of limited partnerships, **co-operatives**, mutual benefit societies (see **mutual societies**), **trusts**, holdings, or other financial entities. In some countries such as France and Germany, association also implies sociability and conviviality, and can be applied to any social group outside the family. In other countries, in particular in Scandinavia, association is closely linked to forms of popular **democracy** and mass move-ments—the *folkrörelse*.

Although the term 'association' is used for many types of organizations, it is also a legal term based on the right of association. In legal terms, an association is a contract among natural and legal personalities that may stipulate any objective, provided it does not violate existing legal, moral or ethical provisions. Associations may be registered, i.e. incorporated, or non-registered and unin-corporated. Incorporated associations are legal personalities endowed with their own rights and obligations, whereas unincorporated associations have no such legal powers and members are personally liable. Although it is a legal require-ment in some jurisdictions, many smaller **non-profit organizations** and asso-ciations do not incorporate—that is, file articles of association or organization with the appropriate government office or the courts.

Associations are not tax-exempt by definition; tax treatments of associations are regulated in respective tax laws such as **Section 501(c)(3)** in the USA or the fiscal code in other countries. Types of membership association typically recognized as tax-exempt are: social welfare and health-related associations, educational and scholarly associations, labour and farmers' associations, **busi-ness** and **professional associations** and religious congregations.

ATD Quarte-Monde
ATD Fourth World

Founded in 1957 by Father Joseph Wresinski, ATD Quarte-Monde is a French-based **international NGO** dedicated to eliminating extreme poverty and exclusion all over the world. The International ATD Fourth World Movement extends to countries in Europe, Africa, North and Central America and Asia. ATD Quarte-Monde, through the members of its international Volunteer Corps, mobilizes poor families and communities in housing estates, slums and isolated shanty towns; researches issues of poverty with the participation of those in poverty; and fosters public opinion.

Website: www.atd-fourthworld.org

ATTAC (Association for Transaction Taxes to Aid Citizens)

Established in 1998 in France, ATTAC is an international **non-profit organiza-tion** working to introduce the **Tobin tax**, a proposal to tax financial market transactions to pay for global **public goods** and opposing free-trade globaliza-tion. ATTAC, which had 40,000 members in France, rapidly expanded through 50 countries and played a role in the climactic protests at the Geneva (1998) and Seattle (1999) World Trade Organization conferences. ATTAC is emblematic of the anti-establishment **organizations** that mushroomed with the deepening of the economic recession of the late 1990s, acting as advocates for the rights of those 'without rights,' and has many links to the wider anti-globalization movement.

Website: www.attac.org

Audits

An audit is an examination of the records or financial accounts of an organization, usually conducted by independent outsiders. Audits are typically done to determine whether the accounting procedures used by an organization are objective, fair, complete and accurate. For a financial audit, auditors will generally look at the organization's expenses and **revenues**, seeking clear evidence that, for example, the expenses were properly authorized and supported by appropriate documents and that the revenues were correctly recorded and classified. The traditional audit does not make judgments about the financial strength of the organization nor confirm that the numbers used are right or wrong; rather an audit gives an opinion about the soundness and merits of the procedures and practices used. By extension, an audit also refers to any systematic inspection of a particular aspect of an entity's operations, even if carried out by internal staff, for example, an internal audit or environmental audit.

B

Backward Integration

Backward integration, i.e. the control of input markets, is one motive for creating an association or entering into an organizational alliance or **partnership** aimed at cost reduction and greater control by cutting out external intermediaries ('the middlemen'). A purchasing **co-operative**, for example, seeks to use its members' combined purchasing power to negotiate better prices and terms. A non-profit food distribution network partnering with local farmers' **co-operatives** to produce food items would be another example of backward integration.

Balanced Scorecards

The balanced scorecard is a tool used to quantify, measure and evaluate the inputs, outputs and outcomes of **non-profit organizations**. Originally developed for businesses, it is based on the idea that traditional measures of performance, which track past behaviour, may not measure activities that drive future performance. Balanced scorecard indicators consider performance over a range of dimensions and force managers to evaluate both outcomes and the status of the organization producing them. There are four types of measures on a balanced scorecard: 'service users/policy changes', which measures achievements of the organization's **mission**; 'internal processes', which measures planning and service delivery processes; 'learning and growth', which measures organizational capacity, **evaluation** and learning; and 'financial', which measures **fundraising**, cost control and productivity improvements. The balanced scorecard shifts the focus from programmes and initiatives to the outcomes they are supposed to accomplish, and brings mission-related measures in contact with operational, learning and financial aspects.

Banking Foundations

'Banking foundation' is a relatively new term of Italian origin, commonly used to describe shareholding entities established as a result of Law 218 of 1990, which restructured and privatized Italy's public banking sector. The law was also known as the '**Amato**-Carli Law', after the Prime Minister and the Finance Minister, respectively, who drafted it. The most common outcome of the restructuring process was the conversion of banks to joint stock companies for actual banking operations, while the banking foundations, which previously managed the banks, kept control of the majority of the shares.

However, with the 'Ciampi Law' of 1998 and Government Decree 153 of May 1999, regulation of the banking foundations underwent a profound revision from both civil-law and taxation perspectives. By changing their statutes to comply with the new regulations, the foundations are now recognized as 'private legal not-for-profit entities endowed with full statutory and managerial autonomy'. This allows the banking foundations to enjoy fiscal benefits, provided that they no longer maintain shareholder control of their respective banks, requiring the foundations to diversify their portfolios.

The final result was the reorganization of the banking system and, simultaneously, the emergence of 89 relatively large private foundations (e.g. **Compagnia di San Paolo** and **Fondazione Cariplo**). At least 10 of the 89 banking foundations have **endowments** exceeding €1,000m., while about 30 of the remainder top €100m. These institutions operate in various ways, but they act primarily as **grant-makers** in education, research, art, culture, health and welfare. Some foundations are also active in the fields of the environment and local development. In response to concerns that grant awards are too heavily focused in the wealthier north and central regions of Italy, several northern foundations have initiated programmes in the southern part of the country

A banking foundation is governed by a **board of directors** consisting, in equal parts, of representatives of local government and **civil society organizations**. The board defines the foundation's guidelines and programmes and elects a 'Management Committee' that decides on grant awards.

Barnett, Samuel Augustus (1844–1913)

A deacon in the Anglican Church and a Canon of Bristol Cathedral, Samuel Barnett was regarded as one of the most influential social reformers in London of his time. Barnett worked with and was inspired by **Octavia Hill** to establish in 1869 the Charity Organisation Society, the first organized, systematic, social relief 'new agency' that brought **stakeholders** from **philanthropy**, government and labour together to address social conditions in London. Barnett's ideas and the **organizations** he helped launch inspired social welfare movements for poverty alleviation, children's assistance and women's rights that extended well beyond the boundaries of London.

Barriers to Entry

Barriers to entry are conditions or circumstances that make it difficult or impossible for competitors to enter a particular market or, more generally, for **organizations** or individuals to enter a specific field. Such obstacles can be raised by government regulations, economic factors, **marketing** conditions, or professional control. Barriers have an impact both on the type or number of **non-profit organizations** in a given society and on the presence or lack of non-profit, for-profit, or governmental entities in particular fields of activity. In some countries like Japan, high capitalization requirements have limited the number of **foundations**. Likewise, in some social service fields, for-profit firms face significant barriers to entry. (See also **Barriers to exit**.)

Barriers to Exit

Barriers to exit are conditions or circumstances that keep too many competitors in a market or quasi-market situation. Such obstacles can be raised by government regulations, economic factors, or **marketing** conditions. In the non-profit context, for example, the tax advantages held by a commercial-type **non-profit organization** provide a disincentive for the organization to become a for-profit firm. Generally speaking, barriers to exit have an impact on the type and number of non-profit organizations as well as on the presence of non-profit, for-profit, or governmental entities in particular fields of activity. (See also **Barriers to entry**.)

Benchmarking

Benchmarking is a comparison-oriented performance measurement tool. Comparisons of productivity, quality and value can be made between activities or units in different departments of a single organization or across different firms in the same industry. Three common techniques are: (1) Best Demonstrated Practice, i.e. comparison of performance between units within one organization; (2) Relative Cost Position, i.e. comparison of every element of the cost structure of two firms; (3) Best Related Practice, i.e. comparison of performance among related firms. Other techniques include site visits to witness different management styles and procedures and the formation of 'clubs' to exchange ideas. In the non-profit field, the benchmarking approach is attractive because **organizations** are believed to share a common philosophy of **social justice** and service and therefore value collaboration and sharing best practices in working towards a common good.

Beneficiaries

A beneficiary is a person, organization or institution that receives or is targeted to receive a benefit, whether from a **trust**, a programme, or a project. Beneficiaries can be either direct (i.e. those who use a service or are the targets of a programme, e.g. school students, hospital patients or the homeless), or indirect (i.e. those who benefit in a secondary way, e.g. the community at large, children of women who receive education, etc.).

Benevolent Organizations

Used in a narrow, legal sense in the USA, the term 'benevolent organization' refers to a local association that operates to provide life insurance coverage to its members. In order to enjoy US federal income **tax exemption**, it may only collect income for the purpose of meeting losses and expenses and therefore tends to provide such coverage at cost. This tax-exempt category is also available to **burial associations**. However, the term is also used both in the USA and internationally in a broader sense in reference to **organizations** engaged in activities which are either benevolent, i.e. organized for the purpose of doing good, or of a charitable nature.

Bequeath

Bequeath, and similarly, bequest, refers to the making of a **gift** of any form and kind, of personal property by means of a will or testament. A bequeathing of personal property is a form of disposition from one owner to another. **Non-profit organizations** are frequent recipients of bequests, and are a major source of asset accumulation and capital funds as well. In 1998, US non-profit organizations received over US \$10,500m. in bequests, representing 7.6% of total private **individual giving** that year.

Bertelsmann Foundation

Established in 1977 by **Reinhard Mohn**, the Bertelsmann Foundation is a German-based **operating foundation** which is dedicated to fostering **innovations** and solutions for societal problems and promoting reform. One of the largest in Europe, the Foundation conducts or commissions activities ranging from research to training to conferences in fields as diverse as the European Union, elementary education, preventative health care and culture. Bertelsmann has also been active in promoting the development of philanthropic institutions similar to **community foundations** outside the USA. The Foundation's income is derived from its holding of the majority of shares of the Bertelsmann publishing house.

Website: www.stiftung.bertelsmann.de

Beveridge, Lord William Henry (1879–1963)

Often referred to as the 'father of the **welfare state**', Lord Beveridge is best known for the 1942 Beveridge Report (officially titled the Social Insurance and Allied Services Report). The report proposed the introduction to the UK of a system of cash benefits, financed by contributions from workers, employers and the state, together with a public assistance 'safety net'. Among the assumptions underlying this system were a national health service and a commitment to state action to reduce unemployment. Critical of shortcomings in social legislation after 1945, his *Voluntary Action* (1948) defended the role of the private sector in the provision of social welfare. Beveridge held posts as, among others, journalist, civil servant and Director of the London School of Economics.

Bibó, István (1911–1979)

A historian and political scientist, István Bibó was one of the greatest Hungarian thinkers of the 20th century, with major works including *The Crisis of Hungarian Democracy, The Distress of the Eastern European Small States, Distorted Hungarian Character, Deadlocks of Hungarian History, The Paralysis of International Institutions and the Remedies,* and *Reflections on the Social Development of Europe.* Bibó's theory on the importance of horizontal social structures was a source of inspiration for comparative European social history and for research on **civil society**. Specifically, his argument about the role of the 'small circles of freedom' has become a common denominator in Eastern European political thinking.

Bloch-Lainé, François (1918–2002)

François Bloch-Lainé was a French civil servant who played a decisive role in the development of French **non-profit organizations** during the 1970s, and in European social policy thinking in the 1980s. He was responsible for the national budget and was later the Director of the Caisse des Dépôts, the state investment bank. Despite this position, he advocated a less statist and more decentralized government by strengthening the **non-profit sector**, which was less developed than in other industrialized countries. Bloch-Lainé implemented public-sector financial incentives and favourable regulations towards non-profit organizations. When he retired, he chaired the **Union of Health and Welfare Non-Profit Organizations (UNIOPSS)**, which became an example of **partnership** between the State and social-service **organizations**.

BlueCross and BlueShield

The BlueCross and BlueShield **organizations** are health insurance schemes and operate forms of prepaid health-care plans throughout the USA and Canada. With the first plans emerging in the 1930s, the 'Blues', all members of the BlueCross BlueShield Association, are now the largest insurer in each US state. Originally tax-exempt non-profit health services corporations (mostly under Internal Revenue Code **Section 501(c)(4)**), many of the US Blues converted in the 1980s to mutual insurance companies and then, beginning in the 1990s, to for-profit companies, amid much controversy about impact on local health care and the disposal of charitable **assets**. The Canadian Blues, organized under the Canadian Association of Blue Cross Plans, are all not-for-profit.

Website: www.bluecares.com; www.bluecross.ca

Board Duties

Members of the **board of directors** or **board of trustees** of a **non-profit organization** have a number of duties that vary by country, jurisdiction and type of organization, but usually include the following: due diligence, i.e. an expectation that a board member exercises reasonable care and follows the business judgment rule when making decisions; avoidance of **self-dealing**, i.e. an expectation that a board member discloses and scrutinizes potential and actual transactions between **trustees** and the organization; loyalty, i.e. an expectation that a board member remains faithful and loyal to the organization; obedience, i.e. an expectation that a board member remains obedient to the central purposes of the organization and respects all laws and legal regulations; and fiduciary control, i.e. a responsibility of board members and the non-profit board as a whole to ensure that the financial resources of the **organization** are sufficient and handled properly.

Board of Directors

A board of directors is a group of individuals elected or appointed to provide overall policy and management directives to an organization; it is the governing body of a **non-profit organization** or a for-profit **organization**, usually incorporated as a corporation or company. The basic responsibilities of the non-profit board include: determining the organization's **mission** and purpose; selecting, supporting and assessing the chief executive; providing proper financial oversight; ensuring adequate resources; ensuring legal and ethical integrity and maintaining accountability; and enhancing the organization's public standing. The method for determining board membership is typically laid out in the organization's articles of incorporation and **bylaws**. In the non-profit organization context, there are three basic models: (1) the directors are elected by the organization's members, (2) the board of directors is a self-perpetuating board, or (3) the directors are elected (or appointed) by another another organization. (See **Governance** and **Board of trustees**.)

Board of Trustees

A board of trustees is made up of people elected or appointed to serve collectively as the governing body of a **trust** or, used more generally, a **non-profit organization**. In non-profit organizations, where no strict equivalents to 'owners' exist, the board is entrusted with the organization, i.e. they are the **trustees**. The task of the board of trustees is to make sure that the organization carries out its designated **mission** without the objective of making profit and with the promise not to distribute organizational **assets** to benefit individuals other than the clients the non-profit was formed to serve. (See also **Board of directors** and **Governance**)

Bodelschwingh, F. V. (1831–1910)

Bodelschwingh was a social reformer and religious entrepreneur who developed one of the largest networks of health and social services institutions in Continental Europe, the Anstalt Bethel (Bethel Institution) outside the industrial town of Bielefeld, Germany. A gifted organizer and preacher, he combined religious devotion, piety and **charity** with a strict work ethic, and demanded a disciplined, frugal lifestyle from his followers. He founded several 'workers' colonies' in response to the growing housing shortage and homelessness problems at the height of the industrial revolution (1880s). The institutions he founded, in particular Anstalt Bethel, are now part of the **Diakonisches Werk**.

Heinrich Böll Foundation

The Heinrich Böll Foundation is a German **political foundation**, established in 1987 in memory of writer Heinrich Böll. Headquartered in Berlin, the Foundation is associated with the Green Party and collaborates with **NGOs** in over 54 countries to strengthen ecology-oriented action and **civil society** exchanges. The Foundation maintains 15 regional offices throughout the world to function as hubs. In particular, the focus of the Foundation's international work revolves around: affirmative action for women and gender **democracy**; ecology and sustainable development; development of democracy, **human rights** and peace; media and critical public debate; and culture and development.

Website: www.boell.org

Bonoficers

The term 'bonoficer' refers to an **organization** that might choose to generate less than maximum profit, while engaging in activities that benefit the public good, but are not necessarily profitable. The organizational behaviour of a bonoficer, therefore, differs from a profit maximizer. For example, a bonoficer might invest in equipment that employs more labour in order to create or keep jobs, whereas a profit maximizer would be more likely to purchase labour-saving machinery as labour costs increase. Similarly, a bonoficer might provide services to the needy in low-income areas, where a profit-maximizing firm would find it unprofitable. According to economist **Burton Weisbrod**, donations supplement the earned income of a bonoficer and constitute, in effect, receipts from the provision of a **collective good**.

Book Value

Book value refers to the value of an asset as recorded in an **organization**'s financial statements. The book value is often different from the current market value.

Boomerang Pattern of Influence

The boomerang pattern of influence refers to an approval by transnational **advocacy** networks to exert pressure on governments (and other entities). The typical boomerang pattern begins when **NGOs** in a country, where communication with or access to government has been blocked, mobilize other like-minded NGOs in other countries for support. These foreign NGOs pressure their own governments or, in some cases, third-party institutions (such as inter-governmental **organizations**) to exert influence likewise on the blocking government. The boomerang pattern is observed most commonly in the case of **human rights** campaigns, but also in environmental and indigenous rights campaigns.

Bosch, Robert (1861–1942)

Robert Bosch, a German businessman and founder of Robert Bosch GmbH in Stuttgart, Germany, was responsible for developing the high-tension magnet and the spark plug. He was a pioneer in improving workers' benefits, providing his labour force with eight-hour working days, five-day working weeks, paid sick leave and a pension plan. He made donations to various causes, most notably to Stuttgart's technical university in 1910 and the Robert Bosch Hospital in Stuttgart. In 1964, the **Robert-Bosch-Stiftung** was established to continue Bosch's philanthropic endeavors by supporting education, science and international understanding.

Robert-Bosch-Stiftung GmbH

Robert Bosch Foundation

Founded in 1964 as a limited liability company, the Robert-Bosch-Stiftung is a **legacy** of entrepreneur **Robert Bosch** to ensure the continuity of his social endeavours. The Stiftung holds 92% of the capital of Robert Bosch GmbH. The Stiftung's focal areas are international understanding (focusing on the USA, France and Poland), public health, education, science in society and social commitment. The Robert-Bosch-Stiftung is one of the very few German foundations that since 1990 has intensely promoted **volunteering**, mainly in former East Germany and Central and Eastern Europe, through grant-making for civic initiatives, the awarding of a journalism prize and the initiation of studies on **voluntarism**.

Website: www.bosch-stiftung.de

Bottom Line

The bottom line refers to the actual bottom line of a firm's profit and loss statement, but is more generally used in reference to 'what really matters'. The bottom line for a business is profit, even though other indicators like market share or community relations are important as well. Such a bottom line allows business firms to set clear and specific goals that are easily monitored and measured. For **non-profit organizations** the notion of a bottom line is more complex. Many scholars suggest that, because there are no price mechanisms in place to aggregate the interests of clients, staff, volunteers and other **stake-holders,** and to match costs to profits, supply to demand and goals to actual achievements, non-profit organizations have multiple bottom lines. Multiple bottom lines require multiple **performance measures** and demand different management models and styles for non-profit organizations. (See also **Triple bottom line**.)

BRAC

BRAC, formerly known as the Bangladesh Rural Advancement Committee, was established in Bangladesh in 1972 as a relief **organization**. BRAC is now one of the largest development **NGOs** in Bangladesh, serving millions of poor households throughout the country and attracting resources from foundations, international development agencies and multilateral institutions such as the **World Bank**. BRAC's main programmes include micro-finance, non-formal and formal education and health services, reaching populations—especially women—who are not served by traditional government-administered pro-grammes. Its activities have expanded both beyond its core programmes to include BRAC University and BRAC Bank, among others, and beyond the Bangladeshi borders to Afghanistan.

Website: www.brac.net

Brands

A brand is an identifying mark, whether a visual design, a name, or a concept, that differentiates a product, service, or **organization** from the competition. The idea of branding stems from the requirement imposed by medieval **guilds** that tradesmen put trademarks on their products to protect themselves and buyers against imitations. In the non-profit arena, an organization's brand should clearly communicate what the organization does and what it represents. For external audiences, a strong brand attracts and enhances loyalty; for internal audiences, e.g. employees, it creates a sense of shared values and **mission**. Examples of strong international brands include **Amnesty International**, Oxford University, the Red Cross (see **International Red Cross and Red Crescent Movement**) or **Greenpeace**.

Bread for the World

Bread for the World (Brot für die Welt) is a large German **NGO** working in the field of humanitarian relief and development assistance. Linked to the Protestant Church, it complements the **mission** and activities of its Catholic counterpart, **Misereor**. In the USA, Bread for the World began as a small group of Christian 'citizen advocates for hungry people' in 1972 and has grown into a nationwide movement to end hunger. Its main activities are to lobby decision-makers on domestic and global anti-hunger policies; to dispel popular misconceptions about federal government welfare spending; and to protect current welfare and anti-poverty programmes from political attacks. Bread for the World also has an affiliate, Bread for the World Institute, which carries out research and education on hunger and publishes an annual *Hunger Report*.

Website: www.bread.org

Break-Even Analysis

Break-even analysis is a popular planning tool for exploring the financial viability of proposed activities. The break-even point is defined as that level of activity where total **revenues** equal total expenditures. At that level, the **non-profit organization** will neither realize a surplus nor incur an operating loss. Conducting a break-even analysis is relatively simple, and requires that the **organization** estimate fixed and variable costs for the time period in question and calculate a price for each unit produced. The very simplicity of this type of analysis can render it of limited value in planning for large, multi-product or multi-service organizations, especially when several activities share costs or when there is a one-time fixed cost that will not be repeated in later years.

Bremner, Robert (1917–2002)

US historian Robert Bremner is acclaimed for having identified **philanthropy** as a topic for historical study. His philanthropy-related books include *American Philanthropy* (1960) and *The Public Good: Philanthropy and Welfare in the Civil War Era* (1980). Bremner also stimulated focus on the history of poverty and social welfare in the USA with *From the Depths: The Discovery of Poverty in the United States* (1956) and *Children and Youth in America: A Documentary History* (1970). Bremner retired as Emeritus Professor of History at Ohio State University in 1980.

Buddhism

Buddhism initially developed based on a symbiotic relationship between **religion** and secular powers. Its spread throughout Asia was made possible mainly through state-supported networks of monasteries, which were run by Buddhist monks and scholars and served as the political, religious and cultural centre of local communities. Over time, the monasteries brought greater cultural unity throughout Asia, which facilitated the transformation of Buddhism into a 'civil religion'. This characteristic was reinforced in the 19th century when Buddhism played an important role in the development of the South-East Asian nation-state as a counter-balance to Western influences, particularly in Thailand. The majority of monasteries co-operated closely with the civil authorities in the process of political and economic modernization, which further strengthened the civil character of Buddhism as a philosophy of life rather than as a theology of salvation. In contrast to **Christianity**, for example, Buddhism appears less expansive in terms of **organization**-building. Local temples and monasteries dominate its institutional landscape while proselytizing activities are absent, as are deep-seated conflicts with secular powers.

Budgets

A budget is the primary financial instrument for a **non-profit organization**. Different from balance sheets, cash flow and income and loss statements, they are comprehensive financial work plans covering a specific project or pro-gramme or the entire organization over a specified period. There are many different types of budgets or budget approaches, all sharing several common line items, including staff or employee-related costs and non-staff costs such as rent, utilities, supplies, transportation and travel, etc.

A very common type of budget for **non-profit organizations** is the line-item budget. The primary objective of line-item budgets is to account for expenditures. Line-item budgets are used for financial and fiscal reporting, for **accountability** purposes, and, from a managerial perspective, for calculating units of inputs for staff hours and materials used. By contrast, performance budgets are used less for reporting purposes than primarily for estimating the minimum inputs needed to achieve a desired standard of output. Thus in addition to input items, a performance budget requires specified output units. The emphasis in a performance budget is on efficiency such as input/output ratios and other **performance measures**.

Both line-item and performance budgeting are incremental in the sense that the organization makes use of past cost behaviour to estimate future cost behaviour. In a sense, the last year's budget becomes the blueprint for next year's budget. Such path-dependent budgeting can create cost increases, as some items are not explicitly examined. To counteract such tendencies, some agencies use zero-based budgets, which require that all line items be reviewed and approved every year, with no assumptions made as to the increments of previous base budgets.

Programme budgeting takes a different starting point, and begins by listing the organization's core programmes based on their **mission** relevance. Each programme is then budgeted separately, using either line-item or performance budgets, even if they share common inputs and cost centres. This assumes no **economies of scope** among programmes, as the intent is to estimate the costs of each programme separately, and the cost advantages that can be achieved by joint production, i.e. running multiple programmes in support of the organization's mission. In a second step, then, these cost links and commonalities are estimated and used to build a cross-programme budget.

Building Societies

A building society is a British financial institution broadly equivalent to savings and loan associations in the USA or *Bausparkassen* in Germany. It functions basically as a mutual savings and loan association (see **Mutuality**) where members receive loans at below-market interest rates and other concessions for the purchase of a primary residence, while the association holds members' savings in the form of dividend-bearing shares to invest in such loans. Their origins lie in the persistent housing crises of the industrial revolution, when local associations were created to help low-income groups purchase property. They continue to play important roles in the creation of property value for low-income families and in making it possible for such buyers to enter the real-estate market. Building societies in the UK as well as in other countries have undergone a wave of demutualization since the 1980s, whereby they converted into commercial firms, losing any tax-exempt status they might have had in the past. (See also **Tax exemption**.)

Bundesverband Deutscher Stiftungen eV

Federal Association of German Foundations

The Bundesverband Deutscher Stiftungen was founded in 1948 to represent the interests of German **foundations** and to raise awareness among its members, politicians, the media and the public about the diversity and significance of German and international foundations. The Association's activities include providing information about German foundations; publishing newsletters, guidebooks and reports about the legal and fiscal environment for foundations in Germany; co-ordinating working groups on emerging issues; organizing an annual conference; and offering training for foundation staff, primarily through its academy.

Website: www.stiftungen.org

Bundy, McGeorge (1919–1996)

McGeorge Bundy led a diverse career in higher education (Dean at Harvard University and history professor at New York University) and foreign policy (special assistant to US Presidents Kennedy and Johnson for national security) in addition to serving as president of the **Ford Foundation** (1966–1979). During his influential tenure at Ford, Bundy put into practice his belief that foundations should play an active role in affecting social policy. For example, under his leadership, the Ford Foundation funded **organizations** such as the National Association for the Advancement of Colored People (NAACP), as well as public-interest law groups such as the Native American Rights Fund, and initiated its own projects such as the Energy Policy Project.

Bureaucracy

Even though many **non-profit organizations** are relatively small and have little organizational structure, some are larger and form bureaucracies. The modern understanding of bureaucracies goes back to Max Weber, who defined them as **organizations** with the following characteristics: activities are divided into a systematic division of labour; employees are selected and promoted on the basis of professional and technical competence; positions and the job descriptions they entail are arranged into a hierarchy; written rules provide guidelines for best practice and job performance; records are kept on administrative decisions, rules and guidelines, and organizational activities; officers are entrusted with responsibilities and receive a salary in return, but they cannot appropriate the positions and offices they occupy.

Weber's central argument was that bureaucracy is best suited for stable, routine task environments. For example, if the task can be divided into a process of separate and relatively distinct steps, if the volume and the nature of the task are stable and predictable, and if the performance of office holders can be easily monitored and translated into reporting requirements, then bureaucracy is a suitable organizational form. Motor-vehicle registration, health-care administration, insurance companies, social-service providers and the Catholic Church are examples of bureaucracies. It is important to keep in mind that for-profits, non-profits and public agencies can be bureaucracies. It is the task environment that matters, and not organizational form in terms of profit status or ownership.

Conversely, bureaucracy is less suited for organizations in changing task environments with high degrees of uncertainty. Examples include the computer industry, research and development, disaster relief agencies, or theatre companies. Of course, elements of bureaucracy, e.g. written rules, formal job descriptions and performance criteria, and hierarchies exist in most organizations. The difference between a bureaucratic versus a non-bureaucratic organization is one of degree, and not a dichotomy. Indeed, organizational age and size are closely related to the extent of bureaucratization: larger organizations tend to have more bureaucratic elements, in particular a more formal administration, and older organizations tend to be more routinized and stable in their task performance.

Burial Associations

Burial associations and similar entities, such as cremation associations, exist in most parts of the world and are a widespread organizational form to provide for the financial and social implications of death, in particular among the poor in developing countries, and historically also among the working classes of 19th century Europe and the USA. Burial societies function basically as a mutual savings and insurance association among members who join voluntarily to make regular contributions to a death fund in return for dignified funeral services and family support. Burial associations tend to benefit from **tax exemption**. (See **Mutuality**.)

Business Associations

Business associations are **non-profit organizations** that serve one or more lines of business, branch or industry, and whose members are typically business firms, proprietors, executives and **trustees**. In market economies, most firms belong to one or more business associations. In the USA, there are over 65,000 **organizations** classified as business associations under Section 501(c)(6) of the Internal Revenue Code. Business associations fulfil a number of roles and collective needs, in particular setting educational standards, certification requirements and performance criteria, addressing ethical issues and establishing rules of conduct. They also represent the collective interest of the business in public relations, and carry out **lobbying** on behalf of the industry at all levels of government. Organizational forms similar to business associations are crafts, chambers of commerce, **professional associations** and **guilds**.

Business Plans

A business plan is a document describing how an **organization** intends to implement a **mission** and set of objectives, usually over a period of several years. It is based on a set of assumptions of how the organization will operate and create value around its stated mission and sets out the needs, rationale, **governance** and financing of the organization. Business plans are generally prepared as part of the start-up of an organization; however, many organizations update their business plans on a somewhat regular basis to incorporate results of **strategic planning** processes.

Bylaws

Bylaws are the rules governing the internal operation of a non-profit corporation or association. Bylaws often set out the methods for the selection of the members of its **board of directors** and officers, as well as their duties; the creation of committees; and the conduct of meetings. These should not be confused with the **articles of organization**, which typically give only the basic legal structure of the **organization**.

C

CAF – *see* **Charities Aid Foundation**

Call for Proposals

A call for proposals is a written text calling on interested parties to submit proposals for a specific project or a specific pool of funds. Such a call for proposals, also referred to as request for proposals or RFP, typically defines the necessary specifications to prepare and submit a proposal, e.g. thematic priorities, deadlines, structure of proposal, etc. Some calls are widely publicized and addressed to any interested party, while others are of more limited scope, sent to a smaller audience of eligible parties. This tool is used by **foundations** and other types of grant-making **non-profit organizations**, as well as governmental and intergovernmental agencies.

Campaigns, Fundraising

A fundraising campaign is an organized, planned effort to raise a specified amount of money for a specified purpose within a specified period of time. Types of campaigns include the **capital campaign**, which is conducted for special projects, e.g. construction of a building, purchase of major equipment, or **endowment**, and the annual campaign, which is held at approximately the same time every year, typically for **revenue** to cover general expenses.

Canadian International Development Agency (CIDA)

Agence Canadienne de Développement International (ACDI)

Established in 1968, CIDA is the Canadian federal agency responsible for planning and implementing 80% of Canada's development co-operation, with the aim of reducing poverty and contributing to a more secure, equitable, and prosperous world. It works with an increasing number of partners, including **NGOs**, think-tanks and universities, to administer a wide variety of aid programmes across the developing world. The agency is represented in the federal cabinet by the Minister for International Co-operation.

Website: www.acdi-cida.gc.ca

Capacity-Building

Capacity-building refers to a process or set of activities (interventions) intended to enhance the target's ability to evaluate and address problems and to build effectiveness and **sustainability**. The set of interventions depends on the target, which could include an **organization** or government agency, or even an entire community or country.

The concept of capacity-building in **non-profit organizations**, for example, is similar to the concept of organizational development, organizational effectiveness or organizational performance management in for-profits. Organization-oriented capacity-building typically focuses on the organization's skills and capabilities, such as **leadership**, management, finance and **fundraising**, programmes and **evaluation**. Capacity-building is facilitated through the provision of a broad range of support activities, including granting operating funds, granting management development funds, providing training and development sessions or funds to participate in them, providing coaching, offering specific technical assistance and supporting collaboration with other organizations, among others.

Capacity-building is also used in the international development field to refer to work at both the micro or community level and the macro policy or country level. At the community level, a variety of training, technical assistance, and related activities can be implemented to increase the ability and willingness of community members to initiate projects, programmes or ventures; to organize them; and to keep them running. The resulting body of talent, skill and experience, known as community organizational capacity, is both the key product and the driving force behind the community's development.

The notion of country or governmental capacity-building is necessarily more complex. As at the organizational level, however, the process focuses on human, technological, organizational, institutional and resource capabilities. It entails the creation of an **enabling** environment with appropriate policy and legal frameworks to allow organizations, institutions and agencies to enhance their capacities; organizational development, including both the design of appropriate management structures and processes and the development of partnerships and other relationships; and human resources development, equipping individuals with the understanding, skills and access to information, knowledge and training that enables them to perform effectively.

Capital Campaigns

A capital campaign is a **fundraising** programme for major capital projects or an **endowment,** typically to augment the **organization**'s physical infrastructure, to acquire equipment, or to accumulate some other capital **assets**. A practice rooted in **religion,** i.e. funds for churches, synagogues, or mosques, and adopted by 19th-century charities, it has become a major and professionalized tool by which large **non-profit organizations** build endowments and special purpose funds parallel to **revenue** needs for ongoing operations. They are most prominent among schools and universities, museums, concert halls and other cultural institutions such as monuments, but are increasingly adopted in most fields of charitable activity, and have become a sign of competition in the **non-profit sector** for **donor** funds. Capital campaigns are usually organized as intensive, time-limited efforts with dedicated events such as fundraising dinners and other social events.

CARE

Founded in the mid-1940s in the USA and Canada following the Second World War to provide relief packages to war victims in Europe, CARE has evolved into one of the world's largest humanitarian relief confederations, headquartered in Brussels. Each of its 12 national member **organizations** is an autonomous **NGO** organized under the laws of its own country. The confederation's members engage in development and rehabilitation programmes to address the causes of poverty; emergency response programming; **advocacy** for effective development policies; and building diverse constituencies to support CARE's vision. As the organization's **mission** broadened, the meaning behind the letters of the acronym CARE changed from 'Cooperative for American Remittances to Europe' to 'Cooperative Assistance and Relief Everywhere'.

Website: www.care.org

Caritas Internationalis

Established in 1950 and based in the Vatican City, Caritas Internationalis is a confederation of 162 Catholic relief, development and social service **organizations** working in over 200 countries and territories to assist the poor and oppressed. Caritas Internationalis serves as a co-ordinating body for its member organizations and mobilizes their responses to emergencies. It also studies the problems arising from poverty; advocates its members' positions particularly with regard to **social justice** at the international level; and collaborates with other international aid and development organizations. Caritas has consultative status with a number of international organizations, including ECOSOC (United Nations) and UNICEF.

Website: www.caritas.org

Carlsbergfondet

Carlsberg Foundation

The Carlsbergfondet was originally founded in 1876 by Danish brewer Jacob Christian Jacobsen to promote the growth of the natural and social sciences in Denmark, to continue the work of the Carlsberg Laboratory, and to establish the Museum of National History at Frederiksborg Castle. It merged with the Tuborg Foundation in 1991. The Foundation works primarily in the fields of science and the arts.

Website: www.carlsbergfondet.dk

Carnegie, Andrew (1835–1919)

Born in Scotland, Andrew Carnegie and his family immigrated to the USA in 1848. Having worked at various odd jobs in his youth, Carnegie went on to make shrewd investments, establishing in 1865 the Carnegie Steel Company and becoming one of the wealthiest men of his time. As he explained in 'The Gospel of Wealth' (1889), Carnegie believed in the moral duty of the rich to give away their fortunes, giving away more than US $350m. personally and through the **Carnegie Corporation of New York**, founded in 1911. His particular interests included adult education (Carnegie Mellon University), the establishment of free public libraries (over 2,500 built) and performing arts (Carnegie Hall). (See also **Carnegie Endowment for International Peace**.)

The Carnegie Corporation of New York

The Carnegie Corporation of New York was created in 1911 by **Andrew Carnegie** as a **grant-making foundation** to promote 'the advancement and diffusion of knowledge and understanding'. Carnegie's bequest stipulated that the majority of **grants** must benefit the people of the USA, although 7.4% may be allocated to countries that are, or have been, members of the British Commonwealth. Andrew Carnegie intentionally created a broad **mission** statement in order that the Corporation evolve and adapt to the changing circumstances and needs of the world and its **beneficiaries**. In the 21st century, the Corporation focuses its grant-making on education, international peace and security, international development and strengthening US **democracy**.

Website: www.carnegie.org

The Carnegie Endowment for International Peace

Established in 1910 with a US $10m. **gift** from **Andrew Carnegie**, the Carnegie Endowment for International Peace is dedicated to improving co-operation among nations and promoting active international engagement by the USA. In his **deed** of gift, Carnegie challenged trustees to use the fund to 'hasten the abolition of international war'. The Endowment does not make **grants**, but rather conducts and disseminates research, convenes decision-makers, establishes international networks, and if necessary, creates new institutions. The Endowment publishes *Foreign Policy,* a leading international politics and economics journal with readers in over 120 countries.

Website: www.ceip.org

Categorical Constraints

'Categorical constraint' is a term used in the political theory of **non-profit organizations**, and is closely related to the **heterogeneity theory** and the notion of government failure. According to James Douglas, who introduced the concept in the 1980s, the democratic state is constrained more than **voluntary associations** in ensuring that goods and services are supplied and distributed fairly and equitably. Furthermore, the democratic state is constitutionally required to treat all citizens equally before the law, whereas **voluntary** organizations face no such constraints. The universalizing demands on democratic government, particularly in the development of the **welfare state**, put categorical constraints on government action, and hence open opportunities for voluntary organizations in the provision of quasi-**public goods** in heterogeneous societies.

Catholic Committee Against Hunger (CCFD)

Created in 1961 after decolonization, CCFD is a French **NGO** devoted to promoting rural and social development projects, mainly in black Africa, as well as fair trade for craft products from developing countries. While Third World development assistance represents CCFD's main **mission**, it is also involved in relief and emergency aid. Linked to the Catholic Church, its main **revenue** source is **individual giving**, especially during Lent. Of its US $37m. **budget**, only 10% comes from government sources. CCFD employs 180 salaried employees and benefits from substantial volunteer involvement and networks of grassroots **organizations** in many developing countries.

Cause-Related Marketing

Cause-related marketing (CRM) refers to commercial activity in which a **non-profit organization** enters into an alliance with a for-profit company to market an image, product or service for mutual benefit. Cause-related marketing campaigns vary in terms of scope and design, types of non-profit partners, and the nature of the relationships between companies and their marketing partners. In the most common type of relationship, also known as a **commercial co-venture**, a company might donate a portion of each purchase made by its customers during a specific period of time to the non-profit entity. An example is the American Express Corporation's initiative to support the lending and training programmes of microenterprise development **NGOs** by, among other elements, allocating 1% of all spending by holders of the Community Business Card. Not all CRM campaigns channel funds to non-profits; some engage principally in educational or awareness-building activities.

Centralization

Centralization can be defined as the act of concentrating power in a central **organization**. In political terms, this centralization of power is made by the central government. The historical roots of centralization in Europe trace back to the Roman Empire, but its modern philosophical origin are in the Enlightenment period, and the thought of Montesquieu, Diderot and **Rousseau.** Rousseau's idea of the general will is the justification for political centralization and the ideology of the 'statist' French Revolution. According to **Marx** and Engels in the *Communist Manifesto*: 'The bourgeoisie has concentrated property in a few hands; the consequence of this was political centralization. Independent provinces with separate interests, laws, governments and systems of taxation became lumped together into one nation... with one government, one code of laws, one frontier.'

A centralized State allows only for limited local power or intermediary interest groups. The centralized State considers that it has a monopoly over public interest concerns, and so **voluntary associations** and **foundations** tend to be viewed with suspicion and either repressed or strictly controlled. Conversely decentralization, which is the spread of power away from the centre to the local branches of government, is favourable to **non-profit organizations** either according to the **subsidiarity principle** or through local partnerships between local governments and the **non-profit sector**. Recently, **new public management** has become a key method of decentralization.

Centre for Advancement of Philanthropy

Established in 1986 in India, the Centre for Advancement of Philanthropy provides resources, guidance and assistance to a wide range of philanthropic institutions in the areas of **charity law**, taxation, resource mobilization, human resource development and effective management. The Centre has a **membership** base of some 400 corporate bodies, **grant-making foundations**, **NGOs** and **philanthropy** professionals. The Centre conducts seminars and training courses; offers technical assistance; publishes a bi-monthly journal on current issues in philanthropy; acts as an information **clearing-house**; and undertakes research, monitors public policy and advocates before the government and the media on behalf of India's philanthropic sector.

Website: www.capindia.org

Centre of Documentation on Foundations – *see* Centro di Documentazione sulle Fondazioni

Centro di Documentazione sulle Fondazioni
Centre of Documentation on Foundations

Founded in 1996 by the **Fondazione Giovanni Agnelli**, the Centro di Documentazione sulle Fondazioni (Centre of Documentation on Foundations) is a research centre specifically designed to track the rapid development of the Italian foundation sector. It monitors the activities of the sector, identifies needs, records trends and monitors any changes in government policy and regulations. It also seeks to build a network and develop relationships among both domestic and international foundations, scholars, government entities and the **third sector**. The Centre offers a database on foundations, maintains a library and publishes a newsletter.

Website: www.fondazioni.it

Centro Mexicano para la Filantropía, AC (CEMEFI)
Mexican Centre for Philanthropy

Established in 1988, the Centro Mexicano para la Filantropía serves as a resource for those committed to philanthropic activity in Mexico. Its members include **non-profit organizations**, corporations, **corporate foundations** and individuals. Member services range from technical assistance in organizational development to a newsletter and information centre. More generally, CEMEFI conducts and disseminates research on the Mexican **non-profit sector**, recognizes socially responsible companies through an annual ceremony, and promotes **volunteering** and charitable giving, among its other activities, to generate a culture of **philanthropy** in Mexico.

Website: www.cemefi.org

Challenge Grants

A challenge grant is a **grant** offered on condition that other grants or **gifts** be mobilized on some prescribed formula, e.g. two dollars to every one dollar raised from other sources, usually within a specified time. Such a grant is made with the objective of encouraging others to give (see **leverage**) as well as encouraging the recipient to continue mobilizing other resources. A challenge grant differs from a **matching grant** in an important respect: because a challenge grant is based on a formula, the amount of money that the recipient **organization** realizes from such a grant may vary widely, depending upon how successful that organization is in meeting the challenge. Matching grants, however, usually award a clearly defined amount and require that a specified sum be obtained before any award is made.

Chalmers, Floyd (1898–1993)

A high school 'dropout' who started his career in publishing during the First World War service, Chalmers eventually joined Maclean–Hunter, the Toronto-based publisher of *Maclean's*, which he elevated to Canadian national significance in his nearly sixty years of service as, among other roles, president and chairman. Canada's 'cultural patron saint', Chalmers made contributions to theatre, opera, music, dance and arts education with donations of money and especially his time and energy. In 1979, Chalmers transferred the **assets** and administration of the Floyd S. Chalmers Foundation, now the Chalmers Fund, to the Ontario Arts Council, establishing the Council's first major capital holding.

Charitable Choice

In the USA, 'charitable choice' refers to a provision (Section 104) in the 1996 Personal Responsibility and Work Opportunity Reconciliation Act that allows religious entities to compete for state Temporary Assistance to Needy Families **grants** without the need to establish separately incorporated **Section 501(c)(3) non-profit organizations**. Previously, religious congregations were barred from receiving public funds, but under Section 104, they became eligible to receive **subsidies** to provide aid to welfare clients without altering their character or internal **governance**. More specifically, religious **organizations** may retain religious symbols in areas where publicly-funded service programmes take place, utilize religious criteria in hiring staff to run these programmes, and use religious concepts in providing services. However, religious organizations are prohibited from using government funds for worship, religious instruction, or proselytizing. They may not discriminate against welfare recipients on the basis of **religion** or their refusal to participate in religious activities; and clients who object to receiving services from religious entities must be provided with secular alternatives.

Charitable Contribution Deductions

The charitable contribution deduction is the portion of the value of a **gift** of property or money that the law allows a **donor** to deduct from its taxable income. The rationale behind such favourable tax treatment of charitable contributions lies in the notion that such gifts devoted to public purposes help offset expenses the government would have otherwise had to make out of tax revenues. Such deductions are available in many countries. Cross-country differences range from the type of **organizations** or purposes eligible to receive tax-deductible contributions (e.g. **Section 501(c)(3)** organizations in the USA; public utility corporations in France; exclusively charitable purposes in the UK), to limits on the deductible amount (in Hungary, no limits; in Taiwan, 20% of income for individuals, 10% of profits for firms), to the persons or entities entitled to take such deductions (e.g. individuals or corporations).

Charities Aid Foundation (CAF)

The Charities Aid Foundation was formed in 1924 in the UK as the Charities Department of the National Council of Social Service, to encourage more efficient giving to **charity**, and was launched as an independent foundation in 1974. Some 30 years later, CAF handles over €1,400m. a year for **donors** and **voluntary-sector organizations**, and has programmes and offices throughout the world. CAF is both a **grant-making foundation**, awarding **grants** to **non-profit organizations**, and an **operating foundation**, providing **capacity-building** and other assistance as well as encouraging debate about non-profit activity through its research, conferences and seminars.

Website: www.cafonline.org

Charity

The common, broad understanding of charity is the **voluntary** giving to those in need, which includes **alms**-giving, the institution or **organization** involved in helping the needy, as well as notions of kindness, benevolence, mercy and tolerance in judging others. In more narrow terms, charity means the relief of poverty or personal distress.

Charity has religious roots, and as a theme or principle is present in virtually all religions. It is one of the three theological virtues of **Christianity** (faith, hope and charity, 1 Corinthians 13:13) to perfect one's love of God and humanity. It is also the third of the Five Pillars of **Islam**, where charity (*Zadaqah*) differs from alms-giving, which is obligatory. An important principle of Islam is that everything belongs to God, and that wealth is therefore held by human beings in trust. The word *zakat* means both 'purification' and 'growth'.

The institution of charity is regulated rather differently in common- and civil-law countries. While charity is rarely defined legally, common-law countries treat charity as part of the law of **trusts**. In countries like the UK or Australia, a charity is essentially an instrument for carrying out the purpose of a charitable trust, and the identification of charitable purposes reaches back to the Preamble to the **1601 Statute of Charitable Uses** (see **Charity law**).

Charity as a term also emphasizes the support **non-profit organizations** receive from private charitable donations and assumes a certain motivation on behalf of both **donor** and recipient. But private charitable contributions do not constitute the only, or even the major, source of their **revenue**; and many non-profit organizations are not 'charitable' but advocate special interests or seek to promote their members' interests through **lobbying**. As a result, the notion of charity as an adequate concept for the much broader array of non-profit activity continues to be challenged. In the early 20th century, the debate was over the distinction between charity (as temporary relief from social problems) and **philanthropy** (as attacking the roots of such problems); today the discussions are about the replacement of charity by the broader concept of **public benefit**.

In 2002, in line with this broader notion, and in an important departure from a narrower concept of charity laid down in charity law, the UK's Cabinet Office suggested that a charity should be defined as an organization which provides public benefit and which has one or more of the following purposes: the prevention and relief of poverty; the advancement of education; the advance-ment of **religion**; the advancement of health (including the prevention and relief of sickness, disease or human suffering); social and community advancement (including the care, support and protection of the aged, people with a disability, children and young people); the advancement of culture, arts and heritage; the advancement of amateur sport; the promotion of **human rights**, conflict resolution and reconciliation; the advancement of environmental protection and improvement; and other purposes beneficial to the community.

Charity Bank

Charity Bank is the first and only general charity to have banking status in the UK. The Bank offers savings accounts for individuals and companies, and lends these resources to charities and **social enterprises** in communities. Its **mission** is to develop financial products for charities and to show that charities and community groups are capable borrowers and that investing in them is sound business practice. An outgrowth of the Investors in Society pilot programme launched by the **Charities Aid Foundation (CAF),** the Bank is supported by banking institutions, other charitable **trusts** and organizations and the UK government.

Website: www.charitybank.org

Charity Law

Charity is an English common law concept that identifies a class of **non-profit organization** by purposes. In contrast, the European civil-law tradition's regulation of similar **organizations** is generally based on the legal structure of the organization rather than its purposes and has a statutory base (see **Civil-law systems**).

The English legal definition stems from the **1601 Statute of Charitable Uses** (Statute of Elizabeth), whose Preamble set out the following charitable purposes:

'The relief of the aged, impotent and poor people; the maintenance of sick and maimed soldiers and mariners, schools of learning, free schools and scholars in universities; the repair of bridges, ports, havens, causeways, churches, sea-banks and highways; the education and preferment of orphans; the relief, stock or maintenance of houses of correction; the marriages of poor maids, the supportation, aid and help of young tradesmen, handicraftsmen and persons decayed; the relief or redemption of prisoners or captives; and the aid or ease of any poor inhabitants concerning payment of fifteens, setting out of soldiers and other taxes.'

The Preamble was not, even in 1601, an exhaustive list of charitable purposes as the advancement of **religion** was omitted. Following centuries of case law, the common law understanding developed. A consolidating milestone was Pemsel's case in 1891, in which Lord Macnaghten classified the categories of charitable purposes under four heads:

'Charity in its legal sense comprises four principal divisions: trusts for the relief of poverty; trusts for the advancement of education; trusts for the advancement of religion; and trusts for other purposes beneficial to the community not falling under any of the preceding heads.' A charitable purpose must also be for the **public benefit**.

The main statute for England and Wales regarding the regulation of charities is the Charities Act 1993 (UK), under which the registration of charities is administered by the Charity Commission for England and Wales according to the common-law definition.

The common-law definition of **charity** has been adopted in other common-law systems to varying degrees, and cases are often judicially noted across jurisdictions. In Ireland, charities are regulated by the Charities Act 1961, as amended by the Charities Act 1973 where the common-law definition applies. The Scottish common law has traditionally not regarded charity as a term of legal significance until Part 1 of the Law Reform (Miscellaneous Provisions) (Scotland) Act 1990 introduced major reforms to the regulation of charities in Scotland. Charities in New Zealand are regulated by the Charitable Trusts Act 1957 (NZ), which provides that the common-law meaning of charity applies.

Australia and Canada are federations where the constitutional power over charities rests with the states or provinces. However, both federal governments' jurisdiction with respect to income tax has ensured that the definition given to charities under the federal taxation statute is of considerable importance and follows the common law. Similarly in the USA, the individual states retain constitutional responsibility with respect to the regulation of charities. While there is a plethora of state legislation regulating charities, most rely upon a modified common-law definition of charity or adopt the definition contained in **Section 501(c)(3)** of the federal Internal Revenue Code (or some modification of it and the common law).

Under the US Internal Revenue Code, tax-exempt status is available for many types of organizations, including those organizations described in Section 501(c)(3), which are commonly referred to under the general heading of 'charitable organizations'. The exempt organization may be a corporation, **community chest,** fund or **foundation** organized and operated exclusively for religious, charitable, scientific, testing for public safety, literary, or educational purposes. Indeed, the regulations determining tax-exempt status have extended the definition of charity beyond the traditional four elements of poverty, education, religion and general community benefit. The regulations provide that:

'The term 'charitable' is used in Section 501(c)(3) in its generally accepted legal sense and is, therefore, not to be construed as limited by the separate enumeration in Section 501(c)(3) of other tax-exempt purposes which may fall within the broad outlines of charity as developed by judicial decisions. Such term includes: Relief of the poor and distressed or of the underprivileged; advancement of religion; advancement of education or science; erection or maintenance of public buildings, monuments, or works; lessening of the burdens of government; and promotion of social welfare by organizations designed to accomplish any of the above purposes; or (i) to lessen neighbourhood tensions; (ii) to eliminate prejudice and discrimination; (iii) to defend human and civil rights secured by law; or (iv) to combat community deterioration and juvenile delinquency.'

Barbados is the only common-law country in the world that has archived a major statutory redefinition of charity. In Barbados, the term 'charity' is defined, in part, as a body that 'is established for charitable objects or purposes, and is intended to and does operate for the public benefit'. 'Charitable purposes' is defined by means of a non-exhaustive list covering 26 main purposes and 14 amplifying sub-headings.

Charter 77 Foundation

The Charter 77 Foundation was established in 1978 in Sweden to support the Charter 77 movement and other independent citizen activities in then communist Czechoslovakia. It distributed over 3m. Swedish kronor (US $90,000) collected from **donors** in Western Europe and the USA, most notably from **George Soros**, to Czechoslovak political activists, intellectuals and artists between 1978—1989. In 1990 the Foundation moved its headquarters to Czechoslovakia, closing its Swedish office in 1999. Since 1990 the Foundation has played an innovative role, and has expanded its operations to the social and health care areas.

Christianity

Christianity is a **religion** based on a belief in Jesus Christ and individual salvation, but with wide variants in theological emphasis, rituals and institutionalization. The tendency of Christian religions to create **organizations** to further their religious and secular objectives has found many expressions over the centuries: from organized **alms**-giving, to monastic orders and missionary societies responsible for poor relief, education and health services, to today's clinics and hospitals, schools and universities, and community centres run by the church. The organizational expansion of Christianity is based on the strong missionary element in most Christian thinking, particularly among the Protestant churches, that encourages active conversion as part of a universal theology.

The tension between church and state is at the core of Christianity's drive to use organizations as a means to further its religious and secular ends. The long-term disengagement of church and state after the Reformation coincided with the colonial expansion of European powers in Latin America (Catholicism), in Africa (Protestantism, Catholicism), and to a lesser extent in Asia. Increasingly, churches, freed from direct control of state authorities, could follow their entrepreneurial aspirations under the banner of religious freedom. Particularly the Jesuit order, in the case of Latin America, and the 19th century Protestant churches in Africa and Asia organized vast missionary efforts in the colonial possessions, which often laid the groundwork for the future educational and health-care systems in those countries.

Church Tax

In several countries, including Germany, Switzerland and Sweden, certain authorized (official) churches have been granted the right to levy a tax on church members. The church tax has long historical roots, and in its modern form developed in the late 19th and early 20th centuries from a political compromise between the emerging secular state and religious powers over the division of responsibilities in the fields of education, social services and health. The level of church tax and the method of collecting it tend to differ from one country to another. In Germany, for example, the church tax is generally collected by the local tax authority, and deducted from an employee's paycheck as income tax is. In practice, the church tax system provides those parts of the **non-profit sector** linked to the official churches with a stable source of income. At the same time, it continues to be politically sensitive, and is generally opposed by advocates of a clearer separation of church and state.

Church Tax Examination

In the USA, the Church Audit Procedures Act lays out the circumstances under which the US Internal Revenue Service (IRS) may investigate a church and the procedures for doing so. According to these rules, if a high-level IRS official has a reasonable belief that the **organization** either does not qualify for **tax exemption** as a church, is engaged in unrelated business, or is otherwise engaged in taxable activities, written notice is given that a church tax inquiry will commence: this can run for a maximum term of 90 days. If the inquiry does not produce conclusive results or if the organization does not respond, a more thorough church tax examination may be conducted. In an examination, the IRS is empowered to audit church records, but only to the extent necessary to determine liability for, and the amount of, any federal tax.

Citizenship

Citizenship has two related meanings. First, citizenship is a legal concept which refers to the legal status of a natural person in respect to a state or nation, and is gained by meeting the legal requirements of a national, state, or local government. The classic approach to modern citizenship is the republican one, which emphasises the double function of citizenship: governing and being governed at the same time, as opposed to historical notions that saw citizens as subjects to the crown or some other aristocratic or theocratic institutions. A nation grants certain rights and privileges to its citizens. In return, citizens are expected to obey their country's laws. Most persons have a single citizenship but some have more than one.

A citizen of the USA, for example, is a native-born, foreign-born, or naturalized person who owes allegiance to the USA and who is entitled to its protection. In addition to the naturalization process, the USA recognizes the US citizenship of individuals according to two fundamental principles: *jus soli*, or right of birthplace, and *jus sanguinis*, or right of blood. In Canada, the concept of citizenship stems from the Citizenship Act. Although the Act does not provide a definition of citizenship, it does note that both Canadian-born and naturalized citizens are entitled to the same rights, powers and privileges and are subject to the same obligations, duties and liabilities.

The 'value' of citizenship varies across countries. In some, citizenship can mean the right to vote, to hold government offices and to associate freely, but citizens may not automatically have the right to social benefits such as unemployment insurance payments, nor are they entitled to education, health care or old-age pensions beyond some minimal standard.

It is the second sense, however, in which citizenship has entered the field of **civil society** and **philanthropy**: the active participation, and caring for, a defined local or national community. In addition to republican notions, this sense of citizenship includes civic virtues like sacrifice for the community and willing obedience to law. It puts emphasis on the self-governing character of citizenship. Having engaged citizens facilitates a sense of trust and social inclusion that is seen as essential for the functioning of modern societies. For analysts like Putnam, citizens who join groups and **associations** generate a vast and complex network of affiliation, which enhances democratic control and **governance**. In this sense, the notion of citizenship is closely related to the **social capital** debate in the social sciences. **Active citizenship** is a key source of social, cultural and political **innovation**, linking the future of **democracy** to its constant renewal through citizen participation and engagement.

These debates also tie in with notions of corporate citizenship, whereby businesses seek to become responsive and responsible members of the communities in which they operate. Many larger transnational corporations have established 'citizenship committees' that seek to provide leadership for corporate philanthropy and monitor corporate performance in relation to community interests.

Civic Culture

As a term, civic culture refers to a country's political culture, characterized by most citizens' acceptance of the authority of the state, and a general belief in active political participation and social engagement in civic duties. The term, introduced by Gabriel Almond and Sidney Verba's influential 1963 book, *The Civic Culture*, was prompted by concerns about the long-term political stability of Western democracies. Specifically, the civic culture model suggested that citizens had to be informed about political issues, involved in the political process, trusting of major social and political institutions, and concerned about the common good, and that they had to be instilled with democratic attitudes for a stable democratic government to sustain itself over time. The term is sometimes used interchangeably with **civil society** and related to notions of **social capital** and interpersonal and institutional trust.

Civic Leagues

A civic league is a community action **organization** engaged in promoting civic betterment and social improvement. In the USA, they are classified as **social welfare organizations** and are exempt from federal income tax under Internal Revenue Code **Section 501(c)(4)**.

Civicus—World Alliance for Citizen Participation

Established in 1993, Civicus is an international alliance of some 650 networks, associations, research institutions, foundations, corporate grant-makers and individuals in 110 countries. Its **mission** is to nurture the growth and protection of citizen action throughout the world, especially in areas where participatory **democracy** and citizens' **freedom of association** are threatened. From its headquarters in Johannesburg, South Africa, as well as its offices in Washington, DC and London, Civicus focuses on five major programmes: Civil Society Watch, the **Civil Society Index**, a Legitimacy and **Transparency** Programme, a Participatory **Governance** Programme and a biennial World Assembly.

Website: www.civicus.org

Civil Disobedience

Civil disobedience is a deliberate, open and non-violent political act involving disobeying governmental authority on grounds of moral objection. It may be practised by individuals, groups or masses of people, who are willing to accept the legal consequences. The term was first used by H. D. Thoreau in his essay *On the Duty of Civil Disobedience* (1849). Examples include illegal gatherings, picketing and 'sit-ins'. While the best known practitioner may be Gandhi, the practice has been used by citizens' movements world-wide, including anti-regime protests in former Soviet bloc countries and anti-globalization demonstrations led by groups such as **ATTAC**.

Civil Law

The term 'civil law', used in contrast with common law, refers to a legal system inspired by old Roman Law, the primary feature of which was that laws were codified following the basic principle that all citizens should be provided with an accessible and written collection of the laws that apply to them and that judges must follow. The civil-law system could be considered disadvantageous for the organizational development of **civil society** institutions, since rights are not recognized and organizational forms are not permitted unless they are codified. However, once such a right is established or such an organizational form is allowed, it can be said that it is easier to protect. Unlike in common-law systems, cases are decided by an expert judge applying the law as written in the code, not based on precedent. Most European countries and their former colonies, Scotland, the province of Québec and the US state of Louisiana are governed by civil law.

Civil-Law Foundation

In civil-law countries such as Germany, Austria and the Netherlands, the essence of a **foundation**, as a legal personality, is its **endowment**, which is the fundamental difference between a foundation and the other major type of **non-profit organization**, the member-based **voluntary association**. In most civil-law countries, however, legal definitions of foundations are usually very broad. In the German and Austrian cases, for instance, the Civil Code falls short of an explicit definition, but mentions three necessary characteristics: Foundations need to have (i) one or more specific purposes; (ii) an asset base commensurate with the need for the actual pursuit of the purpose(s); and (iii) some kind of organizational structure for carrying out activities. Similarly broad is the Dutch legal definition, according to which foundations are **organizations** without members with the purpose of realizing goals specified in their charters by using property allocated to such objectives.

Civil-Law Systems

Civil-law (as opposed to common-law) systems are based on the fundamental distinction between private law, which regulates rights and responsibilities among individuals and private legal personalities, and public law (e.g. administrative and fiscal law), which deals with the relations between individuals and the state, public agencies and public law corporations. The central point is that the state is regarded as a legal actor—*sui generis* and in possession of its own legal subjectivity—that requires laws and regulations qualitatively different from those addressing private individuals.

The civil-law systems have two principal types of **organizations**: private law associations and corporations. To achieve legal personality, an association must be registered in some association registry which, depending on the country's administrative system, is typically maintained either locally, at city or county courts, or nationally, at the Ministry of the Interior. To register, an association must pursue a non-commercial objective and have a specified minimum number of members, a charter and a governing board. A non-registered association possesses no legal personality; the board legally represents it, and members are personally liable.

However, registration does not necessarily imply **tax exemption** for the organization. In most civil-law countries, the distinction between public and private law equates the state with the **public good** and puts the burden of proof of **public benefit** on private law associations only. As a result, the law around public benefit is more complex than in common-law countries and involves a legal act separate from registration. What is more, while many civil-law countries have relatively simple registration procedures for associations and corporations, the achievement of public benefit status is much more demanding. In France and Japan, for example, there are many more **non-profit organizations** than tax-exempt non-profit organizations.

Civil Society

The term 'civil society' has many different definitions, and there is little agreement on its precise meaning, though much overlap exists among core conceptual components. Definitions typically vary in the emphasis they put on some characteristics of civil society over others; some definitions primarily focus on aspects of state power, politics and individual freedom, and others more on economic functions and notions of **social capital** and cohesion. None the less, most analysts would probably agree with the statement that modern civil society is the sum of institutions, **organizations** and individuals located between the family, the state and the market, in which people associate voluntarily to advance common interests.

Civil society is primarily about the role of citizens and the society they constitute in relation to that of both the state and the market. The intellectual history of the term is closely intertwined with the notion of **citizenship**, the limits of state power and the foundation as well as the regulation of market economies. The prevailing modern view sees civil society as a sphere located between state and market—a buffer zone strong enough to keep both state and market in check, thereby preventing each from becoming too powerful and dominant. In the words of **Ernest Gellner**, civil society is the set of 'institutions, which is strong enough to counterbalance the state, and, whilst not preventing the state from fulfilling its role of keeper of peace and arbitrator between major interests, can, nevertheless, prevent the state from dominating and atomizing the rest of society'. Civil society is not a singular, monolithic, separate entity, but a sphere constituted in relation to both state and market, and indeed permeating both.

Civil society is the self-organization of society outside the stricter realms of state power and market interests. For **Jürgen Habermas**, civil society is made up of more or less spontaneously created associations, organizations and movements, which find, take up, condense and amplify the resonance of social problems in private life, and pass it on to the political realm or public sphere. **Ralf Dahrendorf** sees the concept of civil society as part of a classical liberal tradition, and characterized by the existence of autonomous organizations that are neither state-run nor otherwise directed from the central political power.

As a concept, civil society is essentially an intellectual product of 18th-century Europe, in which citizens sought to define their place in society independent of the aristocratic state at a time when the certainty of a status-based social order began to suffer irreversible decline. The early theorists of civil society welcomed these changes. For Adam Smith, trade and commerce among private citizens created not only wealth but also invisible connections among people, the bonds of trust and **social capital** in today's terminology. Others, like John Locke and **Alexis de Tocqueville**, saw civil society less in relation to the market but more in political terms and emphasized the importance of democratic association in everyday life as a base of a functioning polity. Friedrich Hegel sounded a more cautionary note about the self-organizing and self-regulatory capacity of civil society, and emphasized the need for the state to regulate society. For Hegel, state and civil society depend on each other, yet their relation is full of tensions and requires a complicated balancing act. The role of the state relative to civil society was also emphasized in the writings of Montesquieu, von Stein and other thinkers, who saw the **rule of law** as the essence of **state–society** and society–market relations.

In the 20th century, civil society became associated with notions of civility (Elias), popular participation and civic-mindedness (Verba), the public sphere (Habermas), social capital (**Putnam, Coleman**), culture (**Gramsci**) and community in the sense of **communitarianism** (**Etzioni**). The various concepts and approaches emphasize different aspects or elements of civil society: values and norms like tolerance in the case of civility; the role of the media and the intellectual; the connections among people and the trust they have in each other; the moral dimensions communities create and need; and the extent to which people constitute a common public space through participation and civic engagement.

The complexity of civil society and the many relations and intersections it has with the economy, the state and institutions like the family, the media or culture, make it not only possible but almost necessary to examine the concepts from different perspectives and orientations. Some analysts adopt an abstract, systemic view and see civil society as a macro-sociological attribute of societies, particular in the way state and society relate to each other. Others take on a more individualistic orientation and emphasize the notions of individual agency, citizenship, values and participation, using econometric and social network approaches in analysing civil society. There is also an institutional approach to studying civil society by looking at the size, scope and structure of organizations and associations, and the functions they perform. The different perspectives of civil society are not necessarily contradictory, nor are the various approaches to understanding it necessarily rival; on the contrary, they are often complementary and differ in emphasis, explanatory focus and policy implication rather than in principle.

Civil Society Index

The Civil Society Index (CSI), developed under the leadership of **Civicus**, is an action-research project that aims to assess the state of **civil society** in countries around the world, with a view to creating a knowledge base and an impetus for civil society strengthening initiatives. The CSI is initiated and implemented by, and for, civil society **organizations**, but also actively involves a broad range of **stakeholders**. The CSI tool assesses four dimensions of civil society (structure, environment, values and impact) and summarizes its findings in the graphical form of a diamond. The civil society diamond helps participants to visualize the current status of civil society where the CSI is applied and to develop appropriate strategies and actions to address emerging issues.

Clearing-Houses

The term 'clearing-house' has two meanings relevant to **philanthropy** and the **third sector**. The first refers to a clearing-house as a group of prospective **donors** that collaborate in determining actions and responses to local **fundraising** appeals. The second describes a service or **organization** established to promote and facilitate the exchange of information. As examples of the latter, the **Grupo de Fundaciones** (Argentina), the **Centre for Advancement of Philanthropy** (India), or the **Foundation Center** in New York maintain libraries and databases with relevant information about non-profits and the philanthropic sector in their countries.

Climate Action Network (CAN International)

The Climate Action Network is an international network of some 300 **NGOs**, both international (e.g. **Greenpeace** and **Friends of the Earth**) and local, working to mobilize governments and individuals to limit the effects of human-induced climate change. Established in 1989, CAN now has co-ordinating offices located in all the major regions of the world and works to co-ordinate information exchange and strategy among member NGOs. CAN's **vision** is to protect the atmosphere while allowing for sustainable and equitable development world-wide.

Website: www.climatenetwork.org

Club Goods

A club good is a **public good** that becomes excludable. In the economic analysis of clubs, pioneered by Buchanan (1965), collective consumption takes place but under the condition of an exclusion principle, such as a **membership** fee, which keeps non-members from benefiting. In this sense, club goods are public goods *sans* non-excludability, and the benefits arise for members primarily—if not exclusively—although positive **externalities** are possible. There are **economies of scale** in that additional members reduce the average cost of the club good, but additional members also lead to crowding. The notion of club goods can be applied to goods and services provided by **co-operatives**, **mutual societies** and **clubs**, but also by many kinds of membership-based and membership-supported **non-profit organizations**, residents' associations, community projects and neighbourhood schemes.

Clubs

Similar to **membership associations**, clubs are also membership-based **organizations** that tend, however, to be more exclusive and restrictive in their eligibility requirements, as in the case of country, sports and social clubs as well as fraternal lodges. In addition to any social functions, direct member control in clubs serves to protect either significant economic **assets** (e.g. club house, grounds) or access exclusivity. Assets are jointly owned by members, who also assume joint responsibility for maintenance and raising capital for improvements and expansions. In the USA, such clubs are tax-exempt to varying degrees, but are typically not considered charitable [see **Section 501(c)(3)**]. More generally, club membership is related to status-seeking and status-affirming behaviour (e.g. gentlemen's clubs in 19th-century London, country clubs in the USA, golf clubs in Europe), or part of a political culture, e.g. the revolutionary clubs in late 18th-century Paris. In economics, clubs are the producers of **club goods**.

Code of Ethics

A code of ethics is a statement of principles established by an **organization** and used to influence the professional conduct of its staff and members. Such a code of ethics is typically developed by a professional body or trade association, monitored by that body, and enforced by it, especially in fields for which little or no governmental regulation is in place. In general, members must adhere to these rules and regulations in order to remain in good standing with the organization. A code of ethics tends to be different from a **code of practice** or standards of practice in that the principles laid out in the code of ethics tend to be more idealistic.

Code of Practice

A code of practice is an agreement among members of a professional association, umbrella group, or a single **organization**, in which they agree to act in a certain way. Such codes are typically developed in professions or trades that are not regulated by a governmental institution. The term is often used synonymously with **code of ethics**. In other cases, a code of practice is distinguished from a code of ethics because its focus is on implementation, i.e. a set of rules and requirements for performing a task or set of tasks.

Collective Goods

'Collective good' is a term used in public choice theory and non-profit price theory, and is in many ways identical to the notion of a **public good**. If a collective good is the true output of a **non-profit organization**, i.e. closely related to its **mission** and objectives, it will be difficult to 'sell' in private markets because of the **free-rider problem** and difficulties in establishing some form of 'market' price. Examples include basic research, treating environmental pollution, or helping the poor. As a consequence, non-profit organizations involved in the provision of collective goods also engage in the production of **private goods**, use **subsidies** and enlist other sources to generate **revenue**.

Coluche (1944–1986)

Michel Colucci, known as Coluche, was born to a working-class family of Italian immigrants in France. He became a very popular author and actor in comedic TV sketches, poking fun at every kind of racial, social or sexist prejudice. He was struck by the contrast between the destruction of food produced in excess in Europe and the fact that many poor people do not have enough to eat. In 1985, one year before his accidental death, he founded *Les Restaurants du Cœur* (Restaurants of the Heart), an initiative which every winter delivers 60 million meals, feeding 550,000 persons, served by 40,000 volunteers.

Comic Relief

Launched live on British television on Christmas Day in 1985 from a refugee camp in Sudan, Comic Relief brought together comedians and entertainers for raising funds to fight poverty and social injustice in the UK and Africa. Comic Relief is best known for its organization of Red Nose Day, a UK-wide fundraiser held every two years that encourages citizens to don a red nose and do something silly to raise funds. The event is capped by a widely-viewed broadcast television show. Red Nose Day and Comic Relief's other activities are also used to raise awareness among the general public about key issues surrounding poverty, including unfair terms of trade and debt. Since its inception, Comic Relief has raised over £220 million.

Website: www.comicrelief.org.uk

Commensurate Test

The commensurate test is an assessment of whether an **organization** distributes funds for charitable purposes in an amount commensurate to its financial resources. The test is applied by the US Internal Revenue Service—primarily to **fundraising** organizations—to determine qualification for **Section 501(c)(3) tax exemption**. The test's purpose is to prevent organizations enjoying tax exemption from spending all their resources on personnel, administrative and similar costs without fulfilling a real charitable purpose. Because circumstances (e.g. labour costs, overheads or start-up costs) differ from organization to organization, there is no **mandatory pay-out requirement** (except for private foundations). Nevertheless, low distribution levels invite close scrutiny. Similar tests or guidelines are in effect in other jurisdictions and legal systems.

Commercial Co-Ventures

A commercial co-venture is an arrangement between a for-profit business and one or more charitable **organizations** in which the for-profit entity agrees to make a contribution to the charitable organization(s) in an amount either pre-determined or determined according to sales of the for-profit company's product or service, usually over a specific time period. An example is the Timberland clothing and shoe company's **marketing** of specially designed infant bootees. Timberland donates 50 cents from the sale of each pair to Share Our Strength, a US **non-profit organization** working to fight children's hunger in the USA and abroad. Such co-ventures are a type of **cause-related marketing**.

Commercial Fundraising Firms

A commercial fundraising firm is a company that regularly engages in **fundraising** activities on behalf of a third party, typically for a **non-profit**

organization or a particular client or cause, in exchange for compensation, usually a fee or percentage of the amount raised. Services offered range from telemarketing and direct mail to major **donor** campaigns.

Commercialization

A dominant force shaping the **non-profit sector** at the present time in a number of countries is the commercialization or marketization of non-profit services, which implies both a wider use of fees for service, charges and dues (and consequently a larger share of such earned income in the **revenue** mix), and the incorporation of business management techniques and planning tools.

While commercialization as such is nothing new, it is the scale of earned income that seems to have grown significantly throughout the 1990s. While integrating market impulses into non-profit operations can improve an **organization**'s revenue situation, it also comes with consequences that can fundamentally change the organization. Some argue that the non-profit sector has gained many advantages from a closer association with the market: a broader resource base, more diversified revenue and greater flexibility. At the same time, market pressures can undermine the value base of non-profits, and also threaten the sector's public support, i.e. reduce donations and political goodwill.

Some of the reasons propelling **non-profit organizations** towards commercialization include declining government financial support, slow growth in **private giving**, increased service demands from widely disparate population groups and growing competition from for-profit and other non-profit organizations. In response, non-profit organizations may seek to increase market-based income streams, in particular related and **unrelated business income**. With greater reliance on related and unrelated business income comes frequently a greater incorporation of market culture into the non-profit field.

Common-Law Foundations

Under common law, **foundations** typically take the form of a **trust**, which is (legally speaking) not an **organization**, but a relationship between property and trustees. Most common-law countries, including the UK and Australia, use this rudimentary legal definition and leave the actual development of foundation law to case law. One exception is the USA, which, in 1969, established a precise, though negative, definition: Foundations are tax-exempt organizations under **Section 501(c)(3)** of the International Revenue Code that are neither **public**

charities nor otherwise exempted organizations. This basically means that under American tax law, foundations are those charitable organizations that receive most of their resources from one source and are as such considered to be **donor**-controlled.

Commons

Generally speaking, a commons is a set of resources that a community recognizes as being accessible to any member and typically without cost. Historically, the commons refers to England's communal lands, which were owned by no one but where all had the right to graze their individually owned livestock. In what is known as the **tragedy of the commons**, each individual increased the amount of livestock knowing that he would gain while the environmental cost would be shared by all. The inevitable result was the destruction of the commons. Today, the term 'global commons' is used to refer to the natural and cultural cycles that underpin the functioning of such systems and that are considered to be threatened by similar abuse.

Communitarianism

The term 'communitarian' was first introduced in 1841, to mean 'of, pertaining to, or characteristic of a community'. Early sociologists such as Ferdinand Tönnies, **Emile Durkheim** and George Herbert Mead often analysed issues of a communitarian nature, although none used the term itself. Communitarianism is a social philosophy that favours social formulations of the public good. It is often contrasted with liberalism, which assumes that the public good should be determined by each individual. Communitarianism seeks to mitigate the excesses of individualism and rationalism and to encourage an ethic of social responsibility. Selzsnick and **Etzioni**, for example, attempt to rise above the liberal–communitarian debate in pointing out that the development of common values presupposes freely-consenting individuals. As such, to the extent that social institutions and policies are required, these should be based on **voluntary** agreements among the individuals involved, expressing their preferences. Communitarians view institutions and policies as reflecting in part values passed from generation to generation. These values become part of the self through internalization and are modfied by persuasion, religious or political indoctrination, **leadership** and moral dialogue.

Communitarianism has risen to prominence in recent decades and has been brought in close ideological proximity to particular notions of **civil society** and social participation. For example, Robert Bellah points out the importance of civic engagement and value orientation for a Good Society, which itself is modelled after some idealized American society. Etzioni stresses the importance of internal **democracy** in local communities to avoid relativism and oppressive values, and sees in communitarian ideas a stabilizing role in the self-reflection of modern societies.

Community-Based Organizations

The term 'community-based **organization**' (CBO) is a general term used to describe **non-profit organizations** engaged in social services that serve a particular geographic community; many **grassroots associations**, for instance, can be considered CBOs. Although there is no precise definition for what constitutes a CBO, defining features are that they are founded for a specific community, run by members of that community, and usually engage in activities such as social services and community organizing. CBOs generally form out of a need to improve community conditions and therefore often also engage in **advocacy**. Additionally, they often take the form of hybrid organizations, with a broader range of services provided. For example, a CBO may run a day-care centre, a job training programme, and a space for meetings/support groups and conduct community organizing to educate and mobilize people regarding community issues. Funding sources for CBOs are generally diverse, with some receiving support from foundations and others being awardees or subcontractors of government social service agencies.

Community Benefit Standard

The term 'community benefit standard' is used in the USA to describe the rationale by which the federal and several state governments judge whether to grant or maintain tax-exempt status for non-profit hospitals and other health-care providers. Originally, the non-profit designation and thus **tax exemption** stemmed from the role of non-profit hospitals in providing **charity** care. As government assumed a greater role in financing health care for the poor in the 1960s, the US Internal Revenue Service crafted an alternative standard, i.e. the 'community benefit' standard, which today can be met through a variety of activities in support of the broader community, including public health education, research, teaching, and needs assessments, as well as the more traditional subsidized or unreimbursed health care. Various US state governments have adopted the community benefit standard, adjusting it to local circumstances and attaching to it varying consequences relating to tax and other privileges. Similar guidelines are in effect in other legal systems.

Community Chests

A community chest typically refers to a **non-profit organization** or fund whose functions are to raise financial resources through an annual campaign for its member agencies and to allocate those resources, most often to local community groups. The idea of co-operative collecting for charitable purposes originated in Liverpool, England (1873), and, in the USA, in Denver (1887), but has spread to Canada, Hong Kong and elsewhere. The term 'community chest' was first used by **fundraising** efforts in Rochester, New York (USA) in 1919, leading to an expansion of community chests throughout the USA. The US national association of community chests, originally founded in 1927, is now known as **United Way** of America. More recently, the term has also been used to refer to small **grants** programmes administered by local groups in the UK and other similar community-based grant-making programmes.

Community Foundations

Banker and attorney **Frederick Harris Goff** was instrumental in creating the first community foundation in Cleveland, Ohio, USA in 1914. The idea and practice of a community foundation was limited primarily to North America until the 1980s. Since then the concept has spread to other parts of the world, thanks in large part to the efforts of major US **grant-making foundations** to establish community foundations outside the USA.

Community foundations have two main characteristics that distinguish them from other foundations. One of these is the function of making **grants** for the local community or geographic area, from which the name is derived. The other distinguishing feature is a structure that entails clusters of smaller funds, sometimes named for the individual **donors** as well as a variety of other instruments that facilitate giving within the community. In Japan, community foundations are sometimes referred to as 'apartment house foundations'.

More specifically, a community foundation is an independent **organization** operating in a given geographic area which, over time, builds up an **endowment**

63

contributed from many donors, provides services to those donors, makes **grants** and undertakes community leadership activities to address a wide variety of current and long-term needs in its service area.

Reflecting the growth and extension of the community foundation phenomenon, the **Council on Foundations** and Worldwide Initiatives for Grantmaker Support–Community Foundations (WINGS–CF) launched a project in 1999 to learn more about these developments. In addition, the **Bertelsmann Foundation** and the **Charles Stewart Mott Foundation** set up the Transatlantic Community Foundation Network (TCFN), the products of which are available on the website of the **European Foundation Centre**.

Community Fund

Founded in 1994 in the United Kingdom as the National Lottery Charities Board, the Community Fund is a non-departmental public body that distributes Lottery money to the **voluntary** and community **sector**. The Community Fund, whose board members are appointed by the Secretary of State for Culture, Media and Sport, is primarily a grant-making organization, providing funds for all sizes of projects and programmes of UK-based charities and community groups working both within and outside the country. In 2004, the Community Fund entered into a gradual merger with the New Opportunities Fund to create a streamlined Lottery distributor (The Big Lottery Fund) that will administer some 50% of Lottery proceeds for **public benefit** causes.

Website: www.community-fund.org.uk

Compact

A compact is essentially an agreement between two or more individuals, **organizations** or countries. Examples of civil-society related compacts on the large scale include the 1998 Compact between the Government and the English **voluntary** and community **sector**, designed to improve their relationship for mutual advantage. The national Compact's principles have been turned into collaboratively developed **codes of practice**, including a standard 12-week consultation period and funding terms such as payment in advance. Another example is the **Global Compact**, an initiative of United Nations Secretary-General Kofi Annan, which seeks to promote responsible corporate **citizenship** so that business can be a part of the solution to challenges of globalization. The Global Compact, a network of international agencies, corporations and **civil**

society organizations, asks participating businesses to embrace a set of ten basic principles in the areas of **human rights**, labour standards, the environment and anti-corruption.

Compagnia di San Paolo

The Compagnia di San Paolo was founded in January 1563 as a charitable brotherhood and later evolved into a major credit institution. Based in Turin, the Compagnia is currently one of the largest Italian **banking foundations** and one of the largest private foundations in Europe. The Compagnia focuses its grant-making and its own programmes on scientific, economic and juridical research; education; the arts and the preservation of cultural heritage; health; and assistance to the socially disadvantaged.

Website: www.compagnia.torino.it

Conflict of Interest

Conflict of interest situations arise whenever the personal or professional interests of a board member or a group of members are actually or potentially in contradiction to the best interests of the **organization**. Examples would be a board member proposing a relative or friend for a staff position or suggesting contracting with a firm in which he or she has a financial interest. While such actions may benefit the organization and indeed find board approval, they still indicate a potential conflict of interest for the individual board member in discharging his or her duties, and can, consequently, make the organization vulnerable to legal challenges and public misunderstanding. Often this type of conflict is remedied through disclosure or consent. It is a growing practice of **non-profit organizations** to have a written conflict of interest policy.

Contract Failure

The concept of contract failure arises in **non-profit sector** theories that emphasize **information asymmetry** as a reason for reliance on 'trustworthy' entities, such as **non-profit organizations**, rather than for-profit corporations. Contract failure exists where consumers may not have sufficient information or other means to evaluate the goods or services provided (e.g. child day-care, overseas relief efforts) and where market mechanisms provide insufficient discipline to prevent the actions of profit-seeking opportunists. In this scenario, consumers will be more likely to rely on non-profit organizations because of the **non-distribution constraint** and other characteristics that instill in the consumer a sense of trust not offered by for-profit entities.

Contract Failure Theory

Contract failure theory is an economic approach for explaining the existence of **non-profit organizations** in market economies, also known as **trust-related theory** or **market failure** theory. It argues that the **non-distribution constraint** makes non-profits more trustworthy under conditions of **information asymmetry**, which makes monitoring expensive and profiteering likely, and in situations that would lead to **contract failure** under market conditions.

Co-operatives

According to the International Labour Organization's definition, co-operatives are autonomous associations of persons united voluntarily to meet common economic, social and cultural needs and aspirations through jointly owned and democratically controlled enterprises. Linked to the labour movement, co-operatives date back to the mid-19th century. In 1844 weavers in the area of Manchester created the first modern co-operative, 'The Equitable Pioneers of Rochdale', under the inspiration of Robert Owen, a social reformer and entrepreneur who became a leader of the textile industry. Co-operatives spread in Europe and in North America at the end of the 19th century, and later, during the 20th century in most of the rest of the world, especially in developing countries.

Specifically, a co-operative is a grouping of persons, physical or legal, who accept the co-operative principles: **voluntary** and open **membership**; democratic member control; member economic participation; autonomy and independence; provision of education, training and information; co-operation among co-operatives; and concern for community. As **mutual societies**, co-operatives belong to the **social economy**, but they are typically outside the **non-profit sector**, since they can share profits among their members in proportion with their activity and are not subject to the **non-distribution constraint**. Relying on self-help, co-operatives do not generally receive public funding, and they do not necessarily benefit from **tax exemptions** as **non-profit organizations** do. In economic terms, co-operatives are firms of independent market participants that through either forward or **backward** market **integration** try to achieve a better market position for themselves. In this sense, co-operatives are a form of organized collective economic action.

Co-operatives exist in many areas of economic activity, primarily: agriculture, especially in Africa, North and South America, and Europe; electricity, telephone and other public utilities; banking, savings and credit, and insurance; health; and housing. Consumer co-ops are numerous in Nordic countries, UK and USA. Workers' co-operatives, the most challenging form, exist in Canada and South Europe.

Recently, new forms of co-operatives have emerged, such as the Italian social co-operatives with staffs including a minimum of 30% of persons with special needs (e.g. drug addicts), multi-purpose co-operatives, including those dedicated to employment creation, and multi-**stakeholder** co-operatives. However, in post-communist countries, co-operatives are suffering a legitimacy crisis as they are viewed as remnants of the past. In 2002, the United Nations published guidelines aimed at creating a supportive environment for the development of co-operatives in the developing world.

Corporate Dashboards

Corporate dashboards are 'snapshots' of key performance indicators. Their development was originally based on the notion that managers, normally overwhelmed with data, need something that is quick to produce and can be read, like a car dashboard, at a glance. Initially developed for for-profit firms, they are increasingly used among larger **non-profit organizations** as well. Dashboards can be produced quarterly and given to board members, staff, volunteers, members and other **stakeholders** such as major financial contributors. Often viewed as an overview of an **organization**'s **balanced scorecard**, the corporate dashboard also incorporates the idea that a range of indicators is needed to get an accurate overview of performance.

Corporate Foundations

A corporate foundation, also known as a company-sponsored foundation, is an independent legal entity established by its parent for-profit company. It is governed by a board that may include members of the corporation board or contributions committee, other staff members, and members of the community. The corporate foundation is a vehicle for promoting corporate **citizenship** or corporate **philanthropy**.

As separate legal entities, corporate foundations typically operate under the same regulations as private foundations. In the USA, this means that corporate foundations are also subject to the **mandatory pay-out requirement**.

In terms of grant-making and operations, there are very few differences between **corporate giving** programmes and the activities of corporate foundations. The main difference, however, is the locus of decision-making and operations: corporate giving programmes are typically administered through the company's corporate affairs or public relations office, whereas corporate foundations tend to have more autonomy from the corporate boardroom.

Corporate foundations often do not have significant **assets** of their own, but depend on the funds paid in by the corporation, and sometimes by its founder and its employees as well. In order to protect their foundations from the swings of the business cycle, many corporations adopt the pay-in and pay-out system. When profits are higher, the company donates to the foundation (pays in) more than the foundation gives to its community (pays out), and vice versa if earnings are lower. This system helps make corporate philanthropy more stable.

Corporate Giving

Corporate giving refers to the contributions businesses make out of their regular **budgets** as part of **corporate social responsibility**. Corporate giving may take the form of cash or in-kind **gifts**, including the company's product, free use of space (buildings or land) and time (loaned executives and employee volunteers), but does not include **grants** and other contributions made from affiliated **corporate foundations**. In some countries, such as the USA, corporate giving accounts for a small portion of total **philanthropy**, whereas in others, especially Japan and other Asia-Pacific countries, corporate giving constitutes a significant segment of philanthropic activity, far outpacing **individual giving**.

Corporate giving has periodically come into question because the resources utilized come from profits attributable to stockholders. In the USA a court decision (*A. P. Smith Manufacturing Company v. Ruth Barlow, et al.*) authorized withholding a portion of profits, channelling it to worthy causes as a demonstration of good 'corporate **citizenship**'.

Corporate Social Responsibility

Corporate social responsibility in the broad sense addresses how companies manage business processes to produce an overall positive impact on society. The

World Business Council for Sustainable Development defines it as the continuing commitment by business to behave ethically and contribute to economic development, while improving the quality of life of the workforce and their families as well as of the local community and society at large.

Corporations engaged in corporate social responsibility tend to follow one of four models. The neo-classical model considers corporate social responsibility to be justified only if it increases profits either directly or indirectly. The ethical model, by contrast, stresses corporate **citizenship** and argues that profit is but one goal among others that may be equally important in the long term for business **sustainability**. The political model assumes that corporations, as self-organizing and self-regulating entities, want to maximize profit and look after the political and social field in which they operate, in an effort to avoid government action. In this sense, social responsibility is pre-emptive business action to avoid government control of free enterprise. Finally, the **stakeholder** model argues that the purpose of corporate social responsibility is to balance competing demands along economic, environmental and social **bottom lines** (see **triple bottom line**). Approaches to corporate social responsibility include **social audits**, corporate **philanthropy** and community outreach plans, among other activities.

In the USA, corporate social responsibility has been defined much more in terms of corporate philanthropy, whereas in Europe, the term puts more emphasis on operating the core business in a socially responsible way. While corporate social responsibility has a long history, dating back to the emergence of the modern business firm in the 19th century, it has assumed new relevance with the rise of the transnational corporation. The **Global Compact** is the most visible effort to date to bring corporate social responsibility to the forefront of international policy debates.

Corporate Sponsorship – *see* **Sponsorship, Corporate**

Corporatism

According to Philippe Schmitter, corporatism can be defined as a system of interest representation in which the constituent units are organized into a limited number of singular, compulsory, non-competitive, hierarchically ordered and functionally differentiated categories. The entities are recognized or licensed (if not created) by the state, and granted a deliberate representational monopoly within their respective categories in exchange for observing certain controls on their selection of leaders and articulation of demands and supports. In this regard, corporatism is often called on to compensate for **market failure** or state failure. But, like all forms of **governance**, it also has its own tendencies to failure. The relative success or failure of corporatism depends not only on its specific institutional form, but also on corporatist actors' ability to compensate for these tendencies.

Corporatism first emerged in modern Europe as a reactionary and utopian politico-ideological critique of liberal capitalism. It reflected movements among feudal and traditional petty bourgeois classes (including artisans and yeoman farmers), Catholic and other religious groups, and traditional intellectual circles. Inspired in part by medieval occupational **guilds** and the old system of estate-based representation, they called for a restoration of social order through co-operation between vocational and **professional associations**. The second main version of corporatism was linked to 'organized capitalism' in the late 19th and early 20th centuries. This version was not opposed to capitalism as such (which was now consolidated and had begun to develop monopolistic and imperialistic tendencies), but was more concerned about the revolutionary threat represented by organized labour. The third phase of corporatism saw the emergence of tripartism in the context of post-war era and its associated Keynesian national **welfare states**, and corporatism was supported by Christian democrats as well as by social democrats.

Corporatism also features in the **social origins theory** as one of the four major non-profit regime types, characterized by high levels of government social expenditure and a relatively large **non-profit sector** in economic terms.

Cost–Benefit Analysis

Cost–benefit analysis (CBA) is a systematic, quantitative method for comparing the costs, both direct and indirect, and benefits, both tangible and intangible, of alternative options for the allocation of scarce resources. For **public sector** and non-profit decision-makers, CBA is a tool for measuring the economic efficiency of a programme or project, i.e. for assessing how costs compare to outcomes.

Assumptions influencing the results of CBA include: the accounting perspective (that of the **beneficiaries**, programme supporters, etc.); the approach used for measuring outcomes (market prices versus shadow prices, econometric analysis, estimation of opportunity costs and of **externalities** and spillover effects); and the timeframe involved, i.e. the choice of an appropriate discount rate to compare costs and benefits occurring at different points in time.

Cost Disease Theory

In the mid-1960s, economists William J. Baumol and William G. Bowen analysed historical data on performing arts **organizations**, showing that the costs of performances had risen faster than prices. The authors attributed the gap to a lack of productivity, i.e. physical output per work hour, in the performing arts, which they defined as the cost disease. Compared to manufacturing industries, where productivity had increased thanks to technology improvements, performing arts had not experienced the same gain: the classic example was that of the performance of a Mozart string quartet, which would always require four musicians. The conclusions of the cost disease model are often used by those making the case for external (public) support of performing arts.

Council on Foundations

Founded in 1949 and incorporated in 1957 as a **public charity**, the Council on Foundations is a **membership** organization of more than 2,000 **grant-making foundations** and giving programmes. Based in Washington, DC, its members are largely US **organizations**, with some foundations from other parts of the world. It provides **advocacy** services, training courses, legal services and networking opportunities. The Council hosts an annual conference and other meetings throughout the year and sponsors research and educational programmes.

Website: www.cof.org

Cream-Skimming

Used in the context of non-profit economic theories and based on the **moral hazard** phenomenon, cream-skimming refers to attempts by **organizations** to serve the most profitable and the least costly clients or users. For example, cream-skimming health-insurance companies may screen out clients in high-risk occupations, those living in high cancer areas, etc. The economic argument is that non-profits have less of an incentive to engage in cream-skimming than do for-profit firms due to the **non-distribution constraint**. Some **non-profit organizations** under pressure to show results to donors or contracting agencies may also engage in cream-skimming, selecting the **beneficiaries** that are most likely to exhibit positive results.

Credit Unions

A credit union is a type of mutual **organization** that first rose to prominence within the financial institutions sector in the late 19th and early 20th centuries, when many commercial banks did not accept customers with low incomes. There are over 1,000 credit unions in the UK, of which about half have been established since 1990, and some 10,000 in the USA. Credit unions are member-owned financial institutions formed to permit members to pool their savings and subsequently lend them to one another. They have limited return on shared capital, with any surpluses belonging to members. Credit unions are tax-exempt in many countries.

Cross-Subsidization

Non-profit organizations primarily produce public or **collective goods** in accordance with their **missions**. Due to the **free-rider problem**, however, it is difficult to extract user payments for the provision of these goods (on occasion, non-profits also deliberately abstain from charging fees for mission-related concerns), and the provision of **collective goods** relies on **voluntary** donations or government **subsidies**. To the extent that these donative **revenue** sources are not sufficient to cover the costs of collective goods at the desired levels, non-profit organizations also engage in the provision of **private goods** for which there is a market and earnings potential. Surpluses generated through private good provision are then used to cross-subsidize the underfunded collective good provision. Cross-subsidization can either take the form of price discrimination, such as sliding fee scales where clients are charged in accordance with their ability to pay, or business ventures and other commercial activity unrelated to the organization's mission.

Crowding Out

Crowding out generally means that increases in government support to **non-profit organizations** lead to concomitant decreases in private donative support—rendering government **subsidies** ineffective. The assumption is that private **donors** tend to reduce their support to governmentally-funded non-profit organizations either because they feel they support the organization already 'through taxes' or because of a presumed 'corrupting' influence of government funding on the organization's private character. Crowding out provided much of the conceptual backdrop for political efforts during the 1980s to reduce government support for public services particularly in the USA, but also in continental Europe, where non-profits typically rely heavily on **public sector** support with relatively little **private giving**. Most empirical studies found that some degree of modest crowding out does occur in the US context, but the evidence is not fully conclusive, and, outside the USA, nearly non-existent.

Cy Pres

Cy pres is a principle based on French law that means as near as possible to the **donor**'s intent (see **donative intent**) when compliance is for some reason illegal, impractical, or impossible. When, for example, a donor's charitable intent becomes impossible to fulfil, a court may substitute another charitable object in order to protect a charitable **trust**.

Czech Donors' Forum

The Czech Donors' Forum is a **grant-makers' association** which was established in 1997 to offer support to foundations and to cultivate **philanthropy** in the emerging Czech **non-profit sector**. It emerged out of informal meetings among foundation representatives to share information and co-ordinate activities. The Czech Donors' Forum is a **membership**-based association with 38 foundations from the Czech Republic and abroad (as of 2004). In addition to providing support and services to foundations, the Forum fosters the development of corporate philanthropy and acts as an advocate in legislation and tax treatment.

Website: www.donorsforum.cz

D

Dahrendorf, Lord Ralf (1929–)

Lord Ralf Dahrendorf was born in Hamburg, Germany and received doctorates in philosophy (Hamburg) and sociology (London). He has had a distinguished career in academia, having served as professor at various universities and as director of the London School of Economics, and in public service as member of Parliament in Germany, Commissioner of the then European Economic Community in Brussels, and member of the House of Lords in London. He has been a pioneer in the study of how social classes affect human behaviour and on the relationship between **civil society** and liberty. His publications include *After 1989: Morals, Revolution, and Civil Society* and *The Modern Social Conflict*.

Danforth, William (1870–1955)

A Missouri native, Danforth founded the Ralston Purina Company, pioneering the animal feed industry. Dared by a childhood teacher to overcome chronic illness, 'I Dare You' became the theme of his life and the title of his book aimed to inspire young people. In 1924, Danforth, who also served as superintendent of Sunday schools in St Louis, co-founded the Christian **leadership organization**, American Youth Foundation, and in 1927 founded the Danforth Foundation, which currently focuses the majority of its **grants** on plant and life sciences, in addition to providing continued support for the American Youth Foundation and other special causes.

Deed

A deed is a legal document signed, sealed and delivered to effect a transfer of property and to show the legal right to possess it. The term is frequently used in reference to the creation of **endowments** and *wakfs*. It binds the donated **assets** to specified purposes and instructs trustees to act accordingly (see **donative intent**). Because a deed cannot easily be modified, care must be taken that it be constructed neither too narrowly nor too broadly. Too narrow a purpose limits the trustees' ability to adapt distributions of income from the asset to changing circumstances. Conversely, a too-broad construction might enable trustees to support activities well outside the **donor**'s original intent.

Democracy

Based on the Greek 'rule by the people', democracy as a descriptive term may be regarded as synonymous with majority rule and with the constitutions and legal–political systems that allow democratic decision-making to take place and be upheld. Linz and Stepan have offered a widely-used definition of democracy as: legal freedom to formulate and advocate political alternatives with the concomitant rights of association, free speech and other basic freedoms of person; free and non-violent competition among leaders with periodic validation of their claim to rule; inclusion of all effective political offices in the democratic process; and provision for the participation of all members in the political community, regardless of their political preferences. In a more practical sense, democracy implies universal suffrage, the freedom to create political parties and political **organizations** more generally, and the conduct of free and honest elections at regular intervals without excluding any effective political office from electoral accountability.

There are a number of different types of democracy, and a variety of empirical and hypothetical models have been proposed by philosophers (Plato, Hegel), politicians (Madison, **Rousseau**) and political scientists (Hirst, Linz, Stepan, Lijphart). **Civil society**, non-profit issues and **philanthropy** do not relate to all aspects of democracy and democratic theory, but are relevant in some, in particular in what Lijphart calls consensual democracy, and what Hirst labels associative democracy, with the latter being the most relevant.

At the core of the concept of 'associative democracy' is the assumption that democracy functionally depends on a vibrant associational life. **Associations** are regarded as a precondition of functioning democracy, including pluralist interest mediation. However, the proper role of associations in liberal democracy has been controversial. Hegel saw in associations a protecting mechanism for citizens from the hegemony of state power, providing a bulwark against an authoritarian use of power. For **Alexis de Tocqueville**, too, civil society organizations play a key role in 'making democracy work': according to de Tocqueville, **voluntary associations** do not just have an external function (i.e. interest mediation vis à vis the state system), but also an internal function, socialising their members in a democratic value pattern.

Whereas for de Tocqueville associations were the 'learning schools of democracy', others are more doubtful about their role and contributions to democracy. James Madison already argued that curbing the 'mischiefs of faction' should be one of the main goals of the US constitution. Until the present day, concern about the role of special interest groups has indeed been a recurring theme in US politics. In contemporary political theory, however, the emphasis is laid clearly on the democratic role of associations. In *The Civic Culture*, Almond and Verba demonstrated the occurrence of a significant and positive relation between **membership** in associations and democratic attitudes. This finding has only been strengthened by the conclusions from Putnam's work on Italy, *Making Democracy Work,* and others, like Hirst, have argued that democratic **governance** is enhanced by a dispersion of power from centralized state structures to open networks of democratic associations.

De Tocqueville, Alexis (1805–1859)

Born in Paris, descendant of a noble Norman family, Alexis de Tocqueville studied law and went to the USA when he was 25 to study the penal system. His main books are *Democracy in America* (1835–40*)* and *The Old Regime and the Revolution* (1856). In the first, he observes this young **democracy** 'in order to learn what we have to fear or hope from its progress' in Europe and especially in France. He noted that Americans of all ages were forming associations, and he thought that 'in democratic countries, knowledge of associations is the mother of all forms of knowledge'. DeTocqueville has become a cultural icon of the American **non-profit sector**.

Deutscher Paritätischer Wohlfahrtsverband (Parity)
German Parity Welfare Association

The Deutscher Paritätischer Wohlfahrtsverband, founded in 1920, is a consortium of non-denominational, non-partisan private welfare **organizations** and hospitals active throughout Germany. Now known as Der Paritätische (the Parity), the consortium was in part an organizational response to the expansion of denominational and partisan welfare provision. What began as a close federation of independent hospitals, called the Fifth Welfare Association, has grown in significance since the 1960s and now includes about 9,000 member organizations in the field of welfare and social services.

Website: www.paritaet.org

Diakonisches Werk (Diakonie)

The Diakonisches Werk (Diakonie) is a large umbrella **organization** for German Protestant welfare, social and health agencies. Founded as the Innere Mission in 1848–49, it began as a welfare-oriented evangelical movement, often in conflict with the secular political world, and developed increasingly outside the official Protestant church structures. Today, the Diakonie groups together more than 27,000 different agencies and organizations, with a total of some 450,000 employees and another 400,000 volunteers.

Website: www.diakonie.de

Diana, Princess of Wales Memorial Fund

The Memorial Fund was established in 1997 in memory of Diana, Princess of Wales. By making **grants** and seeking to change public attitudes and policy, the Fund continues the work begun by Diana—especially in the areas of palliative care, landmines, HIV/AIDS, prisoners' families and young refugees. Its primary **revenue** source has been revenue from the sale of commercial products world-wide, and it expects to continue raising money by licensing special products that are linked to Diana. In order not to compete with its grantees, the Fund does not actively seek funding from the public, but it does accept contributions. In December 2004 an out-of-court settlement between the Fund and a US company ensured the future of the Fund which had, in mid-2003, frozen all grant-making activities pending the result of a lawsuit.

Website: www.theworkcontinues.org

Diaspora Philanthropy

Diaspora philanthropy refers to philanthropic giving from migrants (or their descendants) living outside their motherland/country of origin to or for individuals, **organizations**, or projects back in their homeland. The most common form of diaspora philanthropy is giving by individual migrants directly to their home community. Increasingly, such giving occurs through intermediary **non-profit organizations** that pool donations from migrants (as well as non-migrants) and remit the proceeds to a community, organization or other recipient in the homeland.

Directory of Social Change

Headquartered in London, the Directory of Social Change is a private charity that offers **non-profit organizations**—primarily in the UK—a variety of information, technical assistance and support services. Among these services are training courses and advice on such matters as **fundraising**, management, networking and legal issues; Charityfair, one of the largest **non-profit sector** fora in the UK; research on a variety of non-profit issues; and publication of a broad range of reference guides and handbooks. The Directory of Social Change recently took over the publishing of the majority of the publications of the **Charities Aid Foundation (CAF)**.

Website: www.dsc.org.uk

Disqualified Persons

In US federal tax law, a disqualified person is a person (individual, corporation, **trust**, etc.) that is in a position to exercise substantial influence over the affairs of the organization in question and is therefore disqualified from certain transactions with respect to the organization. Examples include a **trustee**, director, officer, executive, or manager, but also a substantial contributor, a family member of a disqualified person, or a corporation substantially owned by a disqualified person. See **self-dealing** for examples of transactions involving disqualified persons.

Ditchley Foundation

The Ditchley Foundation is an **operating foundation** established in 1958 by Sir David Wills, originally to advance Anglo-American links. The Foundation's broadened current objectives are pursued by organizing conferences bringing together decision-makers from the worlds of politics, business and industry, academic life, the civil service, the armed forces and the media, primarily from the European Union and the USA, but also representing other countries. The conferences, most held at Ditchley Park in the UK, but also in the USA and

Canada, focus on contemporary topics as diverse as prisoner reintegration, biogenetics, and the future of **democracy** and **civil society**.

Website: www.ditchley.co.uk

Donative Intent

Donative intent refers to the purpose of a **donor**'s **gift** or bequest, as well as stipulations attached to it. Conflicts may arise when a donor's intent is not laid out explicitly, or when an **organization** applies the funds to other, even perhaps related, purposes. Donative intent is usually spelled out in a **deed** or similar instrument.

Donor-Advised Funds

A donor-advised fund is a fund created by an irrevocable contribution to a **public charity**, for which the **donor**, or designees, may recommend eligible charitable recipients for **grants** from the fund. The fund-holding **organization**'s governing body must be free to accept or reject the recommendations. Such funds provide a vehicle for donors wishing to remain involved but not wishing to establish their own foundations. Pioneered in the USA by **community foundation**s, this type of fund has been adopted by community-type founda- tions world-wide and by other **non-profit organizations** such as hospitals and colleges, as well as financial firms.

Donor-Designated Funds

A donor-designated fund is a fund, usually held by a **community foundation**, for which the **donor** has specified that the fund's income or **assets** be used for the benefit of one or more specific purposes. These funds are sometimes established by a transfer of assets by a **public charity** to a fund designated for its own benefit, in which case they may be known as grantee **endowments**.

Donors

Generally speaking, a donor is an individual, **organization**, corporation or foundation giving money or other resources. In many languages, a distinction is made among different types of donors. In German and other languages, for example, the term *Stifter* (or donor) refers only to individuals, organizations or corporations giving **assets** that enable a foundation to generate income; whereas the term *Spender* (or giver) refers to a donor more or less regularly giving money or other resources to cover an organization's daily operations or a special project.

Drucker, Peter F. (1909–)

Born in Vienna and educated in Europe, Peter Drucker pioneered modern management, having developed management concepts such as **management by objectives** and other approaches. Currently Clarke Professor of Social Sciences at Claremont Graduate University in California (USA), he has consulted with numerous corporations, non-profits and governments on management and organizational strategy. In 1990 he founded the Peter F. Drucker Foundation for Nonprofit Management, whose operations were transferred in 2003 to the Leader to Leader Institute, and developed numerous organizational tools, including the 'five questions' for self-assessment. He is also the author of more than 30 books, including *Managing the Nonprofit Organization: Practices and Principles*.

Duke, James B. (1856–1925)

James B. Duke was a pioneer in **corporate social responsibility**, who co-founded Duke Power Company, one of the largest utility companies in the USA. In 1924, he created the Duke Endowment with a 'Grand Design'. The Endowment confines its operations to the Carolinas (Duke's birthplace and location of company headquarters), and its **deed** of trust allocates its income to specific **beneficiaries** (the largest being Duke University) rather than stating a broad **mission**.

Dunant, Jean Henri (1828–1910)

Henri Dunant was a Swiss businessman travelling in Italy when he witnessed the 1859 Battle of Solferino. Horrified by the medical inattention soldiers received, he wrote *A Memory of Solferino*, which inspired the 1864 signing of a twelve-nation treaty, known as the Geneva Convention, ensuring neutral treatment to wartime medical personnel. His book also prompted his appointment to the committee of the Geneva Society for Public Welfare that created the **Red Cross** to provide aid to soldiers in wartime and civilians in times of natural disaster. Ultimately, he ignored his business ventures and went bankrupt,

81

disappearing from the public eye until receiving the first Nobel Peace Prize in 1901 for his efforts in creating the Red Cross. (See also **International Red Cross and Red Crescent Movement**.)

Durkheim, Émile (1855–1917)

Émile Durkheim, son of a rabbi and professor at the Sorbonne, established sociology in France as an academic discipline and is considered the founder of functionalism. In his book *The Suicide*, he views suicide as the result of anomie, a state in which norms have broken down, and advocates for social cohesion through association. In *The Division of Labour*, he distinguishes between mechanical **solidarity**, which prevails when individuals are similar, and organic solidarity, which is the modern consequence of the division of labour. Organic solidarity creates a more flexible form of social cohesion.

E

E-philanthropy

The term 'e-philanthropy' originated during the dot.com boom of the 1990s in the USA, and relates primarily to the use of the Internet as a tool or platform of **fundraising** and fund distribution. Potential **donors** either search grantee/applicant websites or solicit proposals. Upon evaluating and selecting grantees, the e-philanthropist would then make a contribution to causes in line with the donor's objectives. The importance of e-philanthropy is likely to grow in the future to become a major fundraising and fund-seeking tool.

Friedrich-Ebert-Stiftung (FES)

Friedrich Ebert Foundation

The Friedrich-Ebert-Stiftung (FES) was established in 1925 in honour of Germany's first democratically-elected president, Friedrich Ebert. A **political foundation** linked to the German Social Democratic Party, FES is dedicated to promoting social democracy by furthering social-democratic and political education, providing university scholarships, and contributing to international co-operation, with roughly half of its **budget** devoted to projects in developing countries. With headquarters in Bonn and Berlin, FES also maintains four academies throughout Germany and representations in 70 countries. FES houses the largest collection of documents on the history of the German and international labour movement.

Website: www.fes.de

Economies of Scale

Economies of scale refer to per-unit cost reductions as output increases. This is the law of mass production, which states that goods will be cheaper when produced in higher numbers, since fixed costs are shared across more output units. The same is true for many services, such as health care, social services, housing assistance, and international development and relief, provided by **non-profit organizations**. In terms of **organization** and management structure, scale economies require a higher degree of product and service integration and managerial **centralization**. (See **Economies of scope**.)

Economies of Scope

Economies of scope refer to overall cost reductions made possible by combining the production or distribution of related products and services. Scope economies take advantage of synergies across products and markets, and thereby reduce combined total costs. Non-profit theatres, for example, can use their stages, as well as their **marketing** and production units, for multiple purposes. The theatre can be rented out to other companies or used for concerts or dance, the production unit can stage performances off-site, and the marketing department can serve other cultural institutions. In terms of organizational structure, scope economies imply co-ordination of decentralized, semi-autonomous units. (See **Economies of scale**.)

Eleemosynary

The term 'eleemosynary' from the Latin root for **alms** is used to describe acts of **charity**, charitable institutions as well as benevolent activities for the common good. Often used interchangeably with charity and benevolence, it none the less embraces a wider range of activities than that encompassed by the word charitable and **charity law**.

Èlovik v tísni – *see* People in Need Foundation

Employee-Matching Gifts

An employee-matching gift is a contribution to a charitable **organization** by an employee that is matched by a similar contribution from his or her employer. 'Invented' by the American GE Foundation in the 1950s, the mechanism is considered an important tool for demonstrating corporate responsibility by encouraging employees to support their communities. Typically, recipients designated as eligible for such matching gifts include educational institutions, community-based non-profit service-providing organizations, or cultural institutions. Some corporations also make 'matching' financial gifts to **non-profit organizations** where employees volunteer.

Empowerment

Empowerment is a term used in social policy and community development to describe the need for individuals to gain power and authority over their own affairs. In welfare reform, it has meant that individuals dependent on public provision of funds and services take on responsibility for their own well-being, including that of their family and wider community. It has also involved a shift in the social relations between public and non-profit providers on the one hand, and the clients on the other. Empowerment implies that the latter become users and consumers rather than passive recipients. The term empowerment is also central to the work of many **self-help groups**, as well as to the notion of **civil society** as a self-organizing entity, and the **active citizenship** approach.

Enabling

Enabling is a philanthropic strategy of grant-making whereby the focus of the **grant** is less on caring and **charity** in addressing a given problem, than on providing the means for the individual or recipient **organization** to achieve independence in making choices and in carrying out its own activities. Helping individuals to help themselves, supporting indigenous solutions to underdevelopment in Africa, or providing **grants** for training and education are examples of this kind of grant-making.

Endowments

The term 'endowment' refers both to a fund, usually in the form of an income-generating investment, intended to produce income for a **non-profit organization**'s operations and other approved purposes, and to the act of endowing an organization with a permanent source of income. Endowments can be 'legal' or 'quasi'. Legal endowments are those that **donors** give with restrictions for particular uses. A donor may specify that the endowment principal remain intact in perpetuity, for a defined period of time, or until sufficient **assets** have accumulated to achieve a designated purpose. Quasi-endowments are assets of a non-profit organization that the **board of directors** or administration has decided to hold as an endowment; subsequent action of another board or administration could change or end a quasi-endowment.

Entrepreneurship Theories

In contrast to the **heterogeneity theory** and **trust-related theories**, which emphasize aspects of the demand for services, entrepreneurship theories try to explain the existence of **non-profit organizations** from a supply-side perspective. In classical economic terms, the entrepreneur is understood as the one who assumes the risk of organizing and managing a new venture. Psychologists who have analysed entrepreneurs argue that entrepreneurs have a persistent opportunity orientation and think in terms of how things can be done instead of why things cannot get done.

In a series of influential papers in the 1980s and 1990s, **Estelle James**, Susan Rose-Ackerman, and Dennis Young laid out the basic argument for what became known as the entrepreneurship theory of non-profit organizations. According to James, non-profits try to maximize non-monetary returns such as faith, believers, or members; they are primarily interested in some form of immaterial value maximization, and the **non-distribution constraint** on monetary profit is only secondary to their organizational behaviour. Indeed, James suggests that entrepreneurs, or ideologues in Rose-Ackerman's terms, populate non-profit fields eager to maximize non-monetary returns.

The motives of the entrepreneur play an important role in the **organization**'s development, outputs and **mission**. Indeed, James points out that non-profits are strategically located throughout the life course in areas of taste formation: in primary socialization (day-care, nurseries, schools), but also in critical life situations (hospitals, hospices, homes for the elderly) and situations of special need (disability, divorce and other major life events). Entrepreneurship theories argue that during such situations, people are more open to questions relating to **religion** than they would be under normal circumstances. Hence, non-profit entrepreneurs seek out such opportunities and combine service delivery with religious or otherwise ideologically-coloured messages in an effort to garner adherents, believers or recruits.

Whether non-profit entrepreneurs try to maximize quantifiable aspects such as members or abstract concepts such as 'salvation' or some ideology is irrelevant; what matters is that they often seek to combine such efforts with service delivery. In this sense, many value-based non-profits bundle products: one that is the true and preferred output (e.g. salvation) and the other the necessary or auxiliary co-product. This suggests that the value-based or ideology-based non-profits tend to develop into multiple product firms and that **product bundling** is a key aspect of the **revenue** behaviour of many non-profit organizations.

In a sense, entrepreneurship approaches complete demand-side theories because non-profit organizations always need an actor or a group of actors to create the organization. Yet it is often difficult to differentiate between entrepreneurship and **non-profit management**. Moreover, it may be difficult to tell if the cause of **innovation** is from entrepreneurship or from other factors.

Environmental Carrying Capacity

Related to the term 'niche', the notion of environmental carrying capacity refers to the number of **organizations** that can be supported by the social, economic and political conditions, given available resources. To the extent that existing or newly-founded organizations can draw on resources without competing against each other, the limits of the environment's carrying capacity have not been reached. However, once resources become scarcer, or some organizational forms become more efficient in resource use, the survival of other organizations will be put in question. For example, the significant growth of **non-profit organizations** in many parts of the world would suggest that the carrying capacity described by social, economic and political conditions has not been reached. However, in countries with severe budgetary problems, **welfare state** and fiscal reforms can change some of the environmental conditions, and thereby also the carrying capacity of the social services and assistance field.

Behind this reasoning is a basic insight of organizational population ecology, which sees organizational forms basically in more or less open competition with each other. While policies define the rules of the game, over time mismatches develop between the potentials and constraints they impose on forms, and thereby either increase or decrease their competitive edge over others. Some of the underlying forces responsible for mismatches are related to **heterogeneity** and **trust-related theories**: changes in the definition of goods and services, changes in **information asymmetries**, and policy changes more generally affect the environmental carrying capacity of given fields, and hence the **sustainability** of non-profit organizations.

Estate Taxes

An estate tax is a tax imposed on the right to transfer property by inheritance and assessed on the net value of a decedent's estate before distribution to the heirs. In the USA, the law has provided exclusions for selected transfers, among them, charitable bequests. It is commonly held that the exclusion of charitable bequests serves as a significant incentive for giving to charities as well as establishing foundations.

Ethical Investment

Ethical investment refers to an investment policy of selecting stocks for a portfolio partly on the grounds of the ethical or environmental code pursued by the companies in question. Although fund and investment practices vary, it is easier to define ethical investment through exclusion rather than inclusion. The major exclusions tend to be arms, alcohol, tobacco, gambling, animal testing, environmental damage and the payment of exploitative wages in developing countries. In 2000 the FTSE International launched a set of stock indices called FTSE4Good, which is a tradable benchmark index which requires member companies to meet certain ethical standards for inclusion. Similar indices exist for other stock exchanges.

Etzioni, Amitai (1929–)

Born in Germany, Amitai Etzioni was awarded a Ph.D. in sociology from the University of California at Berkeley and was a sociology professor at Columbia University (New York) for 20 years. In 1980, Etzioni was named the first University Professor at the George Washington University (Washington, DC), where he currently directs the Institute for Communitarian Policy Studies. A leading proponent of contemporary **communitarianism**, he founded and led numerous organizations dedicated to promoting communitarian ideas, including the Communitarian Network. Etzioni is also known for major contributions to organizational analysis, which examines how **organizations** evolve, change and interact with individual and social units.

European Anti-Poverty Network

Established in 1989, the European Anti-Poverty Network is an independent coalition of national and international **NGOs** dedicated to eliminating poverty and social exclusion in European Union member states. Based in Belgium, its activities include **lobbying** European Union institutions to address poverty issues, supporting existing campaigns against social exclusion and advocating on behalf of groups affected by poverty.

Website: www.eapn.org

European Citizen Action Service (ECAS)

The European Citizen Action Service (ECAS), headquartered in Brussels, is a non-profit **membership** organization created in 1990 to assist **NGOs** in strengthening their relationship with, and making an impact on, the European Union. ECAS members are involved in various areas of activity including civil liberties, culture, development, and health and social welfare. ECAS has three main objectives in service to its members: to strengthen the European strategy of NGOs in member states and applicant countries of the EU; to defend free movement rights and promote a more inclusive European **citizenship**; and to campaign for **transparency** and reform of the EU institutions.

Website: www.ecas.org

European Cultural Foundation

The European Cultural Foundation was established in 1954 to promote a cultural and human dimension to the processes of European integration. The Foundation, based in Amsterdam, advocates for cross-cultural co-operation between European countries, respect for cultural diversity and the social responsibility of cultural policy. In addition to awarding **grants**, it initiates and manages its own programmes and projects. The European Cultural Foundation also serves as the central secretariat for a network of independent associated institutions dealing with topics as diverse as social policy, education and the environment, and a network of national committees based in 23 European countries.

Website: www.eurocult.org

European Foundation Centre (EFC)

The European Foundation Centre is a **membership association** of over 200 European **foundations** and grant-makers. Established in 1989 by seven of Europe's leading foundations, the EFC is dedicated to strengthening **philanthropy** in Europe and beyond. Its activities and services are focused on three areas: representation of member interests to institutions at the European level; promotion of collaboration and joint projects among members who share common sectoral interests; and dissemination of information on foundations.

Website: www.efc.be

European Voluntary Service (EVS)

The European Voluntary Service is a programme within the framework of the European Union's YOUTH programme designed to encourage the employ-ability of youths by working as volunteers in another European country. Launched in 1996, the programme is open to participants aged 18-25 from EU member states, South-Eastern Europe and the Mediterranean, with indivi-dual service projects being administered by designated government agencies in participating countries. EVS projects are based on **partnership** between the volunteer, a sending **organization**, and a host organization and are co-financed by the European Union.

Evaluation

The term evaluation refers both to the process of determining the merit, worth and value of an output or outcome and to the product of processes involved. Although evaluation expertise may be required during project or programme design and implementation, evaluation is primarily concerned with effects (see **impact evaluation**). The ultimate goal of an evaluation is to assess whether, how, and under what conditions a project or programme has achieved the changes or results it intended to produce. Obviously, there is no evaluation method providing a single answer to these questions. Different theories on evaluation put varying stress on the questions one can ask: while the mainstream experimental and quasi-experimental model rests on the observation of a 'test group' and a 'control group' at the beginning and end of a 'treatment' (the so-called OXO approach), other methods prefer to look into the 'black box', asking more about the conditions under which a particular outcome is observed or about the role of specific actors within the process. Others see evaluation as the result of a process of negotiation between key **stakeholders**.

In the world of **philanthropy** and the **non-profit sector**, the interest in evaluation has been growing since the 1980s. In the case of **foundations**, in particular, this rising interest has accompanied the increase in attention founda-tions pay to the effectiveness of their activities.

In the case of **grant-making foundations**, for example, the ultimate goal of evaluation is to show that funding went to the right **organization** for the right purpose. Similarly, **non-profit organizations** seek to demonstrate that their resources are achieving the desired objectives. Learning is the essential goal of evaluation when foundations and non-profit organizations intend to act as agents of change and **innovation**, wishing to learn from their own achievements and failures.

Externalities

Externalities exist when either a benefit or a cost is not directly accounted for by the market price but passed on to third parties. For example, transmission of infection from a blood donor to recipient in a market situation can yield 'negative' externalities, and others not party to the initial blood transaction might get infected. Air pollution from automobiles is another example of a negative externality, as the sales price of a car does not include the car's lifetime contribution to lowering air quality. A private arboretum in a densely populated urban area would be an example of a positive externality, as the costs for maintaining the park would be borne by the owner but the fresher, cleaner air would benefit a much wider group of residents in the area. Externalities are related to the concepts of **market failure** and **transaction costs**, and closely related to major non-profit theories as well.

F

Esmée Fairbairn Foundation

Established in 1961, the Esmée Fairbairn Foundation is one of the largest independent **grant-making foundations** in the UK. It is dedicated to supporting initiatives to improve communities in the UK, with particular focus on the fields of the arts, national heritage, education, economic and social research, the environment and social development. The Foundation supports innovative programmes that require core funding, and has initiated a pilot loan programme offering financing to **voluntary** organizations and other entities with charitable aims.

Website: www.efct.org.uk

Faith-Based Organizations (FBOs)

Faith-based **non-profit organizations** (FBOs) have achieved greater importance in social policy debates, in the USA in particular (see **charitable choice**), because they are being called upon to play an even larger role in the solution of society's problems. FBOs are specialized **organizations** formed by church clergy to help meet the human service needs of their congregations. They tend to be multi-purpose organizations that perform a wide range of functions, from operating homeless shelters, food banks and neighbourhood centres, to running job-training and transportation programmes.

There are several types of FBOs:

- Church service agencies are semi-autonomous service arms of a single denomination or confessional tradition, e.g. **Caritas** and **Diakonisches Werk**. They often contract with government agencies and have **budgets** that may exceed those of large congregations. Church service agencies are multi-purpose organizations and focus primarily on co-ordination and supervision of various social service activities.

- Ecumenical or inter-faith coalitions are also multi-purpose organizations that range from single neighbourhood coalitions to hundreds of congregations spanning a metropolitan area.
- Direct-service ministries are local organizations operating in specific neighbourhoods and offering a particular service such as a soup kitchen or homeless shelter.
- Church-sponsored ministries have informal and formal connections with their parent organizations through funding, board memberships, or staff.
- Church-initiated organizations are ones that were initially sponsored or aided by a church but have become sufficiently autonomous that their **mission** and **governance** are almost entirely secular.

Family Foundations

A family foundation is an independent private foundation whose funds are derived from members of a single family. Family members often serve as officers or board members and have a significant role in their grant-making decisions. In the USA, 'family foundation' is not a legal or tax designation, and such foundations can support a wide range of charitable and non-charitable purposes. In Europe, family foundations tend to have dynastic elements and serve members of the family primarily.

Federal Association of German Foundations – *see* Bundesverband Deutscher Stiftungen eV

Federated Fundraising Campaign

Federated fundraising campaigns are charitable solicitations organized to support a wide range of social, community and welfare needs. They are usually community-based and are directed particularly at local businesses, seeking annual **gifts** from them and their employees; automatic payroll deductions for these gifts are encouraged. Such efforts tend to be organized by **community chests** and similar federated **fundraising organizations**. The largest network of such organizations is the **United Way** of America, a system of payroll-deduction campaigns that has been replicated in numerous other countries as well. In 2002–2003, United Ways in the USA generated an estimated US $4,400m., which included $3,930m. in **revenue** from the annual fundraising campaign.

Fédération Internationale des Ligues des Droits de L'Homme (FIDH)

International Federation for Human Rights

The Fédération Internationale des Ligues des Droits de L'Homme is an international **NGO** established in 1922 dedicated to upholding the doctrines of the Universal Declaration of **Human Rights**. FIDH represents 116 national **human rights organizations** in nearly 100 countries. In addition to creating a human rights network, the Federation conducts campaigns, provides its members with a voice at the international level, issues publications, provides information services, and works directly to fight human rights abuses.

Website: www.fidh.org

Feeney, Charles 'Chuck'

Philanthropist behind one of the wealthiest **foundations** in the world, Chuck Feeney made his fortune from duty-free shops. In 1982 he transferred his interest in his business to several foundations based in Bermuda and began an 'alternative career' as a secret giver, only outing himself in 1997. He has since adopted a 'giving while living' strategy, announcing in 2002 that his foundation, the Atlantic Philanthropies, would convert its **assets** to cash and spend it within 15 years. Credited with transforming Irish third-level education through his giving, he also played an instrumental role in reconciliation efforts in Northern Ireland as one of a group of Irish-Americans who encouraged republicans to end violence and sit at the negotiating table.

Ferguson, Adam (1723–1816)

Published in 1767, Adam Ferguson's *An Essay on the History of Civil Society* is widely regarded as setting the benchmark for the non-religious justification for the existence of **civil society**, an irony given his own background as a church chaplain. Beyond this, scholarly opinion is divided as to his overall legacy in terms of the conceptualisation of civil society, although it must be said that he wrote primarily about his native Scotland. His name entered civil-society folklore in 1991 when an anonymous collector bought a copy of the first edition of his *Essay* for a record US $1,870.

Filer, John (1924–1994)

John Filer served as chairman of the USA-based Aetna Life & Casualty insurance company from 1972 to 1984. In the early 1970s, Filer inspired the creation of Aetna's **Corporate Social Responsibility** department and the Aetna Foundation. In 1973, he was appointed by US President Nixon to lead the Commission on Private Philanthropy and Public Needs, better known as the **Filer Commission**, which studied the function of **foundations** in America and reported strategies for strengthening non-profits and philanthropies in *Giving in America*. He later chaired **the Independent Sector**, a non-profit umbrella **organization** that works to encourage **philanthropy**, **volunteering**, not-for-profit initiative and citizen action.

Filer Commission

The Commission on Private Philanthropy and Public Needs (known as the Filer Commission, after its chairman **John Filer**) was formed in November 1973 to study the role of philanthropic giving in the USA and its relationship to government. Convened through the initiative (and, in part, financing) of John D. Rockefeller III and composed of religious and labour leaders, former Presidential cabinet members, foundation and corporate executives, federal judges and representatives of several minority groups, the Commission sought to reach its goal through research and debate. Although few of its recommendations were acted upon, the Commission and its report, *Giving in America: Toward a Stronger Voluntary Sector*, are often referred to as the milestone in the development of the American **non-profit sector** and the initiation of philanthropic and non-profit studies.

Flexner, Abraham (1866–1959)

Born in Louisville, Kentucky, Abraham Flexner is best known for revolutionizing American medical education in the early 20th century as well as pioneering innovative methods of philanthropic giving. Flexner influenced the work and direction of well known American philanthropists including Paul Mellon, **John D. Rockefeller, Jr** and **Julius Rosenwald**. In the early 20th century, when American **philanthropy** was struggling to find a role in addressing social issues, Flexner's unprecedented use of funds to reform American higher education demonstrated that philanthropy can effectively partner with government and academia to bring meaningful change.

Folkrörelse

Folkrörelse is the Swedish word describing broad-based, democratic popular mass movements. Older, more traditional movements include the labour movement and the temperance movement, while the women's, sports and environmental movements are among the more recently formed groupings. There is debate among researchers whether *Folkrörelse* refers to the movements as such or to the movement **organizations**, which are more formal and hierarchical. *Folkrörelse* has had significant impact on the development of Swedish society, in particular the democratic **welfare state** and the highly participatory nature of Swedish **civil society**.

Fondation de France

Created in 1969 on the initiative of André Malraux, the first Minister of Culture, the Fondation de France received its first **endowment** from the Caisse des Dépôts et Consignations, a public agency that pools the funds of public savings banks, and from 17 other public or private banks. Independent from government, but with some civil servants as board trustees, the Fondation de France had two original **missions**: encouraging **philanthropy** and housing individual and **corporate foundations** (which numbered more than 500 in 2003). From the late 1990s, it developed its own programmes, especially in the fields of health, social services and culture. Indeed, the Fondation de France represented a new concept, that of the multi-purpose foundation, in contrast to the majority of French foundations which tend to have narrowly defined and fixed objectives.

Fondazione Giovanni Agnelli

Established in 1966 by an **endowment** from FIAT and Istituto Finanziario Industriale to celebrate the centenary of the birth of FIAT's founder, the Fondazione Giovanni Agnelli is an **operating foundation** with headquarters in the Italian city of Turin. The Foundation promotes research and activities aimed at furthering and spreading knowledge of the conditions on which Italy's progress in the economic, scientific, social and cultural fields depends. In light of the rapid expansion of the Italian foundation community, the Agnelli

Foundation established the **Centro di Documentazione sulle Fondazioni**, a foundation dedicated to keeping track of foundation developments.

Website: www.fga.it

Fondazione Cariplo—Cassa di Risparmio delle Provincie Lombarde

Originally founded in 1823 and re-established in 1991 as a private foundation under the Italian **banking foundation** regulations, the Fondazione Cariplo supports work in the areas of arts and culture, health, the environment, education, scientific research, **community foundations** and social services. In addition, the Fondazione funds projects that focus on ways in which technology affects business and public administration systems. It is among the largest European foundations in terms of **endowment**.

Website: www.fondazionecariplo.it

Fondazione Adriano Olivetti

The Fondazione Adriano Olivetti was established in 1962 to support the continuation of the research set in motion by Adriano Olivetti, known for his leadership of the Olivetti office equipment and telecommunications company. With headquarters in Rome, the Fondazione is primarily an **operating foundation**, engaging in conferences, workshops, publications, and other activities focusing on four main areas: institutions and public policies, processes of economic and social development, cultural and social policies, and art, architecture and urban studies.

Website: www.fondazioneadrianolivetti.it

Ford, Henry (1863–1947)

Twentieth-century American industrialist and founder of Ford Motor Company, Henry Ford revolutionized the automobile industry by introducing new car assembly and manufacturing techniques. Ford, having amassed a fortune with the Ford Motor Company, was also a noted philanthropist who established the **Ford Foundation** in 1936 and subsequently donated millions more to the foundation. Despite testy relations with organized labour, Ford negotiated, in 1913, a profit-sharing plan for Ford Motor Company workers that revolutionized management within the industry. Workers now had a stake in company profits and thus worker turnover decreased. At the same time productivity and sales increased because workers, who now had a 'living wage', could afford the products they assembled. Observers at the time called these techniques 'Fordism' and 'human engineering'.

The Ford Foundation

Established in 1936 with a **gift** of US $25,000 from car manufacturer **Henry Ford**, the Ford Foundation is today one of the largest foundations in the world dedicated to establishing peace, strengthening **democracy**, advancing human achievement and reducing poverty and injustice. Primarily a grant-making **organization**, the foundation has, since its inception, granted or lent over US $12,000m. and has invested significantly in the mapping and development of **civil society** world-wide. True to the foundation's belief in having a strong field presence, approximately half of its staff works outside its New York headquarters, in offices in Africa, the Middle East, Asia, Latin America and Russia.

Website: www.fordfound.org

For-Profits in Disguise

The term 'for-profits in disguise' was coined by economist **Burton Weisbrod** and refers to 'false' **non-profit organizations** that are guided by pecuniary rather than charitable or altruistic motives. They may try to maximize profits that are then redistributed in disguised form such as higher wages or generous benefits and perks. They may also try to maximize **revenue** that can lead to more influence and prestige for managers, with the hope for professional advancement and lucrative outside offers. These for-profits in disguise are attracted to the **non-profit sector** by tax and subsidy advantages.

Fosdick, Raymond (1883–1972)

A graduate of Princeton University and New York Law School, Raymond Fosdick was a close associate of many prominent US political and philanthropic figures of his era including **Abraham Flexner** and **John D. Rockefeller, Jr.** Fosdick's relationship with Rockefeller began as one of client–lawyer, but he eventually became president and trustee of the **Rockefeller Foundation** over a

27-year period and, later, Rockefeller's biographer. Fosdick led the Rockefeller Foundation through its international campaigns against hookworm and yellow fever and its advances into psychiatry and human relations study. Earlier, Fosdick served as one of two Under-Secretary-Generals of the League of Nations, the predecessor to the United Nations.

Foundation Center

Established in 1956 in the USA, the Foundation Center serves grant-seekers, grant-makers, researchers, policy-makers, the media and the general public as an information resource on US **foundations**. It seeks to support and improve **philanthropy** and promote public understanding by collecting, organizing and disseminating information on US philanthropy; conducting research on trends in the field; providing training and education on the grant-seeking process; maintaining five library/learning centres located in major US cities, as well as print and electronic publications, to ensure public access to information.

Website: fdncenter.org

Foundation Investment Fund (FIF)

The Foundation Investment Fund has served as an instrument to the Czech government to donate to **foundations** 1% of the proceeds from the second stage of **privatization** of state-owned enterprises. Established in 1991 but inactive for several years due to an unfavourable political climate, the Fund distributed US $99m. to 73 Czech foundations between 1999 and 2004. The foundations that benefited from the FIF had to meet strict criteria concerning payout rates and transparent grant-making. Through FIF, the Czech government enhanced the financial self-sustainability of Czech foundations by more than doubling the total volume of their **endowments**.

Foundations

Foundations have a long history, reaching back to antiquity, and with equally long traditions in most world cultures. Despite this long heritage, the modern foundation is often associated with the rise of the large **grant-making foundation** in the USA in the early 20th century, and its replication in other parts of the world, in particular in Europe after the Second World War. In terms of numbers and material wealth, the foundations of most developed market economies are a product of the last three decades, having benefited from prolonged economic prosperity, political stability and, in many countries, more favourable legislation. In this sense, as non-profit institutions, foundations are both an old and a recent phenomenon.

The various legal systems define foundations rather differently, and registration, legal practices and oversight regimes vary accordingly. Despite these differences, the basic concept of a foundation shares common images: a separate, identifiable **asset** (the root meaning of the Latin-based *fund* or *fond*) donated to a particular purpose, usually public in nature (implying the root of **charity** or **philanthropy**). In fact, most legal systems incorporate the ancient Roman law differentiation between foundations (*universitas rerum*) based on some core asset and associations (*universitas personarum*) based on **membership**.

A basic definition sees a foundation as a private asset that serves a public purpose, with five core characteristics:

1. Non-membership-based organization based on an original **deed**, typically signified in a charter of incorporation or establishment that gives the entity both intent of purpose and permanence;
2. Private entity institutionally separate from government, and 'non-governmental' in the sense of being structurally separate from the **public sector**;
3. Self-governing entity equipped to control its own activities in terms of internal **governance** procedures;
4. **Non-profit-distributing** by not returning profits generated by either use of assets or the conduct of commercial activities to its owners, members, trustees or directors; and
5. Serving a public purpose that goes beyond a narrowly defined social group or category, such as members of a family, or a closed circle of **beneficiaries**.

The nature of the assets can be stock and other shares in business firms, financial, real estate, patents, etc. There are basic categories that group the most common types of foundations according to:

a) Type of activity

- Grant-making foundations, i.e. endowed **organizations** that primarily engage in grant-making for specified purposes;
- **Operating** foundations, i.e. foundations that primarily operate their own programmes and projects;

- Mixed foundations, i.e. foundations that operate their own programmes and projects and engage in grant-making on a significant scale.

Other types include the **family foundation**, grant-seeking foundation, church foundations, **fundraising foundations** and **political foundations**, among others.

b) Type of founders

- Individual, i.e. foundations founded by an individual, group of individuals or family whereby **donors** bring their private assets into the foundation.
- **Corporate foundations** such as the company-related or company-sponsored foundation based on corporate assets, vary by the closeness to the parent corporations in terms of governance and management.
- **Community foundations**, i.e. grant-making and operating foundations that pool **revenue** and **assets** from a variety of sources (individual, corporate, public) for specified communal purposes.
- **Government-sponsored/government-created foundations**, i.e. foundations that either are created by public charter or enjoy high degrees of public sector support for **endowment** or operating expenditures.

Foundations, Functions of

Research on foundations has identified a number of distinct functions they can perform in society. While some overlap exists among these functions or roles, they lead to different implications for foundation impact and policy:

- complementarity, whereby foundations serve otherwise under-supplied groups under conditions of demand heterogeneity and public budget constraints;
- substitution, when foundations take on functions otherwise or previously supplied by the state and become providers of public and quasi-**public goods**;
- redistribution, whereby foundations engage in, and promote, redistribution of primarily economic resources from higher to lower income groups;
- promoting **innovation** in social perceptions, values, relationships and ways of doing things;
- social and policy change, whereby foundations promote structural change and a more just society, fostering recognition of new needs and **empowering** the socially excluded;

- preservation of traditions and cultures, whereby foundations oppose change, preserving past lessons and achievements that are likely to be swamped by larger social, cultural and economic forces; and
- promotion of pluralism, by which foundations promote experimentation and diversity in general, protect dissenters/civil liberties against the state, and challenge others in social, economic, cultural and environmental policy.

Franchises

The term 'franchise' is most typically used in the private sector to mean a smaller, semi-autonomous business entity, i.e. the franchisee, in a contractual relationship with a larger business entity, i.e. the franchisor. The relationship usually involves the franchisee paying both a lump sum of money to use the larger **organization**'s **brand** and a portion of **revenues** each month. The larger organization, in turn, allows the franchisee autonomy in management and retention of revenues, providing technical or business assistance when needed. Some scholars such as Sharon Oster have argued that the franchise system would work in the **non-profit sector** as well and cites the YMCA (see **Young Men's Christian Association**), among others, as an example of a non-profit franchise system. Oster concludes that the franchise form is most effective in dealing with the four common dilemmas of **non-profit organizations**: 'the kind of product or service produced, the dependence of most non-profits on at least some **fundraising**, the inadequate access to capital, and the absence of quantitative criteria for managerial performance'. In order for the franchise form to work in a non-profit setting, however, there needs to be some degree of control by the national or larger organization over its affiliates in order to maintain trust relationships.

Freedom of Association

Freedom of association refers to the right to peaceably assemble, to form societies, clubs and other groups of people, and to meet with people individually, without interference by the government. This right is essential for creating a space within which **non-profit organizations** can function. Generally speaking, the more clearly laws and regulations establish and protect the freedom to associate, the more likely individuals will be to take the risk to organize. In common-law systems, the right to associate is assumed to exist, even if it is not codified. In civil-law systems, by contrast, the right must be spelled out; on the one hand, this leaves room for the State to hinder or interfere with associative efforts, while on the other hand, it provides stronger protection for the right.

Freemasons

Freemasonry is one of the world's oldest secular fraternal societies, established formally in the United Kingdom in 1717. However, it is often speculated that its origins are much older, possibly stemming from the Knights Templar of the 12th century. It is currently estimated to have four to five million members worldwide. Freemasons consider their guiding principles to be brotherly love, relief (**charity**) and truth. While not a **sect**, 'the essential qualification for admission' is a belief in a Supreme Being. In North America, charitable Masonic activities include a number of children's hospitals, run through the affiliated **organization**, the Shriners.

Free-Rider Problem

Identified by **Mancur Olson** in *The Logic of Collective Action* (1968), the free-rider problem highlights the difficulties inherent in the provision of **public goods**. Olson argues that theories of interest groups, which state that people with common interests will join together to accomplish common goals, are flawed because they fail to identify the free-rider problem, i.e. that it is not in the self-interest of an individual to contribute to the group if he or she can still enjoy the goods produced by the group. In situations where goods flow to all members of the group regardless of their participation, people will 'free-ride' because the cost of contributing is higher for the individual than the small increase in overall goods that may result from that individual's participation. Similar to the **tragedy of the commons**, the free-rider problem explains that if each member of a group acts to maximize his or her own self-interest instead of the group's interest, the common good will eventually fail.

French Muscular Dystrophy Association – *see* Association Française contre les Myopathies (AFM)

Friendly Societies

Friendly societies are **voluntary**, mutual **organizations** that exist to provide members and their relatives with benefits such as life and endowment insurance and with relief or maintenance during sickness, unemployment and retirement. Some societies provide not only contractual benefits but also discretionary benefits to members who find themselves in financial difficulties. They are primarily found in the UK, but other Commonwealth countries have equivalent institutions. There are 293 registered friendly societies in the UK, regulated by the Friendly Societies Commission. They make up a considerable proportion of the UK insurance market, with funds amounting to over US $18,000m. and with a **membership** of several million.

Friends of the Earth

Founded in 1969 in San Francisco (USA), Friends of the Earth (FoE) is an environmental 'watchdog' organization dedicated to ecological preservation; social, economic and political justice; and promoting sustainable environmental policies. Friends of the Earth International (FoEI), whose secretariat is based in Amsterdam, was established in 1971 as a federation of autonomous environmental groups, joined by the conviction that championing the environment requires both strong grassroots activism and effective national and international campaigning and co-ordination. Local FoE groups and FoEI challenge government agencies and officials, corporations and international bodies by exposing practices that impact the environment. FoEI has consultative status with the Economic and Social Council of the United Nations (ECOSOC).

Website: www.foe.org

Fugger, Jakob (1459–1525)

Jakob Fugger was born into a wealthy merchant family in Augsburg, Germany. In 1514, together with his brothers, Fugger started construction of the Fuggerei, the first social settlement in the world where the needy could reside for nominal rent. Fugger wanted the settlement to represent Renaissance ideals, with every family having its own private house, equipped with individual rooms, a kitchen and a garden for subsistence, if necessary. The Fuggerei, which consists of 67 buildings and 147 apartments, is still in operation today. Fugger, who was also responsible for the construction of numerous churches in Augsburg, became one of the icons of Central European **philanthropy**.

Fundación ONCE para la Cooperación e Integración Social de Personas con Discapacidad

The Spanish National Organization for the Blind's Foundation for Co-operation with and Integration of Persons with Disabilities

Fundación ONCE is an **operating foundation**, established in 1988 by ONCE, the Spanish National Organization for the Blind, in co-operation with other leading organizations representing and serving persons with disabilities in Spain. Its main objectives are integrating persons with disabilities into the labour force, providing them with training and employment, and working to overcome all types of barriers faced by the disabled. Fundación ONCE facilitates worker placement both through its own subsidiaries and through close co-operation with business firms. Its financial stability is secured through the dedication of a portion of the proceeds from ONCE's national lottery.

Website: www.fundaciononce.es

Fundraising

Fundraising is the mobilization of **assets** and resources from a variety of sources for a particular purpose, be it an **organization**, a project, or a cause. Fundraising has become an increasingly important aspect of non-profit operations, fuelled, in great measure, by the **professionalization** of fundraisers. Many larger non-profits maintain fundraisers on their staff, and smaller ones often hire **commercial fundraising firms**. Initially, fundraising was linked primarily to **private giving**, but now includes seeking **grants**, contributions and contracts from government agencies as well as generating various forms of earned income.

A UK study of the top 500 fundraising charities found that non-profits make use of a wide range of fundraising tools and activities: about two-thirds used direct mail solicitation, 25% telemarketing, 30% door-to-door collections, 35% direct response press advertising, 86% approached corporations, two-thirds contacted **foundations** and charitable trusts, and 57% engaged in major **gift** fundraising. One reason for the multiple approaches is the attempt to reach both general audiences, e.g. via telemarketing and direct mail solicitation, and special populations that have a particular affinity to, and commitment for, the cause or organization. In the latter case, fundraisers use targeted approaches and develop relationships with **donors** over time. Other fundraising tools used by non-profits include newsletter subscriptions, fundraising dinners (with and without VIPs), sale or rental of mailing lists, small games of chance, raffles, auctions, wills and bequests, and social events. (See **Campaigns, fundraising.**)

Fundraising Foundations

A fundraising foundation is to be seen in contrast with a foundation that operates on the basis of income derived from its **assets**. In general, a fundraising foundation takes the legal form of a foundation, but is created without substantial assets. Its success, therefore, depends on its agenda, its communication strategy, and the reputation of the personalities representing the foundation. One advantage of a fundraising foundation is its strong link to the general public due to the need to raise money or other resources on a continuous basis. In a way, a fundraising foundation transforms ideas, **social capital**, individual reputation, or media access into money. For example, Jürgen Fliege, the founder of the successful German fundraising foundation that bears his name, is present every day in German television with his own talkshow. More generally, **community foundations** tend to be organized as fundraising foundations.

G

Gardner, John (1912–2002)

A champion of community building and renewal, John Gardner was instrumental in identifying the role of government in propelling social causes to action. As US President Johnson's Secretary of Health, Education and Welfare, Gardner structured Great Society programmes, including Medicare health programmes, the Public Broadcasting System and the Civil Rights Act. In 1970, he founded Common Cause, a citizens' group that aims to increase government **accountability** and oversight. In 1979, he co-founded **the Independent Sector**, a national association of non-profits and foundations. Gardner was also a professor at Stanford's business and education schools and President of the **Carnegie Corporation of New York** and the Carnegie Foundation for the Advancement of Teaching.

Gates, Frederick T. (1853–1929)

A Baptist minister, Frederick Gates served as executive secretary of the American Baptist Education Society, which attracted the philanthropic interest of **John D. Rockefeller, Sr**, a follower of the Baptist faith. It was Gates who enticed Rockefeller to support the establishment of the University of Chicago as the only Baptist university in the American Midwest. Eventually, Rockefeller looked to Gates to guide and manage his philanthropic activities, as well as his investments. Gates can be given credit as being the impetus behind many of Rockefeller's **gifts**, including the creation of the Rockefeller Institute for Medical Research in 1901 and the establishment of the **Rockefeller Foundation** in 1913.

Bill and Melinda Gates Foundation

Created in 2000 through the **merger** of the Gates Learning Foundation and the William H. Gates Foundation, the Bill and Melinda Gates Foundation is an outlet for the philanthropic activities of Microsoft chairman and chief software architect, Bill Gates and his wife Melinda. Headquartered in Seattle (USA), the foundation works both locally—in particular, in Washington state and Oregon—and globally in over 100 countries. With its US $27,000m. **endowment**, the Gates Foundation has made significant contributions in its four main programmatic areas: global health (e.g. $750m. to the Vaccine Fund), education (e.g. $1,000m. to the United Negro College Fund to provide higher education opportunities for minorities), public libraries (e.g. in USA and elsewhere, **grants** to ensure public access to the Internet), and local support of at-risk families in Washington state and Oregon.

Website: www.gatesfoundation.org

Gellner, Ernest (1925–1995)

Although Ernest Gellner's scholarship spans a wide range of subjects, it is *Condition of Liberty: Civil Society and its Rivals* that has become the touchstone for a culture-bound (i.e. Western) imagination of **civil society**. Gellner was clear about the futility of using civil society to analyse social and political realities outside the West, and his thesis has provoked a bitterly divided body of knowledge. He was strident in his analysis of African and Islamic societies, which, he argued, are 'usually underwritten by ritual and a whole set of inside relationships'. Many hold him responsible for international development agencies' attempts to impose a **vision** of civil society in the developing world.

The German Marshall Fund of the United States

The German Marshall Fund of the United States was established in 1972 through a gift from the Federal Republic of Germany (renewed in 1986) as a permanent memorial to the Marshall Plan, the US assistance programme that helped rebuild Europe following the Second World War. The Fund is dedicated to promoting greater co-operation and understanding between the USA and Europe through **grants** to individuals and institutions, convenings and research. Headquartered in Washington, DC, the German Marshall Fund also maintains offices in Paris, Berlin, Brussels and Bratislava.

Website: www.gmfus.org

German Parity Welfare Association – *see* **Deutscher Paritätischer Wohlfahrtsverband (Parity)**

Getty, J. Paul (1892–1976)

American-born J. Paul Getty managed his father's oil business, inheriting what became known as the Getty Oil Company in 1956. From his residence in England, he controlled a vast business empire and, at the time of his death, was the richest man in the world. In 1953, he opened a small antiquities museum in his California house. The J. Paul Getty Trust was established in 1982 with US $1,200m. from his estate. Today the Trust operates the Getty Center in Los Angeles, which houses the J. Paul Getty Museum, the Getty Research Institute, the Getty Conservation Institute, and institutes dedicated to art history and museum management, and supports a **grant** programme for art history research, cultural conservation, and art education and professional development.

Gifts

A gift is a **voluntary**, irrevocable transfer of money, property, or something of value by one person to another or to an **organization**. It is made without consideration as to the amount transferred or any notions of **reciprocity** for the gift. In the context of **philanthropy** and charitable giving, a gift is also referred to as a contribution or donation.

Girard, Stephen (1750–1831)

An immigrant from France, Stephen Girard contributed to the early development of the American shipping, construction and banking industries and, at the time of his death, was the richest man in the USA. In his will, he **bequeathed** more than US $2m. and land in Philadelphia to build and operate a boarding school for poor, orphan boys, now known as Girard College. The money he left to create Girard College was the largest private charitable donation up to that time in American history. He was also considered generous during his lifetime, giving significant sums to the City of Philadelphia for public improvements and contributing resources and volunteer effort to combat a yellow fever epidemic.

Giving Circles

A giving circle, also known as a **donor** circle, is a pooled grant-making fund, which enables members to combine their charitable contributions, learn together about issues of interest and possible recipients, and decide jointly on distributions. Each giving circle is unique, reflecting the character and interests of its members. Thus, giving circles vary in structure, focus and size. They can be very informal, nothing more than a group of friends pooling their donations and meeting in each other's homes to discuss community issues and decide where their donation can do the most good. Or giving circles can have many members and a governing board and may use their local **community foundation** to manage financial and administrative aspects. Membership typically requires a minimum annual contribution.

Global Civil Society

Global civil society, like **civil society,** is a complex term with differing definitions and little agreement about its precise meaning. Anheier, Glasius and Kaldor define the term descriptively as the sphere of ideas, values, institutions, **organizations**, networks and individuals located between the family, the state and the market and operating beyond the confines of national societies, polities and economies. Similarly, Keane in *Global Civil Society?* attempts to define global civil society as a dynamic non-governmental system of interconnected socio-economic institutions that straddle the whole earth and that have complex effects that are felt in its four corners. Keane further elaborates on this definition and argues that there are five features that make the present form of global civil society different from past instances of 'transatlantic' or 'international' co-operation such as the abolitionists in the 18th century or the work of the **International Red Cross and Red Crescent Movement**. The five features are: (1) that the organizations, institutions and activities are non-governmental in nature; (2) that global civil society is a form of society, i.e. it is a dynamic ensemble of more or less tightly interlinked social processes; (3) that it entails civility, i.e. respect for others expressed as politeness towards and acceptance of strangers; (4) that it contains both strong traces of pluralism and strong conflict potential; and (5) that global civil society is transnational and stretches across state boundaries and governmental forms.

Scholte suggests that deterritorialization sets the 21st-century form of global civil society apart from past examples of international movements. That is, issues, activities and organizations can truly be global because territorial location, territorial distance and territorial borders do not have a determining influence on social connections. In global space, 'place' is no longer territorially fixed, territorial distance is covered in effectively no time, and territorial frontiers present no particular impediment. For Scholte then, global civil society encompasses civic activity that: (1) addresses trans-world issues; (2) involves trans-border communications; (3) has a global organization; and (4) works on a premise of supra-territorial **solidarity**.

Scholars agree that a new terminology, of which 'global civil society' is a byproduct, arose in the late 1980s to early 1990s from discussions concerning globalization and the end of the cold war.

Anheier, Glasius and Kaldor argue that global civil society is difficult to measure using standard systems of social and economic accounts. By and large, all these systems tend to be territorially bounded, whereas global civil society is not.

Global Civil Society Index (GCSI)

The Global Civil Society Index (GCSI) allows for a comparative ranking of countries and regions in terms of their participation and inclusion in **global civil society**. The index complements the existing range of international indices like the **Human Development Index (HDI)** and more economic measures of globalization. The index is based on three components: 1) the organizational infrastructure of global civil society, as measured by the density of **international NGOs** and associations over a given population; 2) the civility of individuals, as a measure of cosmopolitan values such as tolerance and commitment to democratic values; and 3) the participation of individuals, as measured both by **membership** in, and **volunteering** for, global civil society organizations and by individual political action.

Global Compact

Through **collective action**, the Global Compact seeks to advance responsible corporate **citizenship** at the international level. It is a network of United Nations **organizations**, transnational corporations and **NGOs**. At its core are the Global Compact Office and five UN agencies: the Office of the High Commissioner for Human Rights; the United Nations Environment Programme; the International Labour Organization; the United Nations Development Programme; and the United Nations Industrial Development Organization.

The Global Compact is not a regulatory instrument—it does not 'police', enforce or measure the behaviour or actions of companies. Rather, the Global Compact relies on public **accountability**, **transparency** and the enlightened self-interest of companies, labour and **civil society** to initiate and share substantive action in pursuing the principles upon which the Global Compact is based.

The Global Compact asks companies to embrace, support and enact, within their sphere of influence, a set of core values in the areas of **human rights**, labour standards, the environment and anti-corruption. Its ten principles enjoy universal consensus and are derived from the Universal Declaration of Human Rights, the International Labour Organization's Declaration on Fundamental Principles and Rights at Work, the Rio Declaration on Environment and Development, and the United Nations Convention Against Corruption.

Global Unions

The term Global Unions is increasingly being used to refer to the 12 major institutions involved in the international **trade union** movement. These institutions include the International Confederation of Free Trade Unions (ICFTU), which represents most national trade union centres; the ten Global Union Federations (GUFs) which are the international representatives of unions organizing in specific industry sectors or occupational groups; and the Trade Union Advisory Committee to the **Organisation for Economic Co-operation and Development (OECD)**. Global Unions is also the name of a website, jointly owned by the 12 trade union institutions mentioned above, which serves as a networking, information dissemination and organizing tool for its members.

Website: www.global-unions.org

Goff, Frederick Harris (1858 - 1923)

In 1914, banker and attorney Frederick Goff established the Cleveland Foundation, revolutionizing philanthropic giving. Goff designed that first **community foundation** with separate investment and distribution arms, allowing banks to invest donated money and entrusting civic leaders to distribute it. By taking advantage of **economies of scale** and allowing the creation of numerous small funds, philanthropic giving was no longer limited to the wealthy. The success of Goff's model sparked the creation of community foundations around the world. Most of Goff's other philanthropic efforts focused on the Cleveland region, supporting programmes for education, health, social service and the environment.

Governance

Governance is the system by which **organizations** are directed and controlled. It is primarily an organizational steering function and is closely related to the notion of stewardship.

The governance structure specifies the distribution of rights and responsibilities among the organization's various participants and **stakeholders**, including the board, founders, managers, clients, grantees and others, and spells out the rules and procedures for making decisions on the organization's affairs. By doing this, it also provides the framework in which the organization's objectives are set and the means of attaining those objectives and monitoring performance.

In **non-profit organizations**, responsibility for governance lies with the **board of directors** (or its equivalents), whereas organizational management is primarily a staff function, although in many smaller and medium-sized organizations both functions overlap. It is useful to think of the board as the focal point of governance, and the chief executive officer as the focal point of management.

In contrast to for-profit businesses, in which the owner/shareholder (the principal) delegates to a board the responsibility to make sure that management (the agent) acts in accordance with the principal's goals and interests (see **principal–agent problem**), it is unclear who should be regarded or function as owner of the non-profit organization. Members or trustees are not owners in the sense of shareholders, and while different parties could assume or usurp the role of principal, such a position would not rest on property rights. The key to understanding the relationship between the special characteristics of non-profit organizations and their governance and accountability requirements therefore is to recognize the special importance of stakeholders rather than owners.

Since the 1990s, the term governance has been used in a much broader sense to refer to the process whereby elements in society wield power and authority, and influence and enact policies and decisions concerning public life and economic and social development. In this context, governance is a broader notion than government, whose principal elements include the constitution, legislature, executive and judiciary. Governance involves interaction between these formal institutions and those of **civil society**.

Government-Owned NGO (GONGO)

Somewhat of an oxymoron, the term government-owned non-governmental **organization** or GONGO, refers to organizations established or controlled by government. There are several reasons why governments seek to establish and control **NGOs**, from a desire to have organizations removed from civil service regulations and oversight regimes to **privatization** efforts and attempts to compete with other NGOs for recognition and resources. Sometimes governments establish GONGOs to 'co-opt' the more independent-minded members of its citizenry, making GONGOs a characteristic element of authoritative regimes in transition.

Government-Sponsored or Government-Created Foundations

Government-sponsored or government-created foundations are independent or semi-independent **foundations** that either are created by public charter or enjoy high degrees of public-sector support for either **endowment** or operating expenditures. Examples include the Inter-American Foundation and the Asia Foundation in the USA, the Federal Environmental Foundation in Germany, the **Fondation de France**, the Government Petroleum Fund in Norway, or the **public foundations** in Turkey. Governments prefer to set up such foundations for a number of reasons, but usually as an instrument to keep certain policy issues and related activities at arm's length from legislators because the matter at hand may be either too controversial (the Swiss Holocaust Foundation to handle bank accounts from the Second World War) or outside core government interest but still important (Deutsche Bundesstiftung Umwelt—the German Federal Foundation for the Environment).

Grameen Bank

The Grameen Bank began its work in 1976 as a project to provide credit to the rural poor in Bangladesh. From this initial experiment, the Grameen Bank (Grameen means 'rural' or 'village' in the Bengali language) has evolved into a financial institution that has redefined banking practices, providing credit and loans to millions without the need for collateral. As of 2002, the Grameen Bank counted over two million borrowers—mostly poor women—who also own 90% of the Bank's shares. The Grameen Bank has also spawned over two dozen **organizations** known as the Grameen Family, engaging in such businesses as venture capital, fishing and textiles.

Website: www.grameen-info.org

Gramsci, Antonio (1891–1937)

Antonio Gramsci was an Italian journalist and politician, known for his theoretical contributions to concepts such as hegemony and **civil society**. Gramsci, leader of the Italian communist party, was arrested by the Fascists in 1926 and was released only to die in hospital. During his imprisonment he wrote more than 30 notebooks of history and analysis of **socialism**, fascism and other topics, including contradictory and ambiguous references to civil society: on the one hand it is the realm where the existing hegemonic social order is maintained, but, on the other hand, it is also the realm of social creativity from which a new social order can emerge.

Grant-Makers' Associations

Grant-makers' associations are non-profit **membership associations** of private and **community foundations**, corporations, individuals and other types of grant-making entities, including in some cases government funding agencies. Such associations provide a variety of information and **capacity-building** services to member grant-makers, offer a forum for them to network and collaborate, and act as a joint voice of **philanthropy**.

Grant-Making Foundations

Grant-making foundations are entities established as independent foundations to maintain or aid educational, social, charitable, religious or other activities serving the public welfare, primarily by making **grants** to individuals or **organizations**. Included among the types of grant-making foundations are private foundations, **community foundations** and **corporate foundations**. The modern grant-making foundation emerged in the USA in the late 19th and early 20th centuries and has since become the prototype of the philanthropic institution. There are over 60,000 grant-making foundations in the USA, and several thousand in countries like England, Germany, or Italy. Grant-making foundations rank among the most independent institutions of modern society in political and economic terms.

Grants

A grant is an award of funds to an **organization** or individual to undertake charitable activities. There is no expectation that the funds be repaid to the grantor organization. Major types of grants include **challenge grants**, used to stimulate resource mobilization by requiring that the donees raise matching funds from other sources; demonstration grants, given to develop or launch a new programme that might function as a model; general-purpose grants, in support of the organization's regular work rather than a specific programme or project; operating support grants, to cover day-to-day expenses; and technical assistance grants, designed specifically to contract outside consulting services.

Grassroots Associations

A grassroots association is a self-organized group of individuals pursuing common interests through a **volunteer**-based, **non-profit organization**. Grassroots associations tend to form because some members of society have goals and interests that differ from those of the broader society. In many cases, they are formed by activists organized around a particular issue as part of a larger **social movement**. In developing country settings, in particular, the term tends to refer to vehicles through which disadvantaged people organize themselves to improve the social, cultural and economic well-being of their families, communities and societies. In general, grassroots associations tend to have a broader purpose, **membership** and set of **stakeholders** than either **neighbourhood associations** or **community-based organizations**.

Greenpeace

With close to three million supporters and presence in some 40 countries, Greenpeace is one of the largest non-profit environmental **advocacy organizations** in the world. Based in Amsterdam, Greenpeace has been campaigning against environmental degradation since 1971 when a boat of volunteers and journalists sailed into Amchitka, an area north of Alaska where the US Government was conducting underground nuclear tests. This tradition of 'bearing witness' in a non-violent manner continues today and is complemented by research, **lobbying** and diplomacy. Greenpeace was instrumental in fighting for the adoption of, among other policies, bans on toxic waste exports to less developed nations and on nuclear weapons testing. Greenpeace accepts no donations from corporations or governments.

Website: www.greenpeace.org

Grupo de Fundaciones

Association of Foundations

Grupo de Fundaciones is an Argentinian **grant-makers' association** with 15 members in 2004. Incorporated in 1995, the Grupo is a **clearing-house** that provides technical, communication and **advocacy** services to Argentina's philanthropic and grant-making communities. Specifically, it aims to promote **philanthropy** and a culture of social responsibility, and to support professionalism in the work of foundations.

Website: www.gdf.org.ar

Grupo de Institutos, Fundações e Empresas (GIFE)

Group of Institutes, Foundations and Businesses

Based in Brazil, the Grupo de Institutos, Fundacões e Empresas (GIFE) was founded in 1995 to establish legitimacy and confidence in the country's philanthropic community. With **membership** consisting of institutes, **foundations** and corporations, GIFE seeks to reduce social inequalities and strengthen Brazil's **third sector**. GIFE provides support to member **organizations** by serving as an information resource, establishing networking opportunities between local and national organizations, and conducting seminars and forums. As one of the first **grant-makers' associations** established in South America, GIFE has since helped launch similar efforts in other countries.

Website: www.gife.org.br

Guggenheim, Solomon Robert (1861–1949)

Solomon Guggenheim was an industrialist, philanthropist and art collector. With his brothers, Guggenheim built one of the largest mining empires in the world by the First World War. Solomon Guggenheim not only had a keen eye for modern art, but was also a strong patron of artists. Guggenheim established the Solomon R. Guggenheim Foundation (1936) for the 'promotion and encouragement of art and education in art and the enlightenment of the public' and the Solomon R. Guggenheim Museum (1959), designed by Frank Lloyd Wright, to exhibit his impressive collection. Guggenheim contributed significantly to the development of the arts in the USA, in particular helping to establish New York City as an international centre for the arts.

Guilds

Guilds are economic and social **associations** of individuals in the same business, craft, or line of trade. They originated in Western Europe in the early Middle Ages and exerted considerable influence on local government, commerce and society. **Membership** was limited to representatives of specific trades or crafts, with the primary function to establish local control by setting standards of workmanship and price, by protecting the business from competition, and by establishing status in society for members of the guild. The guilds set wage rates, hours of work, apprenticeship terms and protected their privileges by holding membership below the demand for their services. By the end of the Middle Ages, guilds became extremely powerful, influencing the economic and political life of towns throughout Europe, as well as international trade. They often had their own patron saint and staged elaborate processions that both honoured their patrons and provided a form of medieval advertising. Guild halls were often the political centre of towns and, at times, the statutes of guilds were adopted by the town as civic statutes. The guild system disintegrated with the rise of free market ideas and the emergence of modern industries. Powerful guilds also existed in the Arab world, Japan and China, where they became, as in Europe, an indication of a rigid, yet ordered and self-organizing local community. Today the term guild is used to refer to certain associations that have little connection with the medieval institution. Many of the major **professional associations** (e.g. in medicine and law) fulfil some of the functions of the old guilds but have different names.

Gulbenkian, Calouste Sarkis (1869–1955)

Born to a wealthy Armenian oil family in Istanbul, Gulbenkian studied in London and gained British citizenship. He co-founded the Shell Group and remained in the oil business his entire life. Gulbenkian was passionate about art, accumulating a valuable collection, which is now housed in the Calouste Gulbenkian Museum in Lisbon. In his final testament, he **bequeathed** a significant sum to create the Lisbon-based **Calouste Gulbenkian Foundation**, which focuses on the arts, education, social welfare and the Armenian diaspora.

Calouste Gulbenkian Foundation

Established in 1956 and now one of Portugal's largest foundations, the Calouste Gulbenkian Foundation is primarily an **operating foundation** focusing on the fields of **charity**, the arts, education and science. It maintains a centre for modern art, libraries, and an institute for biomedical research and education. The Gulbenkian Foundation also provides **grants** to **organizations** and individuals for activities within its main fields of focus, such as research, library modernization, art restoration, and provision of home-based assistance to the ill. In addition, in recognition of the origins of its founder, the Foundation provides scholarships to members of the Armenian diaspora.

Website: www.gulbenkian.pt

H

Habermas, Jürgen (1929–)

A German philosopher, social theorist and leading intellectual, Habermas was a professor at the Universities of Frankfurt and Heidelberg, led the Max Planck Institute in Starnberg (1971–1983), and later directed the University of Frankfurt's Institute for Social Research, from which he retired in 1993. Initially a representative of the Frankfurt School of critical theory, his work on *The Structural Transformation of the Public Sphere* (1962) became one of the leading statements on the importance of **civil society** institutions. Habermas describes civil society as made up of spontaneously created **associations**, **organizations** and movements, which find, take up, condense and amplify the resonance of social problems in private life, and pass it on to the political realm or **public sphere**.

The Hague Club

Established in 1971, the Hague Club is an informal association of European foundation chief executives and other prominent philanthropists. The Hague Club facilitates discussion and co-operation among its members and meets once a year. The Club served as a precursor **organization** to the **European Foundation Centre**.

Hammer, Armand (1898–1990)

Armand Hammer was a US entrepreneur, philanthropist and art collector, and president of the Occidental Petroleum Corporation. Throughout the Cold War, Hammer conducted business activities in the Soviet Union, while making himself a promoter of cultural exchange between East and West. Less controversial were his exceptional donations to such institutions as Columbia

University, the National Gallery and the Metropolitan Museum of Art, and the establishment in 1990 of his own art museum, the Armand Hammer Museum at the University of California—Los Angeles.

Hansmann, Henry

Henry Hansmann, Augustus E. Lines Professor of Law at the Yale Law School, is one of the leading law and economics scholars of his generation. He has written about a broad range of subjects, from markets for human organs to artists' moral rights, but has focused most extensively on the structure and economic functions of organizational law, including not just the law of business corporations but also the law of **non-profit organizations**, **mutual societies** and **co-operatives**. In the non-profit field, he is credited with the development and application of **trust-related theories**, which state that due to the **non-distribution constraint**, non-profit organizations appear trustworthier under conditions of **information asymmetry**. One of his most influential books, *The Ownership of Enterprise*, was published in 1996.

Harrar, Jacob George (1906–1982)

A plant pathologist, J. George Harrar moved from positions at several universities to become local director of the **Rockefeller Foundation**'s Mexican Agricultural Program—the seed of the 'green revolution'—from 1943 until 1952 when he moved to the Foundation's New York headquarters. During his tenure, from positions as deputy director of agriculture, director of agriculture, vice-president, and ultimately—until 1972—president, Harrar led the Foundation down new roads: joining with the **Ford Foundation** to create the International Rice Research Institute (Philippines) to develop improved basic food crops, launching the Foundation's grant-making programme in Africa, and initiating **grants** to enable disadvantaged minorities in the USA to attend university.

Havel, Václav (1936–)

Human rights activist, writer, former dissident, and Czechoslovak and Czech President, Václav Havel contributed significantly to the development of **civil society** in Central and Eastern Europe. In his essays during the 1970s and 1980s, Havel developed the idea of society's self-organization and autonomy, thus laying theoretical groundwork for the gradual renewal of Czech civil society since the late 1980s. As the country's President, Havel defended the **vision** of a strong civil society against both nostalgia for the state socialist model and neo-liberal zealots. A number of **foundations** and other **NGOs** have been established directly by Havel and his family, friends and collaborators.

Heterogeneity Theory

The heterogeneity theory is an economic theory that explains the existence of **non-profit organizations** in market economies. Also known as **public goods theory** or governmental failure theory, it stipulates that unsatisfied demand for public and quasi-**public goods** in situations of demand heterogeneity leads to the emergence of non-profit organizations.

Hewlett, William (1913–2001)

William Hewlett was born in Michigan (USA) and earned engineering degrees from the Massachusetts Institute of Technology in 1936 and Stanford University in 1939. Made successful through his partnership with **David Packard** in forming the Hewlett-Packard Company in 1939, Hewlett encouraged creativity and individual accomplishment among his employees. In 1966, his dedication to people was formalized in the shape of the William and Flora Hewlett Foundation, an independent **foundation** that offers **grants** promoting the arts, population research, nature conservation and US–Latin American relations.

Hill, Octavia (1838–1912)

Victorian philanthropist Octavia Hill is perhaps best known for her innovative methods for managing housing for the poor in England. In the mid-1860s, with help from friends, she acquired dilapidated houses in London for rehabilitation and renting to the poor and introduced communal amenities such as meeting halls and savings clubs. Her approach and her use of trained **volunteers** laid the foundations of the modern profession of housing management. Hill also co-founded the National Trust for Preservation of Historic Buildings and Natural Beauty, which ensured that open spaces and historic buildings could be held in perpetuity.

Hinduism

Hinduism encompasses a variety of rites, customs and beliefs, united by three aspects that clarify its overall integration: individual devotion as a path toward personal liberation, a complex system of deity structures and worship practices, and the extension of religious thinking into the social organization of society into different castes. In contrast to **Islam**, Hinduism does not insist on the strict following of religious doctrine in everyday life, thereby encouraging a sectarian, loosely-knit **religion**; and in contrast to **Christianity**, no formal organizational structures developed over time. Moreover, in the absence of a pronounced proselytizing element, Hinduism has traditionally put little emphasis on expansion and growth. Over the centuries, the relationship between the Brahman religious *élite* and the ruling class was generally symbiotic, with no systematic conflict between the secular state and the religious community. Recently, however, religious reformers have tried to increase the influence of Hinduism either by influencing the political agenda, e.g. Hindi nationalism, or by creating special **organizations** such as the pan-Indian Ramakrishna Mission or the Hare Krishna movement. Overall, and compared to Christianity, Islam and **Buddhism**, Hinduism is the least 'organizational' religion.

Hlávka, Josef (1831–1908)

19th-century Czech philanthropist Josef Hlávka was born to a poor family, but made his fortune as an architect and building entrepreneur. Partially paralysed from continuous overwork since 1869, Hlávka turned his attention to the support of Czech culture and education. He funded, among others, the Czech Academy of Sciences, Literature and Arts (1890), the Hlávka College, a student dormitory in Prague (1904) and Hlávka's Economic Institute (1906). He also supported the creative work of many artists, writers and scientists. Having no children, Hlávka **bequeathed** his property to a foundation that still bears his name (**Hlávka Foundation**).

Hlávka Foundation

Established in 1904 with the bequest of the entire estate of Czech philanthropist **Josef Hlávka**, the Hlávka Foundation dedicates 70% of its yearly income to the support of scientific, literary and artistic efforts of the Czech nation and 30% to talented university students, in accordance with the founder's original will. It was perhaps the gratitude among former Hlávka scholars that saved the

Foundation from dissolution during the communist era, although it lost both its **assets** and autonomy. After 1989, the Foundation resumed its activities and is now the oldest among major Czech foundations.

Human Development Index (HDI)

The HDI is a widely-used measure for international comparisons of the social and economic development of countries. Introduced by the United Nations Development Programme in the 1990s, the HDI complements gross domestic product (GDP) and other purely economic measures in gauging a country's level of development. HDI is a composite index based on three indicators: 1) longevity, as measured by life expectancy at birth; 2) educational attainment, as measured by a combination of adult literacy (two-thirds weighting) and the combined gross primary, secondary and tertiary enrolment ratio (one-third weighting); and 3) standard of living, as measured by GDP per capita at purchasing power parity in US dollars.

Human Rights

Ideas akin to human rights can be found in cultures throughout history, but the first catalogue of individual rights was the Declaration of the Rights of Man and of the Citizen adopted by the French National Assembly in 1789. The idea of individual rights became an important ingredient in the foundation of constitutional states in Europe, and catalogues of civil and political rights entered many national laws and constitutions in Europe and the Americas.

The Holocaust, and other gross human rights violations associated with the Second World War, gave birth to the idea that these rights needed to be formulated and protected at the international and global level. As a result of pressure from a small number of **NGOs**, the United Nations (UN) Charter obliges the UN and its member states to promote 'universal respect for, and observance of, human rights and fundamental freedoms'. At the request of the General Assembly, Eleanor Roosevelt and a group of legal experts drafted the 'Universal Declaration of Human Rights', adopted in 1948.

The Universal Declaration was meant to be the prelude to the swift adoption of a comprehensive UN treaty on human rights, but the Cold War rift stymied these efforts. Political leaders in the Soviet bloc states realised that the idea of human rights, including freedom of expression, freedom of assembly, and freedom to enter and leave one's country, posed a threat to their political system.

Instead of rejecting human rights outright, however, they argued that economic and social rights, such as the right to food, health, housing and education, deserved priority over civil and political rights. Developing countries were also attracted to this argument. The USA, on the other hand, adamantly opposed—and continues to oppose—the suggestion that such 'aspirations' have equal status to civil and political rights. Therefore, two separate treaties were concluded in 1966, the International Covenant on Civil and Political Rights and the International Covenant on Economic, Social and Cultural Rights. While ratification of these two treaties initially ran along the dividing lines of the two Cold War blocks, nowadays both treaties enjoy almost universal ratification. A number of other regional and specialist human rights treaties were also adopted in the post-war years.

Initially, states did not really pursue the promotion and protection of human rights as a foreign policy goal. Human rights became more prominent in the mid-1970s due to several factors, including the agreement of the Helsinki Accords between East and West in 1977, which offered a framework for discussing human rights in the Eastern bloc, and legislation adopted by the US Congress that linked US aid to the human rights record of recipient countries. These and other factors were closely linked to the rise of an international human rights movement in the 1960s and 1970s. Nowadays, many states all over the world profess to consider the promotion and protection of human rights as an important goal not just domestically, but in foreign policy too.

The main criticism levelled against human rights is that they are a Western construct, and not universal. It is undeniable that the idea of human rights is Western in origin. Whether the root idea behind human rights, human dignity, is Western or universal will remain a matter of philosophical debate. However, the vast majority of states have ratified the most important human rights treaties, and most legal experts believe that at least some human rights obligations have passed into customary law. Hence, state respect for human rights is a legal obligation, not a matter of culture.

Human Rights Watch

Human Rights Watch was established in New York in 1978 as Helsinki Watch, monitoring the compliance of Soviet bloc countries with the Helsinki Accords. While remaining a member of the **International Helsinki Federation for Human Rights**, the **organization** grew to cover other issues and regions until all USA-based 'watch' committees were united in 1988 to form Human Rights

Watch (HRW). With its team of nearly 200 professionals, HRW conducts fact-finding investigations into **human rights** abuses and discrimination abroad and in the USA and publishes these findings in books and reports, thereby exposing the abuses and 'shaming' the perpetrators. Human Rights Watch, the largest international human rights organization based in the USA, accepts no government funds.

Website: www.hrw.org

Jan Hus Educational Foundation

Jan Hus Foundations, named after the Bohemian religious thinker and reformer, were organized first in Great Britain and France (1978) and later in the USA, Canada, Benelux and Germany in reponse to Czechoslovak dissidents. The network funded visits by foreign lecturers and supported publication of books and journals as well as creative work of banned artists. In 1990 the Czechoslovak Jan Hus Educational Foundation was established to serve the needs of Czech and Slovak educational institutions. Its programmes include Cursus Innovati, which sponsors the development of new university courses and curricula; Novicius, which supports talented young teachers; and Res Publica, which fosters grassroots civic activism.

Website: www.vnjh.sk

I

Imagine Canada

Formally launched in January 2005, Imagine Canada is an alliance between two of Canada's leading non-profit and **voluntary sector** organizations: the Canadian Centre for Philanthropy (CCP) and the Coalition of National Voluntary Organizations (NVO). Imagine Canada focuses on three main issues: helping charities and non-profit organizations with their respective **missions**; promoting corporate **citizenship** as well as businesses and community partnerships; and increasing public awareness of the impact and work of Canada's non-profit and voluntary sector as well as the importance of community-minded businesses to the sector, communities, and Canada's future. Imagine Canada not only provides service to its 1,200 members but also serves to bring non-profit, business, and government organizations together around common issues.

Website: www.ccp.ca

Impact Evaluation

The impact of an activity is usually defined as the difference the activity has made in producing the desired changes in a target group. The main challenge encountered in trying to measure the impact of a programme is separating the changes caused by the activity itself from those due to other causes.

The basic approach to testing a cause-and-effect relationship dates to the early years of **evaluation**: it consists of determining what would have been observed for the same target group in the same period had the activity not been implemented, i.e. a counterfactual situation. A wide array of quantitative and qualitative methods have been developed to estimate impact using the counterfactual approach: these range from interviews with **beneficiaries** or expert witnesses who are asked 'what if' questions to statistical models aimed at extrapolating the counterfactual from the historical trend of the outcome variable. These methods can prove useful under particular time, skill or **budget** constraints, but give only an approximate measure of impact.

Experimental impact evaluation with random assignment of subjects to 'target' and 'control' groups is the strongest tool for excluding extraneous confounding factors such as 'selection bias' affecting the composition of the two groups, 'secular drift', i.e. long-term trends, and 'maturational changes', i.e. changes determined by natural developments in the target population. Despite its theoretical simplicity and elegance, experimental impact evaluation is not exempt from criticism. From an ethical perspective, one can see the policy-maker and the evaluator as cynical social engineers, indifferent to the moral problems raised by the arbitrariness of the choice between people included in the 'target' group and those excluded. On the epistemological side, some have complained that experimental evaluation, with its exclusive focus on the relation between an activity and its outcomes, overlooks the mechanisms of causation that are inherent in the activity and in the subjects involved, thus giving up any attempt of explaining the phenomenon it seeks to measure. On a more practical level, the main problem with experimentation remains its relatively high cost and the difficulty of even approximating 'laboratory conditions'.

The picture emerging from this short description of the challenges of impact assessment is one of a trade-off between the methodological rigour of experi-mentation and the practical and ethical advantages of other methods. None the less, the notion of impact embedded in the experimental logic may be of great help to social actors wishing to analyse the results of their activities within a rigorous theoretical framework.

Inamori Foundation

Based in Kyoto, Japan, the Inamori Foundation was established in 1984 by Kazuo Inamori, founder and chairman emeritus of Kyocera Corporation, an international consumer products firm. It aims to promote international under-standing, peace and prosperity by annually awarding the Kyoto Prize to those who have contributed significantly in three fields (technology, basic sciences, and arts and philosophy); by supporting projects conducted by young research-ers in Japan in the fields of natural, human and social sciences; and by proposing and implementing programmes with a global perspective, and facilitating international exchange.

Website: www.inamori-f.or.jp

Income Test

Operating foundations in the USA are required to spend at least 85% of their adjusted net income or minimum investment income, whichever is lower, on programmes and activities that are directly related to the tax-exempt purpose of the **organization**. The purposes of this requirement are to check if the operating foundation does in fact carry out programmes and activities in accordance with its stated objectives, to guard against goal diversion, and to help detect inoperative and defunct entities. This requirement is often referred to as an income test.

Independent Sector

The term 'independent sector' was introduced in the USA in the 1980s and is also the name of an influential umbrella **organization** of some of the largest US charities and foundations (see **The Independent Sector**). The term highlights the role these organizations play as a 'third force' outside the realm of government (i.e. political power) and private business (i.e. the profit motive). However, the term has been criticized since many **non-profit organizations** are far from independent, politically as well as financially. Politically, many are engaged in **advocacy** for special interests on which they depend for support, and in financial terms, they depend heavily on both government and private business for **revenue**.

The Independent Sector

Founded in 1980, the Independent Sector is a Washington, DC-based association representing a diverse collection of mostly American **non-profit organizations**, **foundations** and **corporate giving** programmes. Dedicated to strengthening **philanthropy** and citizen action, The Independent Sector acts as a forum for member **organizations**, as an information resource, as the voice of the sector to the media and government, and as a mediator between the grant-making and grant-seeking communities. In addition, it encourages the sector to meet high standards of ethical practice and effectiveness, works to encourage **volunteer** work and community action, and conducts research on non-profit initiatives and public policy.

Website: www.independentsector.org

Individual Giving

Individual giving is a form of **private giving** distinguished from **corporate** or **foundation giving**. It can be defined as a **voluntary** act by which an individual gives money, time (**volunteering**), goods and services, and resources to other individuals, **civil society organizations,** or public bodies without receiving something in exchange. In economic terms, giving is a transfer and does not involve a quid pro quo in monetary or material terms, even though the **donor** may receive psychological benefits and moral satisfaction. Consequently, such giving excludes market transactions, as well as payments required by law or expected due to strong social customs and obligations, e.g. the money parents spend for the marriage of their daughter.

Information Asymmetry

Information asymmetry exists when either the provider or the client/recipient knows more about the true quality of the product or service offered. Under market conditions, there would be strong incentives to use such knowledge to one's advantage. Examples include situations in which the ultimate **beneficiaries** of a service are unknown to **donors**, e.g. a campaign to raise funds in the USA for refugee relief in Sudan, or situations where inadequate feedback loops exist between the actual recipient of and the customer demanding and paying for a service, e.g. parents seeking care for a mentally handicapped child. For these **donors** or customers, such situations pose a dilemma, leading to a search for trust-engendering signals such as the **non-distribution constraint**. Most trust-based theories of non-profit development are based on such information asymmetries between supply and demand that could be exploited to the disadvantage of the customer or recipient.

INGOs (International Non-Governmental Organizations)

Some authors use the term INGO or international non-governmental **organization** instead of **NGO** to refer to a subset of **non-profit organizations** that operate across national borders to a significant extent (in terms of their operating expenditure), and see themselves less as domestic actors. Philanthropic **foundations** that support causes and meet needs abroad complement this set of organizations. Together, they are part of the internationalization of the **non-profit sector** and linked to the process of globalization.

The internationalization of the non-profit sector is, however, not a recent phenomenon. Indeed, the Catholic Church and **Islam** have long had transnational aspirations and maintained far-reaching operations for centuries. The modern INGO emerged in the 1800s from missionary societies, anti-slavery societies, most notably the British and Foreign Anti-Slavery Society (see **Anti-Slavery International**) and the International Committee of the Red Cross (see **International Red Cross and Red Crescent Movement**). By 1874, there were 32 INGOs; by 1914 this number had increased to 1,083, including political organizations like the Socialist International, peace movements, learned societies, and business and **professional associations**. Today, there are over 50,000 INGOs by some accounts, mostly in the field of economic development and co-operation, humanitarian assistance, research and science, and arts and culture.

What seems new, however, is the sheer scale and scope that international and supranational institutions and organizations of many kinds have achieved in recent years. **Oxfam**, Save the Children (see **International Save the Children Alliance**), **Amnesty International**, **Friends of the Earth**, the Red Cross and **Greenpeace** have become the '**brand**-names' among INGOs with significant **budgets**, political influence and responsibility. Indeed, by the late 1990s, the 10 largest development and relief INGOs alone had combined expenditures of over US $3,000m.

Innovation

Joseph Schumpeter defined 'innovation' as the act of putting into practice a recently invented process, product or idea. He distinguishes between two types of innovation: radical innovations that shape major changes in the world, and incremental innovations that occur and shape the process of change continuously. Other scholars have focused on what is being introduced and where to identify three different types: evolutionary innovation, where there is a new process or product; expansionary innovation, where there is a new market; and total innovation, where there is a new process or product and a new market.

Literature on the **non-profit sector** generally attributes an innovation role to **non-profit organizations**. Because they are not driven by a single, financial **bottom line**, they have at least the potential to be more flexible than other types of **organizations** and more willing to take on the risk of trying something new. Non-profit organizations are therefore expected to identify unaddressed issues and develop new problem-solving approaches.

Institut Pasteur

Founded by Louis Pasteur and incorporated as a private foundation in 1887, the Institut Pasteur promotes research into infectious and parasitic diseases and furthers the study and teachings of all aspects of microbiology. The Institute engages in three spheres of activity: research in biology, specifically viral, bacteria and parasitic diseases; educating young scientists and trainees from around the world; and promoting public health through vaccinations, screenings and other services provided at its medical centres world-wide. Headquartered in Paris, the Institut Pasteur has an international network of Institutes, some of which have been granted the status of regional, national, or international centres by the World Health Organization.

Website: www.pasteur.fr

InterAction—American Council for Voluntary International Action

Formed in 1984, InterAction is a Washington, DC-based coalition of more than 160 US **private voluntary organizations** dedicated to international development and humanitarian issues. InterAction's main activities are organizing members to speak in unison in order to influence policy; enhancing the effectiveness and professional capacities of its members; and fostering partnership, collaboration and **leadership** within the private voluntary organization community.

Website: www.interaction.org

Interdependence Theory

Whereas other non-profit theories establish some notion of conflict between governmental provision and non-profit provision, most clearly in the case of the **heterogeneity theory**, the interdependence theory takes a different starting point and begins with the fact that government and the **non-profit sector** are more frequently partners rather than foes—as indicated by the significant portion of public funding that is made available to **non-profit organizations** in many countries, as well as by the increasingly frequent use of public–private **partnerships**.

The thrust of Salomon's (1987) argument is that government does not 'supplant' or 'displace' non-profit organizations; rather, he argues that government support of non-profit organizations is extensive and that government is a 'major force underwriting non-profit operations'. He outlines the scope and extent of government support for non-profits in terms of direct monetary support, indirect support, and variations in support with regards to where the non-profit is located and the type of service it provides.

Salamon criticizes economic theories in their failure to describe this symbiotic relationship between the non-profit sector and government, in particular the **public goods theory** and **trust-related theories**, which view non-profits as institutions apart from government and perhaps even better than government—in essence, picking up the pieces in areas where government fails. Opposite of the **market failure** theory in which non-profit organizations exist where the **public sector** fails, the **voluntary failure** theory argues that **voluntary** action exists because of people's natural tendencies for collective action and sense of social obligation. However, voluntary action is limited, sporadic, unorganized, and at times inefficient. Government therefore steps in to assist the **voluntary sector** in areas of weakness (see **philanthropic insufficiency, philanthropic particularism, philanthropic paternalism,** and **philanthropic amateurism**).

In short, the voluntary sector's weaknesses correspond well with government's strengths, and vice versa. The government can provide a more stable stream of resources, set priorities through a democratic process, discourage paternalism by making access to care a right and not a privilege, and improve quality of care by setting benchmarks and quality standards. The interdependence theory moves away from the zero-sum thinking that characterized some of the economic theories, shows **non-profit–government relations** less in a competitive light and emphasizes collaboration instead. Government and the non-profit sector complement each other and compensate for each other's strengths and weaknesses.

Intermediary Organizations

Intermediary organizations play a variety of roles in the **non-profit sector,** including engaging, convening and supporting critical **stakeholders**; promoting quality standards and **accountability**; brokering and leveraging resources; and advocating for effective policies. They exist primarily in the social service delivery fields, where they tend to connect smaller **organizations** and the people they serve to the local delivery system, as well as in the field of international development and humanitarian relief, where they often mediate between foreign funding agencies and local government agencies or community organizations. Such intermediaries may also be called upon by funders, whether

foundations or government agencies, to help allocate large sums to a variety of recipients within a particular community or for a particular purpose, and to monitor the use of the funds. A different meaning of intermediary organizations is prevalent in Europe, where they refer to institutions located between more centralized government bodies and the more decentralized **civil society** organizations at local levels.

International Campaign to Ban Landmines (ICBL)

Launched in 1992 by a diverse set of **NGOs** sharing a common objective, the International Campaign to Ban Landmines (ICBL) is today a flexible network of over 1,300 **human rights**, humanitarian, peace, veterans' and environmental groups working in over 90 countries. The Campaign's primary goal is to encourage countries to sign and ratify the Mine Ban Treaty; as of 2004, 143 countries had ratified the Treaty. In addition, the network seeks to focus international attention—and financial resources—on the need for mine clearance, mine awareness programmes, and survivor assistance. In 1997, the ICBL and its then co-ordinator, Jody Williams, were awarded the Nobel Prize for Peace.

Website: www.icbl.org

International Center for Not-For-Profit Law

The International Center for Not-For-Profit Law (ICNL), based in Washington, DC, is dedicated to promoting 'an **enabling** environment for **civil society**, **freedom of association**, and public participation around the world'. Specifically, it works in over 90 countries to strengthen the legal framework for civil society through technical assistance; the expertise of a multinational staff and global network of legal specialists; and **partnerships** with civil society representatives, government officials, scholars and business leaders.

Website: www.icnl.org

International Classification of Non-Profit Organizations (ICNPO)

The International Classification of Non-Profit Organizations (ICNPO) is a classification system designed to differentiate the various types of

organizations included in the **non-profit sector**. Developed through a colla-borative process involving the team of scholars working on the Johns Hopkins Comparative Non-profit Sector Project, the system took shape by beginning with the International Standard Industrial Classification (ISIC) System devel-oped by the United Nations and elaborating on it as needed to capture the reality of the non-profit sector. The ICNPO's main features include a focus on the entity's main economic activity rather than purpose and a modular framework of 12 main groups and numerous subgroups that allows users to regroup **non-profit organizations** to suit their analytical purposes.

International Council on Social Welfare

Based in Canada, the International Council on Social Welfare was founded in 1928 and now represents international, national and local **organizations** in over 50 countries. Member organizations work in the fields of social development, social welfare and **social justice**. The Council supports members through dissemination of information, publications, **advocacy**, policy development, research and training. The Council also provides funding for member organiza-tions to attend international meetings and conferences. The Council has the highest level of consultative status with the United Nations' Economic and Social Council.

International Council of Voluntary Agencies (ICVA)

Established in 1962, the International Council of Voluntary Agencies is a global alliance of some 70 non-profit umbrella **organizations** and **international NGOs** focusing on **human rights**, humanitarian assistance and development. ICVA's main objectives are to act as a catalyst and tool for information exchange; to strengthen networks among **NGOs**; to strengthen working rela-tionships with agencies; and to support NGO **advocacy** and **capacity-building** efforts. It facilitates NGO advocacy on the main international body for huma-nitarian co-ordination, the United Nations Inter-Agency Standing Committee, and on the Standing and Executive Committees of the United Nations High Commissioner for Refugees (UNHCR).

Website: www.icva.ch

139

The International Helsinki Federation for Human Rights

The International Helsinki Federation for Human Rights (IHF) is a self-governing non-profit group established in 1983 to provide a structure for independent Helsinki country committees created subsequent to the 1975 Helsinki Accords. A primary goal of these Helsinki groups, including USA-based **Human Rights Watch**, is to monitor compliance with the **human rights** provisions of the Helsinki Final Act. The IHF gathers and analyses data on human rights, particularly in Europe, North America and Central Asia. It acts as a **clearing-house** for human rights information, and disseminates it to governments, **NGOs** and the media. Based in Vienna, the IHF secretariat supports the 42-member Helsinki committees, representing them at the international level.

Website: www.ihf-hr.org

International NGO Training and Research Centre (INTRAC)

Established in 1991 as a registered charity, Oxford-based INTRAC is dedicated to enhancing the role of **civil society organizations** in issues of sustainable development, **social justice**, **empowerment**, and participation. INTRAC's consulting, training and research activities focus on strengthening the organizational and management capacity of **NGOs**, analysing and disseminating information on global trends, and supporting the institutional development of the sector as a whole. Over the years, INTRAC has shifted its emphasis from support mainly for NGOs from the North towards the building up of local institutional capacity in the South and East and the examination of North–South relationships in the **voluntary sector**.

Website: www.intrac.org

International Planned Parenthood Federation—IPPF

Founded in Bombay in 1952 and now headquartered in London, the International Planned Parenthood Federation links autonomous family-planning associations in over 180 countries world-wide. IPPF campaigns locally, regionally and internationally to increase support for reproductive health and family planning world-wide and to improve national health services. IPPF works to set standards in contraceptive safety, programme management, service provision and gender equity through its expert international advisory panels. IPPF enjoys consultative status with the United Nations and works closely with other **voluntary**, inter-governmental and UN agencies that share its concerns.

Website: www.ippf.org

International Red Cross and Red Crescent Movement

The International Red Cross and Red Crescent Movement is composed of the 181 National Red Cross and Red Crescent Societies, the International Federation of Red Cross and Red Crescent Societies, and the International Committee of the Red Cross, the movement's 'mother' **organization** established in 1863 and now headquartered in Geneva, Switzerland. The movement's **mission** is to prevent and alleviate human suffering wherever it may be found and to protect life and health and ensure respect for the human being, in particular in times of armed conflict and other emergencies, and to encourage **voluntary** service and a universal sense of **solidarity**. It is an impartial, neutral and independent movement. The movement also works to strengthen humanitarian law and universal humanitarian principles.

Website: www.icrc.org

International Save the Children Alliance

Save the Children was founded in the UK in 1919 to alleviate children's suffering caused by the aftermath of the First World War. Its message and method inspired others around the world. Headquartered in the UK, the International Save the Children Alliance was established as the international arm of Save the Children, linking 29 national member **organizations** world-wide which operate programmes in more than 100 countries. Member activities include promoting children's rights, assisting children involved in war or natural disasters, campaigning for an end to child labour, and promoting the International Convention on the Rights of the Child.

Website: www.savethechildren.net

International Society for Third-Sector Research (ISTR)

The International Society for Third-Sector Research (ISTR) is a USA-based international scholarly society established in 1992 to promote research and education in the fields of **civil society**, **philanthropy** and the **non-profit sector**.

With members from more than 80 countries, ISTR is committed to building a global community of scholars to discuss and conduct research on the impacts of the **third sector**. ISTR also seeks to enhance the dissemination and application of knowledge about the third sector and broaden the participation of researchers throughout the world. ISTR holds international conferences every two years, facilitates regional networks and affinity groups, and publishes *Voluntas*.

Website: www.istr.org

Interphil—International Standing Conference on Philanthropy

Established in 1969 and headquartered in Geneva, Switzerland, Interphil is an international association that promotes the development of **civil society**, specifically the idea and practice of modern **philanthropy**. Interphil works towards the advancement of the **non-profit sector** in the fields of research, education, the arts and social welfare. Its activities include conferences, lectures, publications and self-conducted programmes.

Intertemporal Price Discrimination

Intertemporal price discrimination, a term from the economics of non-profit pricing, describes a situation in which consumers are charged different fees at selected times. Examples are free entrance days at museums or zoos, or free concerts for children in order to maintain future **membership** in classical music societies. **Non-profit organizations** are more likely to use this mechanism to reach those unable to pay or to reach new and potential users, whereas for-profit **organizations** use it to attract customers at prices at or below marginal cost during low-demand periods, and then use top-up fees during high-demand periods.

Islam

Islam developed in the 7th century as a universalistic religious community established by the prophet Muhammad. From the beginning, religious and secular functions were—and remained—closely linked. The universalistic aspect of Islam was functional for suppressing local and regional political conflicts and for directing efforts toward outward expansion and conquest of neighbouring territories under the rule of Islam. Unlike **Christianity**, where theology was the most important discipline, sacred law (*sharia*) played the central role in Islam, and doctrinal aspects were subordinated to the interpretation of Islamic law.

Because of the close fusion between **religion** and authority, Islam did not develop separate religious institutional structures at levels comparable to those of most Christian religions. However, there are two historical exceptions. First, the monastic *Sufi* orders, initially limited to intellectual *élites*, formed large networks of hospices and educational establishments. Often suppressed during the colonial and independence periods in countries with Islamic majorities, the orders are experiencing a revival in Muslim urban centres in reaction to the alleged excessive materialism of modernity. Second, the *Wakfs* are traditional charitable institutions under which some form of capital is allocated to serve a charitable purpose such as health or education. The *Wakfs* are complemented by *al-zakat*, the traditional notion of charitable giving in Islam. In recent decades, the popular and political revival of Islam has led to an increase in missionary activities throughout the world, but particularly in Africa, the Middle East and Asia.

Isomorphism

Since all **organizations** in particular organizational fields such as health or social services are subject to similar constraints and outside forces, they will tend to become more similar over time, a process that is called isomorphism, according to a theory proposed by Walter W. Powell and Paul DiMaggio. They differentiate between three mechanisms of institutional isomorphic change: (1) coercive isomorphism, which appears as a reaction to direct or indirect pressure to abide by expectations of, e.g. **donors** and other **stakeholders**; (2) mimetic isomorphism, by which organizations in situations of technological or environmental uncertainty model themselves after other organizations that are perceived as successful; and (3) normative isomorphism, which derives from professional norms and standards that guide the work of professionals in organizations and thus shape organizational behaviour.

J

Jacobs, Klaus (1936–)

Klaus Jacobs, a Swiss entrepreneur and philanthropist, led the conversion of his father's coffee company into a major European concern, Jacobs Suchard. Since its sale, Jacobs has founded, acquired, and merged with a number of other enterprises, held under the Jacobs AG holding and investment company. In 1988, he created the Jacobs **Foundation** to provide opportunities for young people in the Americas and in Europe to develop professional skills and to be in tune with nature. In 2001, Jacobs donated all his rights regarding the financial **assets** of Jacobs AG, estimated at US $1,129m. (1,400m. Swiss francs), to the Foundation.

James, Estelle

Estelle James, a Visiting Fellow at the Urban Institute (Washington, DC, USA) and a consultant to the **World Bank**, is best known in the non-profit field for her contributions to the economic theory of **non-profit organizations**. She is noted in particular for advancement of supply-side approaches such as the **entrepreneurship theory** of non-profit origin and organizational behaviour. Prior to joining the World Bank where she was Lead Economist in the Policy Research Department and to serving on US President Bush's Commission to Strengthen Social Security, she was Professor of Economics at the State University of New York, Stony Brook.

Japan Center for International Exchange (JCIE)

The Japan Center for International Exchange (JCIE) seeks to promote policy dialogue and co-operation, build networks between independent research institutions and **civil society organizations**, and enhance Japan's role in international affairs. JCIE provides international forums for policy research and dialogue through its Global ThinkNet network; facilitates the development of civil society in Japan and Asia-Pacific and promotes greater interaction between civil society organizations and their counterparts abroad through its CivilNet; and promotes political exchange among Japanese political leaders and those from other developed nations.

Website: www.jcie.or.jp

Japan Foundation Center

Established in 1985 by executives of private **grant-making foundations** in Japan, the Japan Foundation Center seeks to provide comprehensive and authoritative information on Japanese foundations as well as raise public awareness about the role and significance of the activities of private grant-making foundations. The Centre serves as a resource to the philanthropic community through its extensive library, publications, meetings, seminars and symposia. The Japan Foundation Center also seeks to promote communication and co-operation between grant-making foundations and other **organizations** as well as grant-making organizations in other countries.

Website: www.jfc.or.jp

Johnson, Robert Wood (1893–1968)

Robert Wood Johnson, II was a business leader, philanthropist and pioneer in **corporate social responsibility**. Under Johnson's leadership, the Johnson & Johnson Company became one of America's largest health-care products manufacturers. Committed to corporate social responsibility, Johnson was one of the few industrialists of his era to incorporate a statement of responsibility to workers and the community as part of the corporate credo and, in the 1940s, led a group of clergymen, businessmen and activists to create the document, 'Human Relations in Modern Business'. Established in 1972, the Robert Wood Johnson Foundation is currently one of America's largest foundations dedicated to health care.

K

Kaiser, Henry (1882–1967)

Born in the USA into a family of poor German immigrants, Henry Kaiser began as a photographer's apprentice, eventually buying the photography business and becoming an industrialist (the 'father of modern shipbuilding') and builder (part of the team that built the Hoover Dam). Called by President Johnson a 'pioneer of the new breed of responsible businessmen', he created a prepaid health plan for his employees, which was the impetus for health maintenance organizations (HMOs) such as Kaiser Permanente, now the largest non-profit health plan in the USA. He also established the Henry J. Kaiser Family Foundation as a source of health information and analysis for policy-makers, the media, health-care providers and the public.

Kellogg, Will Keith (1860–1951)

Will Keith Kellogg worked as a broom salesman until becoming a research assistant at the Battle Creek Sanitarium in Michigan (USA) where his brother worked as a physician. Finding his flakes to be a success among patients, he successfully marketed Kellogg's Corn Flakes, which quickly became a household breakfast item across America. Passionate about providing stimulating opportunities for youth, Kellogg helped build a school for handicapped children and a youth recreation centre. He established the **W. K. Kellogg Foundation** in 1930 to provide opportunities for young people.

W. K. Kellogg Foundation

The W. K. Kellogg Foundation, based in Battle Creek, Michigan (USA), was established in 1930 by cereal industry pioneer **Will Keith Kellogg**. Originally called the W. K. Kellogg Child Welfare Foundation, its **mission** is to promote the health, happiness and well-being of children and youth. **Grants** are made for projects in the USA, as well as Latin America, the Caribbean and southern Africa in the areas of health, education, rural development, food systems, **philanthropy**, volunteerism and **leadership**. The W. K. Kellogg Foundation is among the largest in the USA.

Website: www.wkkf.org

Keppel, Frederick P. (1875–1943)

The son of Irish immigrants, Frederick P. Keppel served as the **Carnegie Corporation**'s fourth president from 1922 to 1942. During his tenure, Keppel led the Corporation into new fields by funding programmes in adult education and fine arts. Keppel was among the first foundation presidents to define the roles and responsibilities of **foundations** and to see the 'modern **(grant-making) foundation** as a distinctively American institution'. One of Keppel's most noted projects was the commissioning, in 1938, of Swedish economist Gunnar Myrdal's *An American Dilemma*, a landmark study of race relations in the USA. The effort was particularly controversial within the foundation community because it represented a foray into social issues.

Kiwanis International

Founded in 1915 in Detroit, Michigan (USA), Kiwanis was originally a business club. By 1919, however, Kiwanis evolved into a **service club,** and at the 1924 Kiwanis International convention, a set of objectives was outlined that has since guided the club's work around three key aspects: evaluating both children's issues and community needs on an ongoing basis; conducting service projects to respond to those identified needs; and maintaining an active **membership** roster of professional business people who have both the desire and the ability to serve their community. Kiwanis became international with the launch of a branch in Canada in 1919 and has since expanded to 8,600 Kiwanis clubs with nearly 300,000 members in 94 countries. A men's club originally, it was not until 1987 that the club allowed women to become members.

Website: www.kiwanis.org

KLON/JAWOR

KLON/JAWOR was established in 1990 as an independent, non-political, **non-profit organization** dedicated to providing information for the development of civil society in Poland. For 10 years, it operated as part of the Regardless of the Weather Foundation and became its own separate entity in 2000. KLON/ JAWOR promotes the development of civil society by supporting and promoting activities of **NGOs**; its other activities include research on NGOs, technical and legal publications, dissemination of information and the maintenance of a database on Polish NGOs.

Website: www.klon.org.pl

Kōeki Hōjin

Kōeki hōjin means, literally, a public-interest corporation. Article 34 of the Japanese Civil Code define it as, 'A *shadan* (**association**) or *zaidan* (**foundation**) relating to worship, **religion**, **charity**, science, art or otherwise relating to *kōeki* (public interest) and not having for their object the acquisition of gain may be made a *hōjin* (a juridical person) subject to the permission of the competent authorities.' As of October 2001, there were 12,889 *shadan hōjin* and 13,294 *zaidan hōjin*, together forming the main core of Japan's **non-profit sector**. Among the **organizations** taking this form are also some **quangos**, which have been criticized for their political and financial closeness to govvernment. In 2003, the Cabinet determined the need to reform the *Kōeki hōjin* system and convened the Fukuhara Commission under the Minister of State for Administrative Reform, with the aim of enacting legislative measures by 2005.

Koning Boudewijnstichting/Fondation Roi Baudouin

King Baudouin Foundation

Established in 1976 to celebrate the 25th anniversary of King Baudouin's coronation, the Koning Boudewijnstichting/Fondation Roi Baudouin is an independent **foundation** dedicated to improving the population's living conditions. Based in Brussels, the Foundation both conducts programmes and makes **grants** using its own resources. In addition, it acts as a national **community foundation**, administering named (for individual **donors**), specific and corporate funds that make it possible for individuals, associations and businesses to contribute to any cause they hold dear. Its activities are currently focused on four major themes: **social justice**, **civil society**, **governance**, and funds and **philanthropy**, especially transnational.

Website: www.kbs-frb.be

Konrád, György (George) (1933–)

A Hungarian essayist and novelist and an advocate of individual freedom and **civil society**, György Konrád's early works (*The CaseWorker, Sociological Problems of Housing Estates, Intellectuals on the Road to Class Power*—the latter co-authored by Iván Szelényi) revealed how the state socialist redistribution system actually worked. In their next book Konrád and Szelényi pointed out that the proletariat was the most oppressed class and the intelligentsia was the dominant force in society. Konrád's subsequent essays (*Temptation of Autonomy, The Slow Work of Independence, Antipolitics*) explored the importance of civil society initiatives under the conditions of limited political freedom.

Körber, Kurt A. (1909–1992)

Kurt A. Körber was a German born philanthropist, inventor and entrepreneur. He founded the Kurt A. Körber Foundation in 1959 and the Hauni Foundation in 1969, which in 1981 merged to create the **Körber-Stiftung**, a private, non-profit **operating** and **grant-making foundation** that seeks to get citizens involved in public discourse on politics, education, science and international communication. Körber left all of his **assets** to the Stiftung, making it the sole shareholder of Körber AG, which develops and produces precision machines and machines tools. In 1983, he was awarded the Medal for Services to Foundations by the Federal Association of German Foundations.

Körber-Stiftung

Körber Foundation

Founded by German entrepreneur **Kurt A. Körber** in 1959, the Körber-Stiftung owns Körber AG and is one of the largest **independent foundations** in Germany. The Stiftung regards itself as a 'Forum for Initiative', initiating discourse within society to identify social problems and to promote measures to find solutions. Organizing competitions and discussions, the Stiftung sets a thematic framework and invites citizens to propose and discuss ideas and thus gives citizens an opportunity to participate in the daily democratic process. Topics include international understanding, culture, history, education and science.

Website: www.stiftung.koerber.de

Kouchner, Bernard (1939–)

Bernard Kouchner served as a medical doctor in the Biafra War from 1968 to 1970. Shocked by the inefficiency of local hospitals and relief efforts, he created **Médecins sans Frontières** in 1971, and Médecins du Monde in 1980, the famous 'French doctors' **organizations**. In 1988 he became Secretary of State at Humanitarian Action and later Minister of Health in several socialist governments. In 1999 Kofi Annan appointed him the High Representative of the United Nations in Kosovo. As a politician, Kouchner advocated the 'duty of meddling' in a country when **human rights** are obviously violated.

L

Law of 1901

This French law legally established in 1901 the **freedom of association**, a principle that emerged later in France than it did in Great Britain (1864 as against 1825). The law defines an **association** as 'the convention according to which two or more individuals permanently pool together in common knowledge or activity with an aim other than sharing profit'. A simple declaration to local government is required to obtain a legal status, and the members choose the **governance** of the **non-profit organization**. This very simple and flexible law still exists in France and inspired the legislation of some other European countries such as Belgium, Spain and Italy.

Leadership

Leadership is the ability of one individual (or, at times, a group of individuals) to exercise influence on people's decisions and behaviours over and above what is required by authority relations and contractual and other obligations. Leadership is a process of influencing others to do what they would not do otherwise.

Non-profit leaders need to focus on four dimensions:

- Internal organizational aspects, in particular the board, staff, volunteers, members and users that the leader has to inspire, encourage and unite behind a common **mission**;
- External organizational aspects, in particular **donors**, policy-makers, the media and other constituencies whose support the leader needs for financial resources and legitimacy;
- Present operations such as organizational performance and service quality, demand, information flows, organizational conflicts and motivation, and community support; and

- Future possibilities, where the leader addresses questions of **sustainability** and potential threats and opportunities that may have important implications for the **organization** and its direction.

There are many types of leadership, each of which is appropriate for **non-profit organizations** at different stages. Charismatic leadership, for example, refers to the personal characteristics of leaders to inspire pride, faith, identification, dedication, and commitment and a willingness to follow directives and accept decisions. This type of leadership is most useful in times of organizational uncertainty. Transformational leadership inspires staff and members to put aside personal self-interest for the common good of the organization and to have confidence in their ability to achieve the 'extraordinary' challenges before them during a transitional stage. By contrast, charismatic leadership can be dysfunctional for organizations that perform in relatively stable task environments. In such circumstances, transactional leadership, which requires maintaining an alignment between the organization's mission and goals on the one hand, and the motivation and interests of employees and members in achieving set objectives, is more appropriate.

League Tables and Rankings

In situations of **information asymmetries**, **quasi-markets** and services provision in which comparisons are complex and difficult to measure and express, league tables and rankings have become a 'second best' device to improve consumer information. They are also used in the context of **new public management** to press for greater **accountability** and improved performance. Examples of 'leagues' using such comparisons include universities and hospitals but also entire local governments or local authorities, and indicators appearing in the tables range from per capita expenditures and capacity, output and **performance measures** to **waiting lists** and reputation factors.

Bernard van Leer Foundation

Established in 1949 in the Netherlands, the Bernard van Leer Foundation (BvLF) supports early childhood development activities in approximately 40 countries. The Foundation's guiding principle is a holistic approach to childhood development that incorporates education, health and nutrition. BvLF both makes **grants** through its Programme Development and Management department and operates its own programmes through its Programme Documentation and Communication department, drawing on the experience of the early child-hood community to inform policy and practice.

Website: www.bernardvanleer.org

Legacies

A legacy is a bequest by will of personal property, financial or otherwise. It is similar in many respects to a gift *causa mortis*. There are several types of legacies. A specific legacy **bequeaths** a designated object, e.g. a named painting or building. A general legacy is a sum of money to be paid out of any **assets** of the **donor**'s estate. A residuary legacy is all of the deceased's personal property otherwise undistributed. Legacies are a significant and growing part of the donative income of **non-profit organizations**.

Leverage

Leverage refers to the intended impact of a **grant** disproportionate to its size, in the same way a properly applied lever can lift a very heavy weight. In the grant-making context, a small amount of money is given to a grantee with the expectation that it will help mobilize additional resources.

Lilly, Eli (1885 –1977)

Born in Indianapolis (USA), Eli Lilly was a philanthropist, industrialist and pharmaceutical chemist. From 1907 onwards, he worked at Eli Lilly and Company, the pharmaceutical company founded by his grandfather. In 1937, Eli Lilly, along with his father and brother, established the Lilly Endowment, which has become one of the largest foundations in the USA. His interests extended to **religion**, history and archaeology, prompting him to author several books. Upon his death, religious and educational institutions in Indianapolis received significant bequests from his estate.

Lobbying

Lobbying, as the term is used in the USA, refers to a specific form of **advocacy**, i.e. efforts to influence legislation. There are two forms of organizational lobbying: direct lobbying, i.e. directly contacting decision-makers in support of or against specific legislation, and grassroots lobbying, i.e. encouraging others to contact legislators in support of or against specific legislation. In the USA, lobbying is legal for **non-profit organizations**, although **Section 501(c)(3)** organizations are restricted in the amount of money they can spend on such activities. This is due to their receipt of tax-deductible donations, in order to prohibit *de facto* subsidization of the political views of major contributors. Regulations regarding lobbying and other political activities of non-profit organizations vary widely internationally. Countries with **common-law** traditions, such as the UK and Canada, have similar regulations to those described above, though not identical. For example, grassroots lobbying is banned for **charities** in the UK. Countries with **civil-law** traditions, such as France and Germany, have tended not to put such restraints on non-profit lobbying.

Local Exchange Trading Networks

Local exchange trading networks (LETS) are locally initiated, democratically organized, not-for-profit **organizations**, which provide an information and 'bookkeeping' service, recording transactions of members exchanging goods and services by using the currency of locally created LETS credits. The LETS credit currency does not involve coins, paper money or tokens of any kind but rather acts as a scoring system, keeping track of the value of individual members' transactions within the system. As there is no interest paid to accounts in credit, and no interest charged to accounts in debit, neither situation is a problem, and both are necessary in order to make transactions happen, although free-riding can be a problem (see **Free-Rider Problem**). LETS have grown in numbers, variety and acceptance since they first became popular in the early 1990s.

Loch, Sir Charles Stewart (1849–1923)

Charles Stewart Loch was born in Bengal, India in 1849. A social reformer of the Victorian era, and known for his keen interest in aged populations and the poor, Loch was a member of the UK Commission on Aged Poor from 1893–1895; he was also a member of the Royal Commission on the Care and Control of the Feeble Minded and the Royal Commission on the **Poor Laws**. Between 1875 and 1914 Loch served as Secretary to the Council of the London Charity Organization Society. His often-quoted writings include *Charity Organization* (1890) and *Charity and Social Life* (1910).

M

MacArthur, John D. (1897–1978)

John D. MacArthur was born in a poor region of eastern Pennsylvania (USA). By the time of his death, however, he was not only one of the three wealthiest men in America and the sole owner of the nation's largest privately held insurance company, but was also responsible for the creation of one of America's ten largest philanthropic **organizations**. That organization, the **John D. and Catherine T. MacArthur Foundation**, began operations in 1978 and has since granted over US $3,000m. to groups and individuals that work to strengthen institutions, policies, and information provision through public interest media for human development.

John D. and Catherine T. MacArthur Foundation

Established in 1978 and based in Chicago, Illinois (USA), the John D. and Catherine T. MacArthur Foundation is a private **grant-making foundation**, providing **grants** domestically and internationally in the fields of global security and **sustainability** and human and community development, among others, and making **programme-related investments**, mostly to US community development financial institutions. It also supports MacArthur Fellows with unrestricted, five-year fellowships in recognition of their promise of continued creative work. With **assets** of more than US $4,000m., MacArthur is one the ten largest private philanthropic foundations in the USA.

Website: www.macfound.org

Macdonald, Dwight (1906–1982)

Dwight Macdonald was an American intellectual, journalist and editor, whose career ranged from assistant editor at *Fortune* magazine, to founding editor of the left-leaning journal, *Politics*, to freelance articles on poverty in America. His 1956 book, *The Ford Foundation*, takes a look at the early years of the **Ford Foundation** and its grant-making activities. Macdonald observed that as Ford grew, it tended toward becoming removed from its intended **beneficiaries**, and its executives reverted to 'foundationese', 'a language that abstracts from reality enough of its life, variety, and general sloppiness to allow it to be embalmed in a staff memorandum'. In his way, Macdonald challenged foundations to be more innovative and more connected to the people affected by their activities.

Maecenas

Maecenas, a word that refers to a wealthy patron of the arts, originated from the Roman statesman and patron of the arts Gaius Maecenas (also known as Cilnius or Caius Maecenas), who was a political advisor to Augustus Caesar and has been reputed to have discovered and supported such writers and poets as Horace and Virgil. Versions of the term 'maecenas' are found in several languages and are used primarily to refer to individual philanthropists supporting arts and culture, such as *Maezenat* in German or *mécénat* in French.

Management by Objectives

Management by objectives (MBO), first outlined by **Peter Drucker** in 1954 in *The Practice of Management*, is a process by which goals are set collectively for the **organization** as a whole and on the basis of consultation and review, optimally involving all units and levels of hierarchy. These goals or objectives then form the basis for monitoring and evaluation of managers, with the focus on achievement of the objective within a specific timeframe rather than on what was done to achieve it. Critics of the MBO system express concern that such objectives restrict creativity and responsiveness to rapidly changing environ-ments, while others point to problems when the manager is not in complete control of necessary resources. The key for non-profits is developing an MBO system, including a set of objectives, that encourages rather than limits the capacity of the work team.

Mandatory Pay-Out Requirement

A mandatory pay-out requirement specifies the minimum amount of resources **grant-making foundations** must expend in **grants** and other related expenses. In the USA, the **Tax Reform Act of 1969** imposed such a mandatory pay-out requirement on grant-making foundations as a means to prevent the misuse of foundations as mere tax shelters. The requirement as modified in 1981 stipulates that US foundations make qualifying contributions (including grants, **programme-related investments** as well as reasonable administrative expenses) of the equivalent of at least 5% of the market value of their **assets**, independent of actual income levels. Different and somewhat less stringent rules tend to be in effect in other countries. For example, foundations must spend at least half of their income on charitable purposes in Finland and two-thirds in Germany. In England, foundations need to provide a justification to the oversight bodies if they choose not to spend their full income in any given year.

Market Failure

In economic terms, market failure occurs where **externalities** or **information asymmetries** exist so that the functioning of the market is not optimally balanced. So-called trust goods like donated blood, child care and social services are prone to such market failures unless market-correcting mechanisms such as a **non-distribution constraint** or government oversight are in place. Non-profit **public goods** theories suggest that market failures give rise to **non-profit organizations** that will provide goods and services that market firms or government cannot or will not provide.

Marketing

Marketing is the analysis, implementation and control of exchange relationships between an **organization** and its external as well as internal **stakeholders**. Since **non-profit organizations** are multiple stakeholder entities, non-profit marketing must be sensitive to different audiences and adjust its communication patterns and other approaches accordingly. Over time, marketing has assumed greater relevance for non-profit organizations and now involves a range of activities such as the marketing of services provided, **cause-related marketing**, image marketing and branding (see **Brands**). The term 'marketing mix' is used to refer to the range of approaches, techniques and tools organizations use to reach their customers, users or audience. The widely used '4-P' classification (Product, Price, Place and Promotion) is increasingly also applied in modified forms by non-profit organizations to chart their competitive position.

Marx, Karl (1818–1883)

Best known as the founder of modern **socialism**, Karl Marx developed a body of theories regarding the relationship between the state and the 'proletariat' and the citizenry, as well as explanations of the economic and social underpinnings of **civil society**, that have directly shaped contemporary theories of civil society (i.e. **Gramsci**), economic interest associations, unions and **co-operatives**. Born in Germany, Karl Marx studied law at Bonn and Berlin and earned a Ph.D. at Jena. Some of Marx's most renowned works include *The Communist Manifesto* (with Friedrich Engels), *Das Kapital,* and the 1859 *Preface* to *A Contribution to the Critique of Political Economy* where Marx outlines his ideas about the 'fundamental structure' of civil society. His writings on the role of private **philanthropy** and **charity**, though far from central in his work, were rather critical and allocated a state-led role to social welfare.

Matching Grants

A matching grant is a **grant** made by a **foundation**, government agency, or individual with the proviso that actual grant disbursement is contingent on the recipient raising a specified amount of funds from other sources to match the offered contribution. Matching grant requirements vary; however, most are one-to-one. From a funder perspective, they are seen as a way to spread risk and responsibilities across multiple investors. From a grantee perspective, they help avoid resource **dependencies** but may increase **fundraising** costs. A **challenge grant** is a version of a matching grant, paid only if the grantee **organization** is able to raise an additional and specified amount of funds from other sources.

McKnight, William L. (1887–1978)

William McKnight, an industrialist and philanthropist, started at 3M Corporation as an assistant bookkeeper and eventually moved up to serve as the company's board chair. His emphasis on **innovation** and employee initiative is credited for 3M's success. In 1953, McKnight and his wife Maude founded the McKnight **Foundation** in Minnesota to provide **grants** to support grassroots action and encourage policy reform. Until 1973, while under McKnight's own leadership, the Foundation had no formal grant-making programme but gave away US $2.3m. Since then, the Foundation has become one of the US's largest foundations while remaining anchored in one state and still under the direction of a family board.

Means-Testing

Means-testing is a way in which selectivity is incorporated into the allocation of public or charitable benefits. In contrast with universal benefits, i.e. those such as primary education that are distributed to everyone equally, regardless of need, selective benefits are distributed on the basis of need, commonly by providing benefits only to those below a certain income level. This income cut-off is called a means test. Examples of selective benefits are public housing, or in the USA, food stamps and Medicaid. Proponents of means-testing argue that it contains costs, ensures that scarce resources are not spent on those that do not need it, and reduces reliance on government and other charitable programmes. Detractors argue that means-tested programmes single individuals out (thus stigmatizing recipients), do little in the way of preventing social problems, and are complex to administer because of eligibility screenings. Historically, the USA has relied on means-tested social programmes to a much greater extent than most of Europe.

Médecins sans Frontières

Doctors without Borders

Médecins sans Frontières (MSF) was founded in 1971 by a group of French doctors, including **Bernard Kouchner** and Francis Charhon, who were previously in charge of emergency hospitals during the decolonization war in Congo. Today, with offices in 18 countries and engaging some 2,500 volunteer health-care professionals working in over 80 countries, MSF provides medical and other assistance and raises awareness about the plight of those they serve. MSF was very active in the Lebanon, Chad, Sudan, Afghanistan and Somalia conflicts. Due to dissent, especially regarding the acceptance of public **subsidies**, a spin-off, Médecins du Monde, was formed. MSF has been awarded several prizes for its work, including the Nobel Peace Prize in 1999.

Website: www.msf.org

Mellon, Andrew W. (1855–1937)

Andrew Mellon, born in Pittsburgh (USA) to a family of Protestant immigrants from Northern Ireland, was a financier, industrialist, public official, art collector, and, by 1914, one of the richest men in the USA. He was Secretary of the US Treasury from 1921 to 1932, when he resigned due to the loss of the President's confidence following the Great Crash of 1929. Mellon gave away nearly

US \$10m. during his lifetime, but is best known for his **gift**, including the donation of his renowned art collection, to establish Washington, DC's National Gallery of Art. Following his death, his children set up the Avalon Foundation and the Old Dominion Foundation, which merged in 1969 to form the Andrew W. Mellon Foundation in their father's memory.

Membership

Membership refers to the state of being a member of a group, **organization**, or **association.** Members are the persons composing a society, community, organization, association or the like.

Membership as a term is also used to delineate between organizations in the **non-profit sector**, such as associations versus **foundations**. In fact, most legal systems incorporate the ancient Roman law differentiation between associations (*universitas personarum*) based on membership, and foundations based on some core asset (*universitas rerum*). In this sense, **voluntary associations** are private, membership-based organizations in which membership is non-compulsory. They are distinct from many **non-profit organizations** like hospitals, social service agencies and art museums, which may have a governing board but no broad membership base. Examples of membership associations include:

- Service organizations like the Rotary Club (see **Rotary International**), the Lions, **Kiwanis** or Zonta International and fraternities like the **Freemasons** and similar societies.
- Special interest associations and **advocacy** groups like the US National Rifle Association, Mothers Against Drunk Driving, Society for the Prevention of Cruelty to Animals, or American Association of Retired People.
- **Self-help groups** such as Alcoholics Anonymous and countless local groups for divorcees, or the sharing of grief and loss, weight loss, or crime victims.

Membership is also used as a measure of **social capital**, which is an individual characteristic and refers to the sum of actual and potential resources that can be mobilized through membership in organizations and through personal networks. People differ in the size and span of their social networks and number of memberships. Social capital captures the norms of **reciprocity** and trust that are embodied in networks of civic associations, many of them in the non-profit field, and other forms of socializing.

Regardless of the strikingly different political and social contexts in which voluntary associations developed historically, recent decades have witnessed a significant expansion in the number of associations and memberships. The number of voluntary associations in the USA, for example, is well over 1.5 million, with 57% of the population being a member in at least one association. America, recalling **de Tocqueville**, is a nation of joiners. Indeed, 92% of the population aged 18 or older belongs to at least one organization, and about 75% to more than one. Two-thirds belong to a religious organization; one-third to an organization active in the field of sports and recreation or education; about one in four is a member of a **professional association** or youth club; and one in five of a political association, social welfare or health-related organization. However, Scandinavia has the highest membership rates in the world, and being a member of social organizations is seen in close relation to a participatory, inclusive and democratic society.

There are different types of membership associations: member-supported organizations and membership-based organizations, each with important implications for decision-making, **accountability** and legitimacy. In the case of member-supported associations, members typically have no vote and little influence on **governance** and decision-making. They are not based on the notion that members form some *demos*; rather members are close to the role of users, clients or **donors**. The contributions of member-supported organizations to **democracy** are mainly limited to their impact on pluralism and diversity. By contrast, membership-based organizations are based on democratic governance and decision-making, and provide formal mechanisms for the representation of different groups. Because some members are more committed than others, member-based organizations have to address the dilemma between the free riding of uncommitted members and the tendency toward elite control by core activists (see **Free-Rider Problem**).

Mergers

Mergers between **non-profit organizations**, i.e. the combining of two independent organizations, have become increasingly common, particularly in the North American context. Mergers are typically seen as a strategic option of last resort that is pursued in reaction to turbulence in funding environments, growing competition, or direct pressures from dominant funding sources. In the non-profit context, a distinction can be made between a takeover and a merger *per se*. In a takeover, the larger, dominant agency retains control of the process and essentially absorbs and assimilates the smaller agency into its own structure. In a more equally-balanced merger, control remains shared between the partners, but the merger requires greater management and structural adjustments. While control issues and restructuring needs differ, both mergers and takeovers require the formation of permanent relationships and resource combinations, and both can be horizontal (between **organizations** providing similar services), vertical (between organizations operating in different parts of a service delivery system), or conglomerative (between organizations in different fields).

Merit Goods

In the context of public choice theory, merit goods refer to situations in which consumer information is poor and the provider likely to make a better decision on the consumer's behalf. For example, public health immunization may be required and sanitation standards maintained irrespective of individual preferences. Likewise, school education is compulsory irrespective of the parents' or children's wishes. The argument is that merit goods are best supplied by government and financed through general taxation when the commodity or service is neither easily tradable, nor fungible within household income, and when it is not easy to reject the good or service. To the extent that these assumptions do not apply, other providers, be they for-profit or non-profit, can enter a market or **quasi-market** for service provision, such as in the field of education and public health.

Mexican Centre for Philanthropy – *see* Centro Mexicano para la Filantropía, AC (CEMEFI)

Michnik, Adam (1946–)

Polish historian, essayist, lecturer and journalist, Adam Michnik was one of the most influential dissidents in Poland during communist times. A **human rights** activist and an advocate for **democracy** and press freedom, he helped found the Workers' Defence Committee (KOR) in 1976 and lectured in the 'Flying University', which brought intellectual and worker activists together in underground seminars. He served as an advisor to **Solidarność** in its struggle for democracy in the 1980s. Following the political transition, he helped launch one of Eastern Europe's most respected dailies, *Gazeta Wyborcza*. Michnik authored countless essays, articles and books, including *Letters from Prison and other Essays*, a collection of his smuggled-out writings.

Mill, John Stuart (1806–1873)

An economist, philosopher and women's rights advocate, John Stuart Mill's writings and thoughts have influenced many philosophical traditions, from positivism and idealism to collectivism and capitalism, and are influential in approaches to **civil society**. Mill was also a leading figure in the women's suffrage movement during the English Victorian era. Although Mill's writings did not generate a new methodology and theory for the social sciences, some have argued that his works on 'social environmentalism' and issues around civil society were a major influence for the development of the applied social sciences and social policy. Some of Mill's most well known works include: *On Liberty, Utilitarianism, Principles of Political Economy,* and *System of Logic.*

Misereor

Misereor is one of the largest Catholic **NGOs** in Germany, providing support for development projects in developing countries, primarily in Africa, Asia and Latin America. It was created in 1958 by the German Bishop's Conference, supported by the German branch of the Pax Christiana lay movement who collected donations and served as volunteers. Its **revenue** for 2003 was more than €150m., of which €60m. represented private donations, €10m. contributions from the Catholic Church, and €81m. from the **public sector**. Misereor co-operates closely with the German government and has assumed an **advocacy** role on behalf of the developing country poor, both in Germany and at the level of the European Union.

Website: www.misereor.de

Mission

The mission is the very reason for the existence of any **organization**. The mission is usually laid out in a mission statement, i.e. a succinct description of the basic purpose of an **organization**. The mission statement brings out the value base of the organization; offers guidance for its operations; helps prioritise objectives and tasks; acts to motivate staff, volunteers and members; and aids in **evaluation** and orientation. A good mission statement articulates the organization's purpose and long-term goals, the needs that the organization fills, the organization's core values and operating principles, and the organization's aspirations for the future (**vision** statement).

Mohn, Reinhard (1921–)

Born in Germany, Reinhard Mohn was the fifth generation to lead the Bertelsmann publishing house, which he expanded to include music clubs, newspapers, television and radio. Currently, he is chairman emeritus of Bertelsmann AG and chairman of the **Bertelsmann Foundation**, which he founded in 1977 to tackle societal problems and foster **democracy** world-wide. In 1993, he transferred 70% of his shares of Bertelsmann AG to the foundation. For his work as a leading businessman and philanthropist, Mohn received the Gold Medal of the Federal Association of German Foundations (1998) and the State Prize of North Rhine-Westfalia (1999).

Moral Hazards

'Moral hazard' is a term used in economic theory primarily to describe consumer behaviour in insurance markets, where the absence of adequate monitoring and regulation can lead to **market failures**. For example, car insurance policies that cover any and all damages create a disincentive to drive carefully, and entitlements to long-term care insurance can lead to moral hazards by lowering family incentives to provide **voluntary** care. The term is important in **trust-related theories** of **non-profit organizations**, since moral hazards arise in situations of **information asymmetry** where providers have incentives to take advantage of consumer ignorance.

Mott, Charles Stewart (1875–1973)

Born in New Jersey (USA), Charles Stewart Mott sold his wheel-making company to General Motors and served on its board from 1913 to 1973, amassing a huge fortune. In 1926, after moving to Flint, Michigan and serving as its mayor for three terms, Mott established the **C. S. Mott Foundation** to respond to the problems of the swiftly growing city. Although the Foundation continues to invest significantly in Flint, it has become a national and international grant-maker. Among his other philanthropic efforts, Mott established a medical and dental clinic for children and helped begin the YMCA (see **Young Men's Christian Association**) and Boy Scouts in Flint.

Charles Stewart Mott Foundation

Charles Stewart Mott established the C. S. Mott Foundation in 1926 to serve and improve the well-being of his adopted hometown of Flint, Michigan (USA). Today, the Mott Foundation operates also nationally and internationally in the fields of social welfare, education, the environment and **civil society**. Primarily a **grant-making foundation**, the Mott Foundation has invested significant grant dollars in building civil society in transitional countries such as Russia and South Africa, as well as in Europe and the USA. In addition to its headquarters in Michigan, the Foundation maintains regional offices in South Africa, England, Ireland and Hungary.

Website: www.mott.org

Muslim Brotherhood

The **Muslim Brotherhood** (*Jamaat al-Ikhwan al-Muslimun*) is an Islamic **organization** with a political approach to **Islam** that opposes secular tendencies. It was founded by schoolteacher Hassan Al Banna in 1928 in Egypt as a youth organization seeking moral and social reform, organizing study circles, public lectures and events, as well as sports activities. During the 1930s the Brotherhood became more political, while in the 1940s it expanded to other countries, and later, in some instances, was accused of taking part in violent actions for which the Brotherhood was ultimately banned, especially in Egypt, Iraq and Syria. Today, with presence in more than 70 countries, the Muslim Brotherhood is viewed frequently as a relatively moderate group, and, where so permitted, has competed in and supported free elections. Yet, in some countries, its members are still subject to stringent government scrutiny and political marginalization.

Mutual Societies

Mutual societies, or mutuals for short, are, like **co-operatives**, organized by individuals seeking to improve their economic situation through collective activity. However, mutual societies differ from co-operatives in that they are mechanisms for sharing risk, either personal or property, through periodic contributions to a common fund. Examples are retirement or sickness funds, **burial associations**, or savings and loan associations. Ideally, mutual societies also hold to the patron-owner principle, whereby depositors formally control their operations. Mutuals in this sense are also similar to **self-help groups** in that individuals join to accomplish goals of mutual support that would be unattainable on an individual level. They differ, however, in that the latter are not principally engaged in commercial activities; moreover, self-help groups tend to be small informal **organizations**, whereas mutuals have developed into very large economic institutions. (See also **Mutuality**.)

Mutuality

Mutual benefit societies are non-profit insurance companies for protecting their members against social risks on a **voluntary** and non-compulsory basis. **Mutual societies** are descendants of the oldest part of the European **non-profit sector**: they appeared in the Middle Ages as charitable brotherhoods and **friendly societies**, linked to the **guilds** in urban areas. These **organizations** helped the needy members of the guild or their families. Mutual benefit societies flourished during the late 19th century in Europe, when the industrial revolution and rural depopulation pauperized the working class. Some of them were linked with the emerging labour-unions, and others were more middle-class oriented. Depending on the country and the period, they were either repressed or encouraged by the state.

Whatever its form, mutuality was the forerunner of the **welfare state**. Mutual societies first detected the main social risks—sickness, disability and old age— that were covered later by public social insurance schemes in all European countries. Nowadays, in many developing countries where public social insurance does not exist, they play a similar role, especially in Asia or Africa. In developed countries, they run the compulsory health insurance (Germany, Belgium, Netherlands) or provide a complementary sickness or old-age insurance (France, Spain, Portugal) or alternatives to the National Health System and offer low-interest loans (UK).

Mutuality relies on principles that are different from commercial insurance companies: fees are paid according to the member's income and not according to personal risk or age; 'bad risks' are rarely rejected; and there is no rate and benefit discrimination among members. Therefore a **cross-subsidization** between bad and good risks occurs. Mutual societies fight adverse selection and moral hazard through the education of their members to prevent social risks and through some financial incentives.

In the United Kingdom, the passage of legislation for the demutualization of **building societies** in 1986 was the beginning of a wave of demutualization in the 1990s as part of a deregulation trend. Of course sharing the collective property of these mutual organizations accumulated by many generations was a windfall gain for the present members, but the increasing costs and prices that followed were an unexpected consequence for consumers. Demutualization was less pronounced in continental Europe, and is forbidden by law in some countries. By contrast, a major demutualization wave took place in the USA in the 1980s and again in the late 1990s. (See also **Mutual societies.**)

Myer Foundation

The Myer Foundation is one of Australia's oldest, largest and highest profile philanthropic institutions. It is a **family foundation** with total **assets** of around $A39m., and expenditures of $A7.7m. in **grants**, special projects and administration in 2003. Sidney Myer, a refugee from Russia arriving in Australia in 1899, founded the Myer retailing business. On his death in 1934 he left one-tenth of his estate to the Foundation for the benefit of the community in which he made his fortune. The Myer Foundation's **mission** is to build a fair, just, creative and caring society by supporting initiatives that promote positive change in Australia, and in relation to its regional setting.

Website: www.myerfoundation.org.au

N

National Council for Voluntary Organisations (NCVO)

Established in 1919, the National Council for Voluntary Organisations (NCVO) is the main umbrella body for the **voluntary sector** in England. NCVO works to support the voluntary sector and to create an environment in which voluntary **organization**s can flourish. Activities include advocating for the voluntary sector to policy makers and carrying out research to promote a better understanding of **voluntary** action. Other services include a free phone helpdesk, policy briefings, information networks, events and a wide range of publications including NCVO's self-published magazine, *Voluntary Sector*. In 2004, NCVO had a **membership** of over 3,400 voluntary organizations.

Website: www.ncvo-vol.org.uk

Friedrich-Naumann-Stiftung

Friedrich Naumann Foundation

Founded in 1958, the Friedrich-Naumann-Stiftung is a German **political foundation** dedicated to promoting a liberal (in the classic European sense) foundation for political and civic education and, at the international level, to enhancing dialogue among countries and providing advisory and vocational assistance to developing countries. Its focal areas include globalization and development, civic education, peace and conflict resolution, economic and international affairs, and law and **human rights**. It is primarily an **operating foundation**, conducting research, organizing conferences and producing publications; however, it also offers scholarships and fellowships. The Stiftung operates in more than 50 countries.

Website: www.fnst.org

Neighbourhood Associations

Neighbourhood associations are generally comprised of home-owners and renters, formed to guard home-owner rights and property, discuss issues pertaining to neighbourhood conditions, respond to safety concerns by, for example, setting up a neighbourhood watch programme, and plan social events. In the USA, neighbourhood associations are generally found in more suburban areas. In Japan, however, neighbourhood associations are close to local authorities and involved in matters of public administration and safety. In some parts of the world, by contrast, neighbourhood associations tend to be informal groupings of people living in the same part of a city. In others, especially developing countries, neighbourhood associations often play the same role as **community-based organizations**, providing services to and advocating on behalf of neighbourhood dwellers.

Nell-Breuning, Oswald (1890–1991)

Born in Trier, Germany, Oswald Nell-Breuning was a Jesuit priest, a sociologist and a Roman Catholic theologian. Considered a leading interpreter of Catholic social teaching, he was involved in some way with nearly all important social policy issues of his time. Before the Second World War, Nell-Breuning played a critical role in drafting Pope Pius XI's social encyclical *Quadragesimo Anno*, which introduced the notion of subsidiarity as a principle of church-state relations in social policy. Following the war, he was called upon by the new German government and church hierarchy to advise on social policy and to develop the **subsidiarity principle** as the cornerstone of social policy and the emerging **welfare state**. He served as professor of ethics at the University of Frankfurt am Main and founded the Oswald Nell-Breuning Institute, a social policy research institute based at the Philosophical-Theological University of Saint Georgen at Frankfurt.

Network Organizations

'Network organization' is a term used to describe the structure of certain **organizations** operating in complex environments. Such network organizations are 'fluid', decentralized forms that try to balance **centralization** and decentralization in complex task environments by emphasizing the autonomy of internal components. Without central co-ordination, decisions are made at the local level with a minimum of costs for consultation and negotiation.

Adaptability is maximized when undertaken by small independent units rather than large bureaucratic organizations.

On balance, and on largely economic grounds, the global organizational environment for **INGOs** would favour the network form with decentralized and autonomous units. Nevertheless, the extreme decentralization of this form invites free riding and therefore tends to constrain identity formation and collective action, and possibly the legitimacy of the organization to speak with one voice. (See also **Free-Rider Problem**.)

New Public Management

New public management (NPM) is an approach that developed in response to what was regarded as inefficient and ineffective government bureaucracies—and that since the early 1990s has changed the way in which public administration operates. Generally, the term is used to describe a management culture that emphasizes the centrality of the client or **beneficiary**, as well as **accountability** for results. It also suggests structural or organizational choices that promote decentralized control through a wide variety of alternative service delivery mechanisms, including **quasi-markets** with public and private service providers competing for resources from policy-makers and **donors**. More specifically, NPM foresees:

1. Reorganization into corporate units organized along product or service lines as opposed to hierarchical management;
2. More contract-based competitive provision, with internal markets and term contracts;
3. Stress on private-sector styles of management practice, including more flexible hiring and firing, greater use of **marketing**, and improved **budget** policies;
4. More stress on discipline and frugality in resource use, including a better cost and **revenue** accounting;
5. More emphasis on visible hands-on top management, fewer middle management levels, and increased span of control for executive management;
6. Greater use of explicit, formal standards and **performance measures**; and
7. Greater emphasis on output rather than input.

These NPM principles have to be seen in the wider context of two factors: first, the degree of distinctiveness from the private sector in the sense that public management is based on equity considerations, and primarily about managing

public and semi-public **goods** that carry the potential of **market failures**; and second, the need for rules separating political and managerial decision-making to establish and maintain some 'buffer' between the world of politics on the one hand, and service provision on the other. These context conditions are similar for **non-profit organizations**, with one major difference, however: that non-profits are much less guided by equity considerations and more by values. In any case, NPM brought to **non-profit management**, among other aspects, concerns about outcomes versus outputs, efficiency versus effectiveness, as well as **accountability** and performance measurement.

New Ventures in Philanthropy

Launched in 1998, New Ventures in Philanthropy is a multi-year initiative of the Forum of Regional Associations of Grantmakers. The goal of New Ventures is to inspire and nurture organized **philanthropy** among high-wealth individuals and emerging **donors**. In its first phase, New Ventures funded 41 regional coalitions of **foundations** and other partner organizations throughout the USA, who used the resources to **leverage** additional monies from other sources and to encourage and organize philanthropy in their respective regions. In its second phase, the initiative will focus on gathering knowledge about what has worked and on disseminating that information to extend the initiative's impact.

Website: www.givingforum.org/newventures.html

NGOs (Non-Governmental Organizations)

The term 'NGO', or 'non-governmental **organization**', is cross-nationally used in rather inconsistent and sometimes confusing ways. It is a somewhat imprecise term that originated in the League of Nations in the 1920s, came to prominence in the United Nations (UN) system, and is today used largely to refer to **non-profit** and non-governmental **organizations** working in the field of international relations, environment, **human rights**, humanitarian assistance and development co-operation. The UN system and similarly the European Union, the **World Bank** and the **Organisation for Economic Co-operation and Development (OECD)** recognize the importance of NGOs in international affairs and award them consultative status that allows them to comment on policy initiatives, participate in plenary sessions, etc. NGOs have become an instrument by which international organizations seek wider social and political participation in an effort to increase their effectiveness and legitimacy.

To some extent, the concept of NGO is too narrow because, as typically used especially in developing countries and in international development literature, it includes only organizations that are explicitly involved in the promotion of social and economic development. This is problematic because the definition of what truly contributes to social and economic development is highly contested, making the term NGO potentially a political and ideological, rather than a scientific, concept. Thus, depending on a particular observer's definition of 'development', the category of NGO may exclude or include schools, universities, hospitals, social **clubs, professional associations**, social welfare agencies, religious groups and cultural institutions—all of which would normally be considered integral parts of the **non-profit sector** in most other parts of the world. NGO thus becomes a term of approbation carrying ideological baggage rather than a neutral term that can reliably be used for description and analysis.

In addition to being too narrow in coverage, moreover, the NGO concept is also frequently too broad. This is so because it embraces not only domestic or indigenous organizations, but also the large number of international agencies headquartered in the North but operating in the South, such as **Oxfam**, Save the Children (see **International Save the Children Alliance**) and others (see **INGOs**).

Furthermore, the distinction is often made—mainly in developing and transition countries—between **intermediary organizations** and member-based grassroots and other **community-based** groups. In this case, the intermediary organizations that act as conduits for external funding to **grassroots associations** and provide technical and other types of assistance to such groups are called NGOs. As noted above, however, the use of the term and the types of organization covered by the term vary from country to country.

Nielsen, Waldemar A.

Waldemar A. Nielsen pioneered the study of **philanthropy** in America. His works, which include *The Golden Donors* and *The Big Foundations*, have influenced not only **foundations**, but also public perception, and spurred debate about philanthropic **accountability** and the role of philanthropy in American society. Nielsen is a former Rhodes Scholar (see **Rhodes Trust**), was a foreign affairs writer for prominent American magazines, was involved in the design and implementation of the Marshall Plan, served on the staff of the **Ford Foundation**, and later led the African-American Institute.

Nippon Foundation

The Nippon Foundation, based in Tokyo, Japan, is a non-profit, **grant-making foundation** established in 1962 by legislation that set aside 3.3% of the **revenues** from motorboat racing to be used for philanthropic purposes. The foundation supports projects in the following areas: public welfare in Japan; **volunteering** programmes in Japan; maritime and shipbuilding projects (promoting both the shipping business and the preservation of marine resources); and overseas co-operative assistance (meeting basic human needs, training and education, and exchanges promoting mutual understanding internationally). The total **grants** made in the 2002 financial year amounted to over US $250m.

Website: www.nippon-foundation.or.jp

Non-Cash Payments

Non-cash payments are a tool in non-profit pricing whereby users supplement cash payment with labour and other non-monetary contributions such as donations in kind. Examples are non-profit housing construction schemes in which future home-owners contribute their labour for no wages and thereby build up 'sweat equity' in their future home. **Non-profit organizations** use labour as payment for service to signal commitment to a cause and regard it as part of their **mission**, while for-profit firms prefer cash income and regard non-cash payments as a less efficient mechanism of generating resources.

Non-Charitable Assets

Non-charitable assets are described by the US Internal Revenue Code as any **assets** other than those that are used (or held for use) directly in carrying out a charitable **organization**'s exempt purpose. Non-charitable assets are typically those held for income production or investment (stocks, bonds, interest-bearing notes, **endowment** funds and leased real estate), whereas a museum's collection, for example, would be considered a charitable asset. The value of a private foundation's non-charitable assets is used to determine its **mandatory pay-out requirement**, i.e. the foundation's annual distributions.

Non-Distribution Constraint

As part of the theoretical arguments for the existence of the **non-profit sector**, the non-distribution constraint refers to the fact that **non-profit organizations** are prohibited by the laws of the state or jurisdiction in which they were formed from distributing residual earnings to individuals who exercise control over the firm, such as officers, directors, or members (see **non-profit distribution**). Non-profit organizations are not prohibited from earning profits; rather, they must simply devote any surplus to financing future services or distribute it to non-controlling persons. Economic theories of the non-profit firm are, then, essentially theories of the way in which the presence of a non-distribution constraint relates to organizational origin, behaviour and output.

Non-Governmental Organizations – *see* NGOs

Non-Preferred Private Goods

Economic theory assumes that **non-profit organizations** produce two basic kinds of goods, **collective goods** and **private goods**. The private good can be preferred, i.e. close to the **mission** of the organization, and non-preferred, i.e. less mission-related and produced primarily for the purpose of generating **revenue** for the preferred collective and private goods. Examples of the latter include restaurants in museums, charity shops, or lotteries. Non-profits typically face significant problems in raising revenue for collective goods; use a variety of mechanisms to generate revenue from **preferred private goods**; and make opportunistic use of non-preferred private goods. The distinction between preferred and non-preferred goods is important for understanding **cross-subsidization** and other instruments of revenue generation in non-profit organizations.

Non-Profit-Distributing

In economics and many tax laws, **non-profit organizations** are essentially firms barred from distributing profits to owners and equivalents. A non-profit organization may accumulate surplus, but the surplus must be reinvested in the agency's basic **mission**, not distributed to the organization's owners, members, founders, or governing board. The fundamental question is: how does the organization handle its surplus? If the surplus is reinvested or otherwise applied to the stated purpose of the organization, the organization qualifies as a non-profit organization, providing the purpose is charitable or in the **public benefit**. In this sense, non-profit organizations are **private organizations** that do not exist primarily to generate profits, either directly or indirectly, and that are not primarily guided by commercial goals and considerations. Thus, the non-profit-distributing criterion of the **structural–operational definition** of a non-profit organization differentiates non-profit organizations from the other component of the private sector—private businesses.

Non-Profit Institutions Satellite Account

Within the System of National Accounts, the set of guidelines used to develop and report national economic statistics, **non-profit organizations** are clearly evident in only one category, **non-profit institutions serving households (NPISH)**, which does not include a significant portion of the entire set of non-profit and philanthropic **organizations**. In order to highlight the entire **non-profit sector** and allow more detailed analyses, the Non-Profit Institutions (NPI) Satellite Account was developed. The NPI Satellite Account consolidates information on non-profit institutions found in other categories of economic actors and suggests data collection methods that capture information specific to non-profit organizations. In addition to standard data on **revenue**, operating expenditures including employee compensation, and transfers such as **grants**, the NPI Satellite Account adds detail on **volunteer** labour.

Non-Profit Institutions Serving Households (NPISH)

According to 1993 System of National Accounts, the set of guidelines used to develop and report national economic statistics, non-profit institutions (NPIs) are legal or social entities created to produce goods and services whose status does not permit them to be a source of income, profit or other financial gain for the units that establish, control or finance them. Any surpluses they happen to make cannot be appropriated by other institutional units. Non-profit institutions serving households (NPISH) are those that receive most of their income from households or individuals in the form of **gifts** and are not substantially financed and controlled by government. This category of NPIs does not include many non-profit entities, including, for example, hospitals that receive most of their income as payments for services and **social welfare organizations** that receive substantial income from government.

Non-Profit Management

Management is the process of planning, organizing, directing and controlling activities to accomplish the stated objectives of **organizations** and their members. Management is different from **governance**, although there is some overlap between both functions. Management makes an organizational **mission** operational and works towards achieving its objectives. There are several core management activities:

- planning (i.e. engaging in long-term **strategic planning**)
- controlling (i.e. allocation of human, financial and material resources)
- monitoring (i.e. developing, measuring and applying **performance measures**)
- supervising (i.e. overseeing the work of subordinates)
- co-ordinating (i.e. co-ordinating with other managers and staff outside direct area of control)
- **marketing** (i.e. 'selling' the product or service to customers; watching the 'market')
- external relations with **stakeholders**, other organizations, government agencies, etc.
- consulting with peers and other professionals.

Non-profit management thinking has been subject to various ideas and concepts emanating either from the business world, such as **social entrepreneurship**, or from **new public management**, such as concerns about outcomes versus outputs, efficiency versus effectiveness, as well as **accountability** and performance measurement.

The modern understanding of non-profit management involves three critical points. First, the chief responsibility of management is 'value creation' in relation to the organization's stated mission. For example, if the mission is to help the homeless gain paid employment, then all management activities are to contribute to the stated objectives around that mission, i.e. 'create value' for the organization in fighting homelessness. In this sense, management is all about how that mission is to be accomplished within the guidelines established by the board. Second, even within the guidelines established by the board, management involves making critical, clear and consistent choices. This means weighing trade-offs and establishing boundaries. Third, the design of organizations and the management styles they entail are contingent upon mission, strategy and task environment. No management model fits all circumstances equally well, and like organizational structure, management approaches are context- and task-specific.

It is useful to think of **non-profit organizations** as organizations consisting of multiple components and complex, internal coalitions among stakeholders. The structure of non-profit organizations may require a multi-faceted, flexible approach to management and not the use of singular, ready-made models carried over from the business world or public management. This is the true challenge non-profit management theory and practice face: how to manage organizations that have multiple **bottom lines** and are therefore intrinsically complex.

While for-profit and public management approaches offer important insights into how to manage non-profit organizations, they fail to provide a more contextual and comprehensive approach. The management concept suggested by Gomez and Zimmermann offers a useful step toward the development of management models that are more fully in tune with the realities of non-profit organizations. Among the key facets of their approach are:

- A holistic conception of organization that emphasizes the relationship between the organization and its environment, the diversity of orientations within and outside the organization, and the complexity of demands put on it.
- A normative dimension of management that includes not only economic aspects, but also the importance of values and the impact of politics.
- A strategic-developmental dimension that sees organizations as an evolving system encountering problems and opportunities that frequently involve fundamental dilemmas for management.
- An operative dimension that deals with the everyday functioning of the organization, such as administration and accounting, personnel and service delivery.

Thus, organizations are seen as economic and political systems that have normative and strategic as well as operative dimensions. As non-profit organizations evolve, their basic structural features reflect choices on how to combine, integrate or control the various component parts. In other words, if organizations are understood to be systems with various component parts, central organizational dimensions can begin to be analysed as a series of choices made (or not made) by management or the governing body over time. This is the key to non-profit management. Multiplicity is the signature of the non-profit form. As such, models must be developed that identify these components, their cultures, goals and operating procedures in an effort to establish some coherence and identity between mission, activities and outcomes.

Non-Profit Organizations

The term non-profit organization, or not-for-profit organization, while often used interchangeably with **voluntary association, charity, NGO** or **third**

sector organization, is primarily economic in nature and refers to the **revenue** behaviour of this set of institutions. It originated in the System of National Accounts (SNA), the set of guidelines used to develop and report national economic statistics which defines non-profit institutions (NPI) as legal or social entities created for the purpose of producing goods and services whose status does not permit them to be a source of income, profit, or other financial gain for the units that establish, control or finance them. In practice their productive activities are bound to generate either surpluses or deficits, yet owners or their equivalents cannot appropriate any surpluses NPIs happen to make.

The reasons cited by the SNA for the creation of such entities are varied—to provide services to their creators, to the poor, or to the community at large or to promote the interests of particular groups. In addition, while they may provide services to groups or individuals, by convention they are—unlike government agencies—deemed to produce only individual services and not collective services. In the SNA, NPIs form a class of institutional units capable, in their own right, of owning goods and **assets**, incurring liabilities, and engaging in economic activities and transactions with other units.

Against this definition, the SNA splits non-profit institutions across a number of different sectors based largely on their principal source of income. Thus, NPIs can be found in four of the five SNA sectors. The rationale for this treatment is threefold. First, NPIs that sell their services at prices sufficient to cover the majority of their operating expenses might be expected to exhibit the same market behaviour as for-profit producers of the same services, and thus are grouped together with those for-profit producers in either the financial or nonfinancial corporations sector. Moreover, the market price provides a measure of the value of the service—and, thus, of the value of output—for both non-profit and for-profit producers in those sectors. Second, in the case of non-market NPIs controlled and financed by government, the measure of output—operating expenses—is the same for both public and private producers. Therefore, the SNA sectoring brings together all service producers financed and controlled by government, whether set up as government agencies or as NPIs. Third, in the case of households, the SNA includes within the production boundary the production of goods for own final use, but not of services. Again, the SNA sectoring groups households with small-scale providers of services to them, including certain small non-profit organizations and **grassroots associations** (see **Non-profit institutions serving households**).

The major difficulty with the 1993 SNA treatment of non-profit institutions is not so much with the definition of the NPI as an institutional unit, but with the aggregation rules used to group them into sectors (see **Non-Profit Institutions Satellite Account**). To mitigate this, the **structural–operational definition**, developed and refined during the Johns Hopkins Comparative Non-profit Sector Project, defines the **non-profit sector** as a set of entities that share the following characteristics:

- Organized, i.e. institutionalized to some extent;
- Private, i.e. institutionally separate from government;
- **Non-profit-distributing**, i.e. not returning profits generated to their owners or directors;
- Self-governing, i.e. able to control their own activities;
- **Voluntary**, i.e. involving some meaningful degree of voluntary participation.

The structural–operational definition has much in common with the definition of non-profit institution in the SNA. The characteristics 'organized', 'private' and 'self-governing' can be interpreted as general characteristics of institutional units: The entity is capable, in its own right, of owning **assets**, incurring liabilities and engaging in economic activities and in transactions with other entities; a complete set of accounts exists or, in principle could exist, for the entity. The other two characteristics—'non-profit-distributing' and 'voluntary'—would seem to be the crucial elements for differentiating NPIs from other types of institutional units. The first, especially, is consistent with the SNA definition.

Thus, non-profit organizations are institutional units that, by law or custom, do not distribute their surplus to those who own or control them and that, in addition, are non-compulsory and customarily receive voluntary contributions of time or money, although these contributions need not constitute the major source of income or employment for the entity.

Non-Profit Organizations, Functions of

Researchers have identified several distinct functions **non-profit organizations** serve, although the extent to which they actually do so, and relative to the contributions of other forms, remains subject to debate. The most widely used functional typology developed by Ralph Kramer includes four basic functions:

- **Service-provider** role: Since government programmes are typically large-scale and uniform, non-profits can perform various important functions in the delivery of **collective goods** and services, particularly for minority preferences. They can also be the primary service providers, where neither government nor business is either willing or able to act. They can provide services that complement the service delivery of other sectors, but differ qualitatively from it, or they can supplement essentially similar services, where the provision by government or the market is insufficient in scope or not easily affordable.

- Vanguard role: Non-profits innovate by experimenting with and pioneering new approaches, processes or programmes in service delivery. Less beholden than business firms to the expectations of **stakeholders** demanding some return on their investment, and not subject to the electoral process as are government entities, non-profit organizations can, in their fields, serve as change agents. If **innovations** prove successful after being developed and tested by non-profits, other service providers, particularly government agencies with broader reach, may adopt them, or businesses might turn them into marketable products.

- Value-guardian role: Governmental agencies are frequently constrained—either on constitutional grounds or by majority will—from fostering and helping express diverse values that various parts of the electorate may hold. Businesses similarly do not pursue the expression of values, since this is rarely profitable. Non-profits are thus the primary mechanism to promote and guard particularistic values and allow societal groups to express and promulgate religious, ideological, political, cultural, social, and other views and preferences. The resulting expressive diversity in society in turn contributes to pluralism and democratization.

- **Advocacy** role: In the political process that determines the design and contours of policies, the needs of under-represented or discriminated groups are not always taken into account. Non-profits thus fill in to give voice to the minority and particularistic interests and values they represent and serve in turn as critics and watchdogs of government with the aim of effecting change or improvements in social and other policies.

Non-Profit Sector

The non-profit sector is a term used mainly in the USA and Canada as shorthand to refer to **organizations** that are exempt from income taxation and serve some kind of **public benefit**. It is a broad and imprecise concept, often used interchangeably with **third sector** and **voluntary sector**, and suggests a demarcation of society into distinct sectors that may be empirically questionable.

The term has its origin in the System of National Accounts, which designated a group of private economic entities, i.e. non-profit institutions that cannot be a source of income to their members or owners. The non-profit sector is thus defined in economic terms based on its **revenue** behaviour, and not in terms of its function or purpose, and exists next to the government, corporate sector and household sector. The **structural–operational definition** developed by Salamon and Anheier defines the non-profit sector as the sum of organizations that are organized, **non-profit distributing**, self-governing, **private** and **voluntary**.

Non-Profit–Government Relations

The relationship between **non-profit organizations** and government has received much attention among researchers, as it refers to one of the most critical aspects in the range of relationships this set of institutions has with outside parties, involving issues of resourcing, legitimacy, **governance** and **accountability**. Widely-known and -discussed models of non-profit–government relations are the system of **third-party government** in the USA, subsidiarity in Germany and *verzuiling* in the Netherlands. Prominent among conceptual models of non-profit–government relations are those introduced by Dennis Young and Adil Najam.

Young suggested a triangular model of non-profit–government relations, i.e. supplementary, complementary and adversarial, and argues that to varying degrees all three types of relations are present at any one time, but that some assume more importance during some periods than in others. Taking the United Kingdom as an example, non-profit–government relations were at the same time (i) supplementary, with **voluntary** organizations providing services not covered by the **welfare state**, e.g. counselling and other services, in response to government cutbacks in the 1980s (**public goods** argument—minority tastes); (ii) complementary, with contracts and **partnerships** between government and non-profit agencies in response to **new public management** and out-sourcing (**transaction costs** argument—greater efficiency); and (iii) adversarial, with groups advocating the rights of needy people left unserved and underserved by the state.

Najam's Four-C's model offers a different view of non-profit–government relations by examining the extent to which their respective organizational goals and means overlap. If the goals and means are similar, then government and non-profit organizations develop a co-operative relationship, e.g. the co-operation between the Canadian government and the **International Campaign** to **Ban Landmines**. If the goals are similar but the means are dissimilar, then a complementary relationship between government and non-profit organizations emerges. For example, many non-profits in the field of social service provision and community health care complement basic government services. If the goals are dissimilar and means are similar, then government tries to build a co-optive relationship with non-profit organizations. An example would be the humanitarian assistance funds channelled to local grassroots organizations in African countries for programmes that are similar to governmental ones. In such situations, government may try to co-opt grassroots organizations and non-profits to further its own goals. Finally, if the goals and means are both dissimilar, then government and the **non-profit sector** are in a confrontational relationship. Examples include **Greenpeace** pressuring governments on environmental issues, an **advocacy** group demanding better welfare services for the urban poor, or the anti-**globalization** groups demonstrating against the World Trade Organization.

Novib

Best known by its acronym Novib, the Nederlandse Organisatie voor Internationale Bijstand (Dutch Organization for International Assistance) was established in 1956 to engage the Dutch population in campaigns to combat hunger internationally. True to the desire to enlist Dutch **civil society**, Novib created an unusual structure as a **foundation** with a general assembly to include civic **organizations** and political parties as members. Today Novib supports projects of local **NGOs** in developing countries, provides emergency relief, lobbies governments and international organizations, and campaigns to increase public awareness about poverty and injustice. Since 1994, Novib has been a member of **Oxfam International**.

Website: www.novib.nl

Nuffield, Lord (1877–1963)

William Morris, who was later called Lord Nuffield, was born in England. He was a successful industrialist, one of the first to introduce mass production methods in England, and the owner of Morris Motors Ltd. Lord Nuffield spent a great portion of his later years engaged in **philanthropy**. In 1943, with a donation of £10m. worth of his company shares, he established the **Nuffield Foundation** with the goal of enhancing social well-being. The Foundation was intended to fund research supported by reliable, practical evidence that aimed at bettering society.

Nuffield Foundation

The Nuffield Foundation was established in 1943 by William Morris (**Lord Nuffield**), the founder of Morris Motors, with the goal to 'advance social well-being' through scientific research. The Foundation, headquartered in London, awards **grants** for experimental or development projects in education and social welfare as well as for scientists and social scientists at the early stages of their careers. The Foundation also develops and runs its own projects, including the Nuffield Council on Bioethics and the Nuffield Curriculum Centre.

Website: www.nuffieldfoundation.org

O

OECD – *see* **Organisation for Economic Co-operation and Development**

Olin, John Merrill (1892–1982)

John Merrill Olin began his career working for his father's company, which later became the Olin Corporation, one of the largest US producers of copper alloys, ammunition and chlorine. John Olin served as the corporation's Chairman of the Board until 1957. He made a name as a conservationist who led efforts to save the Atlantic salmon and as a philanthropist who founded the John M. Olin **Foundation** in 1953. Through the foundation, Olin wished to preserve, strengthen and further cultivate principles and institutions of political and economic liberty. In accordance with Olin's wishes, the foundation has begun a process to cease operations over the next few years.

Olson, Mancur (1932–1998)

Professor at the University of Maryland, Mancur Olson is the author of the *Logic of Collective Action*, in which he explains that when interests are shared, rational actors should prefer free-riding to co-operation. Consequently private incentives are necessary to make a **collective action** possible. A collective action is also more likely in small **organizations** where the free-rider can be identified and forced to pay. (See also **Free-Rider Problem**.)

One Percent Provision

The 1% provision is a method of supporting non-profit and charitable activities that was introduced first in Hungary in 1996 and then in other countries of

Eastern and Central Europe. This scheme enables taxpayers to support **non-profit organizations** with **1% of their personal income tax**. Though it is connected to the tax system, the 1% provision is not a classical form of tax advantage. When taxpayers designate a recipient organization, they do not make any sacrifice; rather, they decide on the use of public money. **Civil society** organizations are eligible for this support if they are engaged in services and activities of **public benefit** (e.g. health and social care, culture, education, research, etc.). Each taxpayer can freely decide which of the eligible organizations should get 1% of his/her personal income tax. This decision is a part of the tax declaration. The transfer itself is made by the tax authority.

Open Society Institute (OSI)

The Open Society Institute (OSI), an operating and **grant-making foundation** with headquarters in New York, was founded in 1993 by **George Soros** to serve as a hub for and to provide support to the network of autonomous Soros organizations in over 50 countries. These organizations were originally created beginning in 1984 to support the transition to democracy in Central and Eastern Europe, but have now been established in Africa, Asia and Latin America, among other areas. OSI and the network undertake a range of activities—from support for economic and legal reform to protection of **human rights**—designed to promote 'open societies,' after a term coined by **Karl Popper**.

Website: www.soros.org

Operating Foundations

Operating foundations are **foundations** that do not (primarily) make **grants** to other institutions. Rather than relying on third parties (grantees), operating foundations pursue their **missions** through their own activities.

There are principally two different types of operating foundations, depending on the nature of the foundation's **assets**. Some operating foundations are established with financial **endowments** or other income-producing assets and utilize proceeds from these assets to support self-administered programmes, projects and other activities. The German **Bertelsmann Foundation** and the US Russell Sage Foundation (see **Sage, Margaret Olivia Slocum**) are examples of such operating foundations.

Particularly outside the USA, the principal assets of the second type of operating foundations are non-monetary, such as art collections or individual institutions. These institutional operating foundations include many private museums, hospitals and nursing homes, some private universities and research institutes. The French **Institut Pasteur** and the US Barnes Foundation belong to the second type of operating foundations.

Historically, the institutional operating foundation is the original foundation form. Plato's Academy in Athens and the Library of Alexandria are cited frequently as early examples in antiquity, and the medieval hospital foundation dominated in Continental Europe until modernity. Similarly, *al-wakf*, the Islamic **endowment**, still tends to support institutions such as mosques and *madrasas* (religious schools) and is the functional equivalent to operating foundations in the Judeo-Christian tradition.

In some European countries, such as France and Italy, the foundation community is still largely comprised of operating rather than **grant-making foundations**. In others, like Germany, operating foundations make up a significant part of the foundation sector and even some of the largest grant-making foundations, such as the **Robert-Bosch-Stiftung**, have some element of the operating foundation in them. In the USA, by contrast, the focus is almost exclusively on grant-making foundations. In contrast to European understandings, many true operating foundations—including internationally prominent private universities such as Stanford, Johns Hopkins and Chicago—are typically not considered to be part of the foundation sector, not least because tax regulations exclude them from the technical definition of foundations.

Organisation for Economic Co-operation and Development (OECD)

The OECD is an international body of 30 countries (as of 2004) and maintains consultative relationships with some 70 other countries as well as numerous **NGOs** and **civil society organizations**. The OECD is a forum for policy dialogue and works to set standards and develop internationally comparable performance indicators in such policy areas as public management, the environment, education, employment, food, development aid and agriculture. The Paris-based OECD is the successor to the Organization for European Economic Co-operation created under the Marshall Plan for European reconstruction following the Second World War.

Website: www.oecd.org

Organization

Several components define 'organization' and set it apart from other forms of regular social activity. For one, an organization is a social entity that includes people, some form of resources and technology; two, it is goal-directed and serves an explicit purpose; three, it is a structured arrangement with tasks that are divided into separate activities and co-ordinated; and four, it is a bounded entity with an identifiable boundary that makes it possible to judge the organization from its environment, e.g. some recognized difference between members and non-members, awareness of the distinction between organizational and individual responsibilities, or an understanding of the difference between the organization and other entities such as family, friendship circles and loose networks among individuals. The **structural–operational definition** of **non-profit organizations** uses the criterion of organization as one characteristic, and requires that the entity have some institutional reality to it. In some countries a formal charter of incorporation signifies this, but institutional reality can also be demonstrated in other ways where legal incorporation is either not chosen or not readily available, such as having regular meetings, officers, rules of procedure, or some degree of organizational permanence. However, purely *ad hoc* and temporary gatherings of people are not considered organizations.

Organizational Test

In the USA, while a **non-profit organization** can be established for any lawful purpose, the organizational test for **Section 501(c)(3)** tax-exempt status requires that the entity's **articles of organization** state that it operates exclusively in one or more of eight functional purpose areas: educational, religious, charitable, scientific, literary, testing for public safety, fostering certain national and international amateur sports competitions, and prevention of cruelty to children and animals. In addition, the articles must not empower the organization to engage in activities that do not further one or more of those purposes (except in an insubstantial way).

Outdoor Relief

Under the British **Poor Laws**, two types of relief for the poor were established. 'Indoor relief', when the poor were sent to **alms**houses, **workhouses**, hospitals or orphanages, was meant for the 'idle poor' or those unable to care for themselves. More common was 'outdoor relief' when the poor were cared for in their own homes, through monetary contributions (the origins of the 'dole') or in-kind donations, such as food and clothing. Outdoor relief was intended for the 'deserving poor' or those who could not work due to disability, age, illness, or caretaking duties. Outdoor relief was provided through taxes upon local property owners and contributions from local parishes, while it was expected that family members would care for indigent relatives. Safeguards were put in place to ensure that the poor from other areas did not migrate to take advantage of more generous localities.

Overseas Development Assistance (ODA)

Official development assistance and net official aid record the actual international transfer of financial resources or of goods or services valued at the cost to the **donor**, minus any repayments of loan principal during the same period. ODA data consist of disbursements of loans made on concessional terms (net of repayments of principal) and **grants** by official agencies of the members of the Development Assistance Committee (DAC) of the **Organisation for Economic Co-operation and Development (OECD)**, by multilateral institutions, and by certain Arab countries to promote economic development and welfare in recipient economies. Loans with a grant element of at least 25% are included in ODA, as are technical co-operation and assistance. ODA flows include transfers to **NGOs** in both donor and recipient countries.

Oxfam International

Oxfam International was established in 1995 as a confederation of 12 autonomous **NGOs** working together in more than 100 countries to combat poverty and injustice. The member NGOs do this individually and jointly by working on projects with local partner **organizations** in less-developed countries, by providing emergency relief in times of crisis, and by campaigning locally and globally for social and economic justice. The Oxfam confederation includes the original Oxfam, established in 1942 in Oxford, England (now also the headquarters for the Oxfam International secretariat) to respond to the humanitarian problems created by the Nazi occupation of Greece, sister Oxfams created subsequently in other countries, and, among others, **Novib**, an independent Dutch **NGO**.

Website: www.oxfam.org

P

Packard, David (1912–1996)

David Packard, born in Colorado (USA), was co-founder of the Hewlett-Packard Company; he retired in 1993 to become its Chairman Emeritus. Throughout his life and career, Packard was active in community and civic affairs. With his wife Lucile, Packard provided US $55m. to create the Monterey Bay Aquarium and attached Research Institute, and $40m. to build the Lucile Salter Packard Children's Hospital. In 1964, the couple also founded the David and Lucile Packard Foundation, which received a major portion of Packard's estate upon his death.

Parallel Summits

Originating largely from transnational **social movements**, and around pivotal policy issues, the phenomenon of parallel summits emerged in the 1980s, since then has achieved global prominence, and is now a key element of the emerging **governance** system. Parallel summits are events organized by national and international groups with international participation, independent of the activities of states and firms. They tend to coincide with or be related to official summits of governments and international institutions (with or without formal contacts with the official summits), addressing the same problems or issues as the official summits. They conduct public information and analysis, engage in political mobilization and protest, and develop alternative policy proposals. Prominent examples include parallel summits at the 1993 Earth Summit in Rio de Janeiro, the 1995 World Social Summit in Copenhagen and the 1997 World Women's Summit in Beijing.

Such parallel summits have widely differing themes (environment, globalization, women, social policy), but the roles and activities of parallel summits include primarily the framing of issues, where summits define the issues of transnational relevance; for example, the parallel summit to the United Nations Conference on Environment and Development in Rio de Janeiro in 1992 helped define the nature of, and solutions to, environmental problems. Other, less pronounced roles include: rule-making, whereby parallel summits help formulate the rules for national policies in internationally relevant fields, from security to trade, from the environment to new technologies, and developing policy guidelines, through which summits define the direction to be taken by policies at national levels and for major **organizations**.

They are a crucial part of the shift in the balance of power from national to international decision-making. Critics point to the missing democratic process and legitimacy of such summits comparable to state-level politics and official summitry.

Partnerships

Partnership is an oft-quoted word in non-profit-related circles and is sometimes considered the magic solution to the ills of **non-profit organizations**. There are different kinds of partnership; it should be understood as both a process and a structure. Partnership can exist as a collaborative process involving non-profit actors, the State and for-profit companies, or it can refer to an actual structure such as a partnership company.

Using Ireland as an example because its recent economic success has been attributed to social partnership, clear cases of both structure and process are evident. First, the social partnership process can be dated to 1987 and the production of the first national programme, *The Programme for National Recovery*, which involved input from three social partners (employers, farmers and trade unions) and the State. The second national programme, *The Programme for Economic and Social Progress*, published in 1991, recommended the establishment of 12 partnership structures in identified disadvantaged areas around the country, which were augmented to 38 in 1996, following the third national programme's recommendations. In the mid-1990s, a new social partner, the '**voluntary** and community pillar', entered the partnership process and has had since that time an input to subsequent programmes such as *Partnership 2000, Programme for Prosperity and Fairness,* and *Sustaining Progress* as well as the *National Anti-Poverty Strategy.* In addition, partnership structures now exist, in various forms, in different policy and geographical areas. So, for example, in an effort to decentralize government, community fora have been discussed as one way to localize decision-making.

What both process and structure have in common is the collaboration between different kinds of actors, all involving non-profit organizations in some form or another. An issue not addressed sufficiently in thinking about partnership, however, is the need for resources so that all partners can collaborate equally. This is particularly pertinent for non-profit actors who do not have excess resources, whether financial, human or technical, to invest in the partnership process or structure in order to make an effective contribution.

Patman, John William Wright (1893–1976)

Born in Texas, John Patman spent his life serving the community as a lawyer and as a US congressman, being elected 24 times. He is most well known in the **philanthropy** field for his investigations of abuse of the private foundation form by wealthy families. He argued that the tax-exempt status of many charitable foundations provided incentives for private gain rather than public good and insisted that there were too many **foundations** in general. Patman was a key witness in the congressional hearings that led to passage of tax reform legislation in 1969 that included a **mandatory pay-out requirement** for foundations and placed limits on potentially fraudulent practices, such as **self-dealing**.

Peabody, George (1795–1869)

Born in Massachusetts and having had only four years formal education, George Peabody achieved financial success first as a merchant in Baltimore, Maryland, and ultimately as an investment banker in London. Considered by some the founder of modern **philanthropy**, Peabody's philanthropic activities were non-sectarian and non-political, mostly devoted to education and the arts. Among his most notable legacies are the Peabody Donation Fund, which continues to this day to provide subsidized housing for the working class in London; the Peabody Education Fund, founded at the close of the American Civil War to educate poor children in the southern states; and the Peabody Institute, a renowned music conservatory in Baltimore.

People in Need Foundation—PINF

Founded in 1992 to help 'people in need' and promote democratic values, *Èlovik v tísni* (PINF) is a **public benefit** corporation (the legal form taken by **operating foundations**) co-founded by the state-owned Czech Television. PINF has run humanitarian aid projects in Bosnia, Chechnya and Kosovo, but also in Czech regions affected by floods. It promotes **empowerment** of the Roma minority in the Czech Republic and Slovakia and organizes a film festival on **human rights**. In partnership with the Czech media, PINF launched several successful **fundraising** campaigns. (See also **Public benefit companies.**)

Performance Measures

Performance measures provide a series of indicators, expressed in qualitative, quantitative or other tangible terms, that show whether current performance is reasonable and cost-effective. Typically, they are classified into four categories: outcome measures (indicators of actual impact or **public benefit**), output measures (indicators that count the goods and services produced), efficiency measures (indicators that measure the cost), or explanatory measures (indicators that show the resources used to produce services). Research has shown that performance metrics have to be tied to **bottom lines**, and as most **non-profit organizations** are multifaceted and have multiple bottom lines, multiple performance measures are necessary. Reliance on performance measures entails a number of risks, among them the possible shifting of an organization's efforts to areas that are more easily measured, but less change-oriented or needy of resources, or the encouragement of 'short-termism' and consequent neglect of longer-term achievements. (See also **Benchmarking.**)

Pew Charitable Trusts

The Pew Charitable Trusts is a group of seven individual charitable funds established between 1948 and 1979 by the children of Sun Oil Company founder Joseph N. Pew and his wife, Mary Anderson Pew. The Trusts seek to provide the public with research and practical solutions in the fields of culture, education, the environment, health, public policy and **religion**. Since the 1970s, Pew has expanded its programmes to cover the entire USA but maintains a special focus on its Philadelphia home base. In 2004, Pew began operating as a **public charity**, which allows it to save resources and engage in activities that are prohibited for private foundations and **trusts**.

Website: www.pewtrusts.com

Philanthropic Amateurism

One of the four regularly cited weaknesses of the **non-profit sector**, philanthropic amateurism points to the fact that **voluntary associations** frequently do not have professional teams of social workers, psychologists, etc., since they can ill afford to pay for such expertise. Therefore, they rely disproportionately on volunteers in dealing with social problems. On the other hand, there is growing criticism that some **non-profit organizations** may have gone too far in the direction of **professionalization**.

Philanthropic Insufficiency

Philanthropic insufficiency, or resource inadequacy, is cited as a general weakness of the **non-profit sector**. The notion suggests that the goodwill and **charity** of a few cannot generate resources on a scale that is both adequate enough and reliable enough to cope with the welfare and related problems of modern society. A reason for this insufficiency, aside from the sheer size of the population in need, is the fact that **third-sector** goods are quasi-**public goods**, and thus subject to the **free-rider problem** whereby those who benefit from **voluntary** action have little or no incentive to contribute.

Philanthropic Particularism

The phrase 'philanthropic particularism' refers to the tendency of **non-profit organizations** and their benefactors to focus on particular subgroups or clients while ignoring others. This can lead to problems such as addressing only the needs of the 'deserving' poor; inefficiency due to duplication of efforts whereby each particular subgroup wants their 'own' agency or service; or service gaps in the population. Furthermore, those who control the organization's resources may have particular groups they favour. Such particularism would be the negative side of the **non-profit sector**'s purported advantage in recognizing and attending to special needs or representing special interests.

Philanthropic Paternalism

Philanthropic paternalism refers to the relationship of dependence that may develop between a **non-profit organization** and its clients or **beneficiaries**. To the extent that non-profit organizations establish privileges rather than rights or entitlements, there is opportunity for the non-profit organization to establish or reinforce dependency on the part of those who rely on its services, which can be used to force the clients or beneficiaries to convert to another **religion** or belief system, to vote for or support political parties or candidates with which they might otherwise disagree, etc.

197

Philanthropy

Philanthropy refers to the use of personal wealth and skills for the benefit of specific public causes and is typically applied to philanthropic **foundations** and similar institutions. Philanthropy, derived from Greek, means love for humankind. Therefore, philanthropic acts are intended to enhance the well-being of humanity, relieve misery, or improve the quality of life through personal acts of kindness, compassion, or financial support. Yet philanthropy is often hard to separate from self-interested behaviour, however subtle and however pecuniary. It is equally difficult to distinguish between genuinely philanthropic and selfless **organizations** and those advocating philanthropy for the common good with some form of self-interest or **lobbying** on behalf of members or third parties.

Philanthropy takes different forms in various countries, cultures and political contexts. A traditional philanthropic ideal of **Christianity** is that of **tithing**, which obligates believers to donate one-tenth of their income to **charity**. Such charity is found in all major world **religions**; it is important in **Islam** (*Zakat*, *Waqf*), Judaism (**Zedaka**), **Buddhism** and other religions. In many developing countries, philanthropy is often expressed in the form of mutual help **organizations** such as the *Wat* in Cambodia. In transitional and post-conflict countries such as Bosnia-Herzegovina, philanthropy stems from the region's religious (Muslim, Jewish, Catholic) heritage and historical customs of mutual help.

Philanthropy in the form of monetary **donations** made by individuals, foundations and corporations represents a significant source of funding for the **non-profit sector**. In the USA, it accounts for about 20% of the **revenue** of the entire non-profit sector. In Israel, philanthropy represents approximately 17%, with most of these funds going to civic and international organizations. In Japan, when looking at monetary contributions strictly, philanthropy only accounts for 3% of non-profit sector revenue, but when **volunteering** is taken into account, that figures jumps to 11%. In Brazil, philanthropy comprises approximately 11% of non-profit sector revenues, with this figure increasing to 16% when volunteers are taken into consideration.

In economic terms, acts of philanthropy can be explained in various ways. Stemming from the basic economic premise that individuals are rational beings and act in self-interested ways, the idea of philanthropy may seem at first in contradiction to economic theory. One explanation is that people value service provided by charities and therefore donate voluntarily so that they can continue to enjoy the service, as in the case of museums or public broadcast stations. Another explanation is that some may be getting something in return for their contributions such as their name on a university building or preferential treatment at the particular organization. A third and more common reason most theorists give is that individuals simply draw an intrinsic satisfaction from giving.

A major distinction is made between **charity**, as the alleviation of suffering, and philanthropy, which refers to a longer term, deeper commitment to **public benefit** that seeks to address the roots of social problems. This distinction was important in the emergence of the modern philanthropic foundation that emerged in the USA in the early 20th century, with the **Rockefeller Foundation** and **Carnegie Corporation of New York** as prime exemplars.

Philanthropy Australia

Philanthropy Australia, headquartered in Melbourne, is a national **grant-makers' association**, with a **membership** of over 220 grant-making **trusts** and **foundations**. Formerly known as the Australian Association of Philanthropy, it was established in 1975 and incorporated as Philanthropy Australia in 1988. It offers **advocacy**, education, networking, information services, publications, and consultancy services to its members.

Website: www.philanthropy.org.au

Pierre, Abbé (1912–)

Born in Lyon to a large Catholic family, Henri Groués became a priest in 1938. During the Second World War, he was in the Resistance with de Gaulle in London and took the name Abbé Pierre. A member of Parliament from 1945 to 1951, he founded in 1949 Emmaus, a community of ragmen devoted to building shelters for the homeless. This emergent **non-profit organization** was initially funded by the recovery and sale of waste products. In 1952, he led a high-profile **fundraising** campaign for the homeless and against the housing shortage, and became one of the most popular personalities in France.

Pithart, Petr (1941–)

A lawyer by education and politician by vocation, Petr Pithart has been an influential advocate of a strong **civil society** in the Czech Republic. Pithart was persecuted after the 1968 Soviet invasion and again after he became one of the first signatories of the **Charter 77** declaration. As Czech Prime Minister in

1990–1992 and two-time Speaker of the Czech Senate from (1996–1998 and 2000–2004), Pithart has exerted considerable influence on the Czech government's policy towards civil society and the not-for-profit sector and, in particular, the landmark decisions concerning the **Foundation Investment Fund (FIF)** and the 1997 Foundations Act.

Pitter, Přemysl (1895–1976)

A Czech social-religious activist and pacifist, Pitter founded and directed the Milíč House (1932) in Prague, an institution that provided assistance to children from poor families. During the Second World War Pitter helped rescue Jewish children, and after the war he took in Czech, Jewish and German children and criticized the treatment of Germans deported from Czechoslovakia. Forced into exile by communist authorities in 1951, Pitter became pastor at a detention camp for *émigrés* in West Germany, and also continued his work as educational activist, publicist in the field of Czech-German reconciliation and organizer of Protestant Czech exile groups.

Planned Giving

Planned giving, also known as charitable gift planning, entails working with individual **donors** to integrate their personal financial objectives with their charitable impulses. There are numerous planned giving vehicles and combinations that take into account factors such as the donor's short and long-term financial objectives, current financial circumstances, age, estate plan, family situation and charitable goals. Planned **gifts** are usually deferred, i.e. arranged now and fulfilled later. They can be revocable (as in a will bequest) or irrevocable (as in a charitable gift annuity). Even though a deferred gift may not actually benefit a charity for many years, the gift arrangement can generate an immediate income tax charitable deduction when the future gift is irrevocable. On the other hand, revocable gifts do not provide immediate tax benefits. Such gifts usually entail legal documents and often require the assistance of a qualified professional advisor.

Political Action Committees (PACs)

Regulated by the Federal Election Commission (FEC) in the USA, political action committees (PACs) are **non-profit organizations** that raise money for, contribute to and otherwise support the election of candidates for public office.

PACs generally represent specific interest groups and are not the same as campaign or party committees. PACs wield considerable power in elections, as a group outspend political parties, and often work very closely with campaign officials. They largely grew out of the Federal Election Campaign Act of 1971, increased rapidly in the 1980s and numbered over 4,500 in 2000. One reason for their popularity is that electioneering, otherwise known as express **advocacy**, is prohibited for **public charities (Section 501(c)(3)** organizations); often PACs are set up by such 501(c)(3) non-profits who wish to be active in electioneering, but cannot under their current tax status. The PAC is then a separate organization but remains affiliated with its sister non-profit.

Political Foundations

In many countries, a political foundation (PF) is a foundation closely linked with a particular political party, although it is generally not involved in the immediate task of electioneering. A PF is active in political education, international relations or policy research. In some cases, it also maintains the historical archives of the parent party or makes **grants** to students. A PF receives most of its **revenue** from the state. Critics of PFs argue that political parties thus disguise from the electors the extent of public funds used for their own purposes. Defenders of PFs underline the impact on **democracy** and the legitimacy of their work.

Political Test

In the USA, to qualify for **Section 501(c)(3)** tax-exempt status, an **organization** may not participate in the electoral process promoting any specific candidate for office. This prohibition includes the preparation and distribution of campaign literature. The political constraints imposed on **Section 501(c)(3)** organizations go beyond actual elections and campaigning and extend to **lobbying** as well, and such organizations are prohibited from making substantial contributions to lobbying activities by third parties. Accordingly, an organization qualifying for 501(c)(3) status may spend only a limited amount of its annual expenditures on lobbying activities relating to the organization's **mission**. Private foundations generally may not lobby except in very limited circumstances, such as on issues affecting their tax-exempt status or the deductibility of **gifts** to them. By contrast, **Section 501(c)(4)** organizations have fewer restrictions on their lobbying activities. The extent of electoral and lobbying activities in which a

non-profit organization intends to engage or actually engages is often referred to as the political test for determining whether the organization meets the criteria for 501(c)(3) status.

Poor Laws

The Elizabethan Poor Law of 1601 and the Poor Law of 1834 changed the manner in which poor relief was handled in Britain, setting the pattern still seen today in anti-poverty policy in the UK and its former colonies, including the USA. Prior to the Poor Laws, relief for the poor was not uniform and was left to local parishes, under the jurisdiction of the Church of England, and other forms of **charity** stemming from the local community. With the Poor Laws, the national government took some responsibility for the poor for the first time, requiring local counties to provide relief when overburdened parishes could not. Notably, these laws made the first distinction between people who were seen as unable to work due to illness or disability and were provided **outdoor relief** in their homes, and those who were seen as 'idle' or 'undeserving' and were sent to **workhouses**.

Popper, Sir Karl Raimund (1902–1994)

Sir Karl Popper's theories on the logic of discovery, scientific methodology and **civil society**, among others, have influenced prominent 20th-century scientific and philanthropic figures including Albert Einstein and **George Soros**. His social and political writings established the framework for subsequent theories and debates on civil society, social science research and the nation-state. Terms he coined, such as open society and social engineering, continue to be redefined and utilized today. Popper's seminal works include *The Logic of Scientific Discovery* (1934), arguably the most important work in 20th-century philosophy of science, and *The Open Society and its Enemies* (1945). Born in Vienna, Popper received his Ph.D. in philosophy in 1928 from the University of Vienna, lectured at Canterbury University College (New Zealand) during the Nazi years, then moved to the London School of Economics.

Preferred Private Goods

In non-profit economics, a preferred private good is a product or service that is related to the **mission** of the **non-profit organization** and can be sold in private markets. Non-profit organizations may decide to make it available to some clients or users independent of their ability to pay. Examples of such preferred **private goods** are education, health care, social services and museums. Economic theory suggests that, in trying to cover the deficit for preferred private and **collective goods**, non-profit organizations can follow two basic strategies, either exclusively or in combination. First, they can turn to government and ask for **grants** for core funding, specific cost **subsidies**, service agreements, reimbursement schemes, or similar contract regimes; second, they can become multi-product firms, seek efficiencies through **product bundling**, and engage in **cross-subsidization**, whereby **revenue** raised from the production of **non-preferred private goods** subsidizes preferred goods.

PRIA (Society for Participatory Research in Asia)

Headquartered in New Delhi, PRIA is an **advocacy** and development **organization** dedicated to empowering and improving the lives of India's poor and marginalized. PRIA focuses on reforming government institutions, mainly local, and building **civil society** through **capacity-building**, policy **advocacy** and knowledge-building. Throughout India and with the help of its partner regional support organizations, PRIA engages citizens as well as other **stakeholders** including academia, media, **donors**, corporate and government institutes, and other civil society organizations in a multi-stakeholder approach to development.

Website: www.pria.org

Prince Claus Fund

The Prince Claus Fund for Culture was established in 1996 in honour of the 70th birthday of HRH Prince Claus of the Netherlands. The Fund's **mission** is to expand insight into cultures and promote interaction between culture and development. In particular, the Fund supports exchange among purveyors of culture in non-Western countries as well as dialogue between artists and academics. The Fund envisages a world-wide platform for the intellectual debate on shared values in the form of meetings, discussions, lectures and publications. It also supports cultural experiments and other novel projects that push people to reflect on their respective cultures. Support is given to artists and **organizations** in Africa, Asia, Latin America and the Caribbean.

Website: www.princeclausfund.nl

Principal–Agent Problem

A key to understanding **governance** and **accountability** issues in **non-profit organizations** is the principal–agent problem. In its simplest terms, the principal–agent problem recognizes that, due to **information asymmetry**, principals cannot adequately monitor the behaviour of their agents, and therefore agents are likely to take advantage of the situation and not act necessarily in the best interest of the principal. In the business world, the principals are the owners/shareholders and the agents are managers; and in public administration, the principals are elected officials and the agents are bureaucrats. In non-profit organizations, since there are no owners or shareholders, it is unclear who should be regarded or function as the principal, a situation that adds a special twist to the basic principal–agent problem. As such, it is necessary to recognize the special importance of **stakeholders** in grappling with the complexities of non-profit governance. In non-profit organizations, the principal–agent problem is considered to be less pronounced than in for-profit firms due to the presence of the **non-distribution constraint** and the presumably higher commitment of **non-profit management** and staff to the organizational **mission** and the underlying values it represents (religious, humanitarian etc).

Pritchett, Henry Smith (1857–1939)

Henry Smith Pritchett was an accomplished astronomer and educator, who served as professor of astronomy at Washington University, St Louis (1881–1897) and as president of the Massachusetts Institute of Technology (1900–1905). It was in his role as president of the Carnegie Foundation for the Advancement of Teaching (1906–1930) that Pritchett was able to help build the prestige of American higher educational institutions. Because he believed that foundations and accumulated wealth were in a unique position to support human improvement, Pritchett advocated for a 'science of giving', in which philanthropic funds would be given for an extended period of time in order to truly address the roots of social problems.

Private Fees and Charges

Private fees and charges or 'programme fees' are a major **revenue** category of **non-profit organizations**. They essentially include four types of business or commercial income: fees for service, i.e. charges that clients of a non-profit organization pay for the services provided (e.g. fees for day-care or healthcare);

dues, i.e. charges levied on the members of an organization as a condition of **membership**; proceeds from sales of products and services, which includes income from for-profit subsidiaries; and investment income, i.e. the income a non-profit organization earns on its capital or its investments.

Private Giving

Private giving is a major **revenue** category of **non-profit organizations** that includes **foundation** giving in the form of **grants** from **grant-making foundations, operating foundations** and **community foundations**; business or corporate donations, which includes giving directly by businesses or giving by business or **corporate foundations**; and **individual giving**, i.e. direct contributions by individuals as well as contributions through **federated fundraising campaigns**.

Private Goods

Private goods are goods to which property rights can be established and that are not available to all irrespective of contribution. 'Pure' private goods have two essential characteristics inherent in the nature of the good or service in question. The first is excludability, i.e. once the good is produced, only consumers with property rights can benefit, and others can be prevented from benefiting at no or little cost. For example, food purchased in a supermarket is typically consumed by household members; others are easily excluded unless invited for lunch or dinner. The second essential characteristic of a private good is rivalry, i.e. individual use limits and can even exhaust potential use by others. For example, food items are consumed by one person only, even if they share the same meal. A basic tenet of economic theory is that markets best provide pure private goods, that the state or **public sector** best provides pure **public goods**, and that **non-profit organizations** are suited for the provision of quasi-public goods, i.e. where exclusion is possible and significant **externalities** exist.

Private Organizations

A private organization is 'non-governmental' in that it is institutionally separate from government and not part of the state apparatus of government. This does not mean that such a **non-profit organization** may not receive government support in cash or in kind, or even that government officials cannot sit on its board. What is important is that the **organization** has an institutional identity separate from that of the state, that it is not an instrumentality of any unit of government whether national or local, and that it therefore does not exercise governmental authority. While such separate institutional identity is relatively easy to identify in most cases, there are numerous borderline cases, the most obvious of which are **quangos** and **government-sponsored foundations**. The critical point in such borderline cases is the extent to which such organizations operate as extensions of government exercising governmental authority, albeit through separate institutional structures. The private criterion is one characteristic of the **structural–operational definition**.

Private Voluntary Organizations

'Private voluntary organization' (PVO) is the term used by the US Agency for International Development (USAID) to denominate overseas relief and development non-profit or non-governmental organizations (**NGOs**) that have registered with the Agency and are eligible to receive USAID funds. In official parlance, the term is reserved for US (PVO) and other, mostly Northern organizations (International PVO—IPVO). Organizations in the South that PVOs work or partner with are usually referred to as local NGOs, not PVOs. As of fiscal year 2001, there were 444 US PVOs registered with USAID, ranging from the Academy for International Development to **CARE**, Catholic Relief Services, Lutheran World Relief, **World Vision** and the Zoological Society of Milwaukee County. The close to 50 registered IPVOs include organizations such as **ActionAid**, the **International Planned Parenthood Federation**, the Terre des Hommes Foundation, the Save the Children Fund UK (see **International Save the Children Alliance**) and the Polish Stefan Batory Foundation.

Privatization

Privatization is a broad policy approach that refers to a shift in ownership of public **assets** and governmental responsibilities to **private organizations** and individuals. Carried by preferences for small government, welfare reform and economic liberalization processes, privatization policies took hold in the 1980s and 1990s to reduce state involvement in economy and society. Among other aspects, it implies a greater role for **voluntary** and **non-profit organizations**, leading to a mixed economy of welfare in many health and social services and social security areas, but also in arts and culture, education, international humanitarian assistance and community development. Specifically, for the **non-profit sector**, privatization of state functions entails replacing tax-based **grants** with fees and charges; assuming greater administrative and programmatic responsibilities for planning, implementation and performance; and competitive bidding for service contracts. Privatization is closely linked to **new public management** approaches.

Product Bundling

Product bundling is a term used in non-profit price theory but also in **marketing**, and refers to a situation where **organizations** combine two or more related or unrelated product or service lines to achieve better **revenue** and cost outcomes. Examples include homeless shelters, where users may receive not only shelter but also counselling services; schools that offer learning but also require the purchase of their own uniforms, meal programmes, etc.; and religious organizations that combine religious teaching with service delivery. **Non-profit organizations** are very likely to bundle products, and do so around their **missions** and to achieve **economies of scope**, whereas businesses bundle goods to achieve scope economies as well, but also to achieve greater profit margins.

Product Portfolio Map

The product portfolio map is a management planning tool designed to help an **organization** find a balance between **mission** fit and economic viability across different programmes and service lines. For each programme, two dimensions are examined: its contribution to achievement of the organization's mission and its contribution to economic viability. Activities with a high contribution to the organization's mission and viability are the preferred **private** and **public goods non-profit organizations** seek to provide; they are also the most difficult ones to establish and maintain, as they are likely to attract competitors. At the other extreme are programmes that rank low in terms of mission fit and economic contribution; the organization should exit such programmes. In other words, programmes around **non-preferred goods** or services should be added or discontinued depending on their contributions to **revenue** and efficiency. Programmes with good mission fit and low economic viability face **budget** problems, and their operations can only be maintained in the medium to long term if counterbalanced by resource-attracting programmes with lower mission fit but greater economic viability. (See also **Value–return matrix**.)

Professional Associations

Professional associations are self-governing **organizations** of members of particular professions and professional areas of expertise, such as medicine, engineering, accounting and law. Professional associations serve the interest of their profession, particularly in public policy matters relating to its practice, but in many cases, they also often raise their voices on broader issues such as **human rights** and democratic reform. Practically speaking, they are usually responsible for licensing practitioners, setting standards, and assuring compliance with ethical and professional expectations. Furthermore, an individual is usually prohibited from advertising as a 'professional' unless he or she is a member in good standing of the relevant professional association. Examples of professional associations include the British or American Medical Association, mainly representing doctors, and bar associations in the USA, both national and locally-based, representing and licensing lawyers. Although their functions are similar, professional associations differ from **business associations** in that their members are individuals rather than corporations or organizations.

Professional Bureaucracy

Mintzberg (1979) introduced the distinction between machine **bureaucracy** and professional bureaucracy. Machine bureaucracies are designed as 'mechanized' systems with high degrees of specialization and formalization. Most decisions are pre-programmed and implemented in the **organization**'s structure, similar to the Weberian notion of bureaucracy. Employees tend to perform highly standardized tasks and have very little autonomy in task performance. By contrast, in professional bureaucracies, e.g. hospitals, universities and social-service agencies, employees have greater autonomy and co-ordinate task performance in more decentralized ways. Moreover, professional bureaucracies tend to be influenced by organized professional interests, such as the medical profession and nursing profession in hospitals, professors at universities, and social workers in service agencies.

Professionalization

Professionalization refers broadly to the development of skills, identities, norms and values associated with becoming part of a professional group. At the individual level, it is traditionally measured by one's level of education and degrees obtained. However, it can also be measured by standards established by a **professional association** in a given industry.

In the context of **non-profit organizations**, at least two types of professionalization are relevant. The first is the professionalization of volunteers, i.e. bringing volunteers in certain service fields up to a certain level of expertise through training or recruiting volunteers that already have such expertise. This is often demanded, for example, where volunteers provide services such as counselling to children or families.

The second type of professionalization entails hiring professionals to manage and run an organization's activities. In environments of uncertainty, non-profit organizations feel greater pressure to professionalize and introduce more technocratic control. But this is also a tendency in organizations as they develop from start-up, volunteer-run organizations into more mature entities that might need to prove their legitimacy before funders. The potential pitfall occurs when professional staff gain control over agency operations and limit the involvement of **stakeholders**.

The trend toward professionalization among many **non-profit organizations** brings with it a number of dilemmas. How does a non-profit organization professionalize without becoming elitist or exclusive and losing touch with its **beneficiaries**? How can an organization demand professionalization from volunteers? Does the professionalization of **voluntary** social work involve the risk of undermining the ethical and moral dimensions of **voluntarism**?

Programme-Related Investments

Programme-related investments (PRIs) are investments made by foundations to support charitable activities relating to their **mission** that involve the potential return of capital (as distinguished from a **grant**). PRIs include financing methods such as loans at no or low interest rates, loan guarantees and equity investments in charitable **organization**s or in commercial ventures for charitable purposes. PRIs can be used to support affordable housing and community development, as well as capital projects ranging from preserving historic buildings to providing emergency loans to social service agencies and protecting and preserving wildlife habitats. The principal benefit to the **foundation** is that the repayment or return of equity can be recycled for another charitable purpose. PRIs are valued as a means of leveraging philanthropic dollars (see **Leverage**).

Proudhon, Pierre-Joseph (1809–1865)

Pierre-Joseph Proudhon was a self-educated French printer and author of numerous books and brochures. He corresponded also with **Karl Marx** who wrote *Misery of Philosophy* in answer to Proudhon's *Philosophy of Misery*. Representative and inspirer of the skilled workers labour movement in Europe, he fought the State and **centralization** and was in favour of a new social contract relying on mutualism (see **mutuality**), federalism and workers' **empowerment** in factories. His new social contract relies on **friendly societies**, mutual credit and consumer **co-operatives**. He foresaw Europe as a federation of nations. The influence of Proudhon remains visible on **social economy** in Southern Europe.

Public Benefit

The notion of public benefit is critical to the tax treatment of **non-profit organizations**, the privileges they enjoy, and the **accountability** requirements to which they must adhere. Broadly speaking, public benefit refers to some cause related to the good of society. What constitutes public benefit varies across countries, across time, and across legal and tax regimes.

In common-law systems, such as the UK, guidelines on what is considered public benefit have developed over time. The UK *Charity Commission Guidelines* offer a useful set of criteria indicative of public rather than private benefit of organizational purposes:

- The organization benefits the public as a whole or a significant segment of it;
- The **beneficiaries** are not defined in terms of a personal or contractual relationship;
- **Membership** and benefits should be available to all those who fall within the class of beneficiaries;
- Any private benefit arises directly out of the pursuit of the charity's objectives or is legitimately incidental to them;
- The amount of private benefit should be reasonable;
- Charges should be reasonable and should not exclude a substantial proportion of the beneficiary class;
- The service provided should not cater only to the financially well off. It should in principle be open to all potential beneficiaries.

In **civil-law systems**, the state typically puts more onerous requirements on private actors that seek to work for the public good, with the French system being among the strictest in trying to limit public benefit to state agencies rather than extending it to private actors. In most civil-law countries, the definition of what constitutes public benefit is essentially defined by provisions in various tax laws. Public benefit status is therefore primarily a fiscal term. Its definition and application serve to differentiate tax-exempt organizations from those liable to various forms of taxation. Using the German tax code as an example, the promotion of the following objectives is covered by the definition of public benefit:

- public well-being in material, spiritual and moral spheres;
- charitable and benevolent activities to support persons in need and unable to care for themselves;
- church-related activities including the construction, maintenance and administration of churches and church property, religious instruction, religious services and training of the clergy.

The tax code goes so far as to provide a list of examples of activities that meet the definition. They include support of science and research, education and instruction, art and culture, **religion**, international understanding and exchange, development aid, environmental protection, historical preservation and local customs; support of youth welfare, the elderly, public health, welfare and sport; general support of a democratic state and community; and support of animal husbandry, plant cultivation and gardening (all non-commercial), traditional customs, veterans' affairs, amateur radios, model airplane clubs and dog shows.

What is more, the tax code stipulates that private activities for public benefit must be carried out in a certain manner:

- selfless, in the sense of altruistic (see **altruism**), whereby members of the organization are neither allowed to receive profits nor other profit-like compensation. This strict **non-distribution constraint** excludes many mutual membership **associations**, as well as business and **professional associations**. It also implies that the cost behaviour of non-profits must be 'reasonable' in terms of salaries and fringe benefits.
- exclusive, in the sense that the organization pursues only purposes defined as public benefit. If an organization carries out other activities, it may lose the non-profit tax status altogether. In practice, the organization may declare some of its activities as public benefit and others as 'commercial'. This has the effect that those activities classified as public benefit receive preferential tax treatment, whereas commercial activities may be subject to taxation.
- direct, in the sense that the charitable purpose has to be served by the organization itself rather than through third parties.

- timely, in the sense that the organization has to spend its resources for the specified purposes within a certain time period, usually a given fiscal year. This implies that many non-profit organizations are not allowed to build up financial reserves or accumulate capital for investment.

Current debates recognize that the more traditional notions of public benefit and public responsibilities have shifted from the state to other actors, which brings in the role of non-profit organizations as private actors for the public good. In particular, the role of the state as 'enabler' and 'animator' of private action for public service has increased, which heightens the role of the **third sector** as a locus of public benefit production.

Public Benefit Companies

Public benefit companies are not-for-profit entities established in order to produce **public goods** and to meet public needs. The profit of their occasional unrelated business activities must also be used to pursue their public purposes. They are not allowed to distribute profit to their owners. In addition to the **non-distribution constraint** imposed by the Civil Code, it is the basic economic regulation of for-profit limited liability companies that applies to public benefit companies. They can be established either by private persons and **organizations** or by government bodies. Many of them are engaged in the provision of public goods and services and contribute to alleviating unemployment problems. They are important partners for municipalities and other government authorities in the process of contracting out welfare services.

Public Charities

In the USA, a public charity is a **non-profit organization** that is exempt from federal income tax under **Section 501(c)(3)** of the Internal Revenue Code. Religious, scientific, medical and educational organizations are considered public charities. Other charitable organizations are deemed to be private **foundations**, unless they pass a public support test. One type of public support test—according to sections 509(a)(1) and 170(b)(1)(A)(vi) of the Internal Revenue Code—requires that, to be classified as a public charity, an organization must receive at least one-third of its total support from the general public (including government agencies and foundations). An organization that does not pass this test may still qualify for public charity status if it can demonstrate that its percentage of 'public support' is at least 10% of its total support and that it has other characteristics, e.g. a broad-based **board of directors**, that make it 'sufficiently public'. Other organizations that receive the largest part of their income from the sale of services must pass a different test—as specified in Section 509(a)(2)—in which they must demonstrate that at least one-third of their total income comes from the sale of services that further their **mission**, and that the income from investment or non-core activities does not exceed one-third of their total income.

Public Foundations

In the USA, the Internal Revenue Service (IRS) distinguishes between **public charities** and private **foundations**, exerting significantly more stringent authority over the latter. The IRS provides no specific definition for a public foundation, but the **Council on Foundations** considers public foundations to be publicly supported **non-profit organizations**, legally classified as public charities, that focus more on grant-making than on providing direct charitable services. In contrast with a private foundation that relies on one source for most of its funds, a public foundation receives support from multiple sources and must continue to seek funds from diverse sources in order to retain its public status.

Public Goods

Public goods are goods to which no property rights can be established and that are available to all irrespective of contribution. 'Pure' public goods have two essential characteristics inherent in the nature of the good or service in question: non-excludability, i.e. consumers cannot be prevented from benefiting except at great cost, and non-rivalry, i.e. individual use does not reduce the amount available for others. If only one of these characteristics is present, and the other either not at all or much less so, the good is considered to be quasi-public. A basic tenet of economic theory is that the state or **public sector** best provides pure public goods, that markets best provide pure **private goods**, and that **non-profit organizations** are suited for the provision of quasi-public goods. The reality is that the area of quasi-public goods allows for multiple solutions: they can be provided by government, by businesses, and, prominently, by non-profit organizations.

Public Goods Theories

In 1975, the economist **Burton Weisbrod** was among the first to publish the **public goods** theory of **non-profit organizations**—a theory that has influenced the development of other theories in the field. It provides an economic rationale for the formation of non-profit organizations to provide public goods and is also referred to as **heterogeneity theory**.

The theory explains the existence of non-profit organizations with the help of two basic concepts: demand heterogeneity for the provision of public goods, and the median voter. Demand heterogeneity refers to the extent to which the demand for public and quasi-public goods is similar across the population (demand homogeneity) or if different population groups have divergent demands for such goods in both quality and quantity (demand heterogeneity). The median voter represents that largest segment of the demand for public and quasi-public goods within the electorate.

In a competitive liberal **democracy**, government officials, in seeking to maximize their chances of re-election, will strive to provide a given public good at the level demanded by the median voter. This strategy of public goods provision leaves some demands unmet. This unfilled demand for the public good is satisfied by non-profit organizations, which are established and financed by the **voluntary** contributions of citizens who want to increase the output or quality of the public good. In other words, non-profit organizations are gap-fillers; they exist as a result of private demands for public goods not offered by the **public sector**. By implication, due to **market failure**, the public good would not be likely to be supplied by for-profit organizations.

Generally speaking, in a heterogeneous society, one would expect more non-profit organizations than in homogeneous societies, where the median voter segment of the demand curve for public goods would be much wider. Thus, the number of non-profit organizations is positively related to the increase in the diversity of a population.

Major extensions of Weisbrod's model concentrate on the output produced by the **non-profit sector**, incorporating the preferences of **stakeholders** (such as managers, volunteers and employees) other than **donors**, and allowing for more than one type of good to be produced. The result of adding other stakeholders and other goods into the model is an explanation of why certain non-profit goods and services differ from those of government-provided goods and services.

Public Law Foundations

Public law foundations are foundations created by public charter and endowed with public funds. They have long been a popular instrument of public policy in civil-law countries, but have gained new prominence in the **privatization** process in Eastern and Central Europe. They are established in order to take over tasks that are defined in law as government responsibilities (e.g. education, health care, public safety, etc.). Their founders can only be the Parliament, the Government and the municipalities, which are not allowed to create private foundations. The boards of public law foundations are appointed by the founders. Their **endowments** come from governmental budgetary sources. Most also receive annual **public-sector subsidies**. The public law foundations are held financially accountable by the State Comptroller's Office (or equivalent). The founders can initiate the dissolution of a public law foundation if they think its function can be more efficiently fulfilled by another type of **organization**. The property of the dissolved public law foundation reverts to its founder. Apart from these special provisions, the basic legal regulation of private foundations applies to public law foundations as well.

Public Sector

The term 'public sector' refers to all branches of government, including the executive, judicial, and administrative and regulatory activities of federal, state, local, or regional political entities. The term is often used synonymously with 'state' and 'government', although each carries somewhat different connotations.

Public Sector Payments

Public sector payments is a major **revenue** category for **non-profit organizations** that includes **grants** and contracts, i.e. direct contributions by the government to the organization in support of specific activities and programmes; statutory transfers, i.e. contributions by the government, as mandated by law, to provide general support to an organization in carrying out its publicly-mandated programmes; and **third-party payments**, i.e. indirect government payments reimbursing an organization for services rendered to individuals (e.g. health insurance, **vouchers**, or payments for day-care).

Public Sphere

The closely related concepts of **'civil society'** and 'public sphere' developed in the early modern era to refer to capacities for social self-organization and influence over the state. Civil society usually refers to the institutions and relationships that organize social life at a level between the state and the family. Public sphere is one of several linked terms (including 'public space', simply 'public' and the German *Öffentlichkeit*, or publicness) that denote an institutional setting distinguished by openness of communication and a focus on the **public good** rather than simply compromises among **private goods**. Located in civil society, communication in the public sphere may address the state or may seek to influence civil society and even private life directly. Key questions concern the extent to which it will be guided by critical reason, and how boundaries between public and private are mediated.

Over the last century, new ideas about public discourse were complemented by the development of new communications media, especially those dependent on print; rising literacy and education levels; growth of the state; and expansion of popular political participation. In this process, the distinction of public and private took on new importance and complexity. On the one hand, the realm of public interaction expanded; cities were the primary setting for this, especially cosmopolitan trading and capital cities. Public spaces appeared literally with coffee houses, parks, theatres, and other places where people who were not bound by private relations gathered and communicated. They also grew metaphorically with printed sermons, pamphlets, newspapers, books in vernacular languages, journals that reviewed them, and other media of public communication. On the other hand, the state also expanded and with it the range of *res publica*, 'public things' that included property held in common and matters of concern to the whole polity. Publicness took on a dual sense, referring both to the openness of access and interaction and to collective affairs as managed by the state. The public referred both to the collective subject of **democracy**—the people organized as a discursive and decision-making public—and as its object, the public good. Today, the notion of the public sphere is changing due to developments in communication technology (internet), information systems (television), and, closely related to these, economic and cultural globalization. The emergence of a **global civil society** is part of this process.

Q

Quakers – *see* Religious Society of Friends

Quangos (Quasi-Non-Governmental Organizations)

Quangos are **organizations** created, largely funded, overseen by, and accountable to government, but given some degree of programmatic and operational independence. Coined by Alan Pifer, then President of the **Carnegie Corporation of New York**, the term describes such organizations appearing in the USA, such as the National Science Foundation, and organizations originating during the Great Society era of the 1960s. In the UK and Europe, the term has been applied to many forms of arms-length public-provision entities with diverse purposes, including the British Broadcasting Corporation (BBC) and some German television networks. Critics point to concerns about power being devolved from elected public bodies to unelected quango representatives, raising legitimacy problems and fear of technocratic dominance amidst a growing democratic deficit.

Quasi-Markets

Quasi-markets are part of **new public management** policies used to improve the efficiency of public providers by introducing market forces, and are now more widely understood as an attempt to either simulate or develop market conditions by controlling sources of potential **market failures**. Quasi-markets differ from conventional markets in a number of ways: on the supply side, they introduce competition, but the providers are not necessarily private, nor necessarily profit-maximizing, but can include a mix of public agencies, **non-profit organizations** and business firms. Examples are schools, hospitals and social service providers. On the demand side, consumers do not necessarily spend cash; their purchasing power is often expressed as an earmarked **budget**. Consumers may make their own choice (e.g. **vouchers**), or the choice may be made on their behalf by professionals (e.g. social workers or medical experts in managed care situations).

R

Reciprocity

Reciprocity is a form of exchange based on mutual obligations to give and to receive. It is a transaction and implies internalized expectations of a long-term equalization of benefits rather than short-term market expectations or enforcement by third parties. Family and friendship relations often involve reciprocity, as do the notions of **active citizenship**, **civic culture** and **civil society**. In social policy terms, reciprocity is important for the operation of **voluntary** schemes such as blood donation, volunteer ambulances or volunteer fire brigades. For example, while individuals may give blood freely, they also expect others to do likewise, consequently ensuring that blood will be available to them when needed.

Redmond, Mary (1950–)

One of Ireland's leading employment lawyers, Mary Redmond founded the Irish Hospice Foundation in 1986 and is also a founding member of The Wheel, which provides support to, and advocates for, community and **voluntary** organizations. Spurred by her father's illness and on realizing that no suitable services existed in Ireland at that time, Redmond provided the motivation to start a hospice to provide palliative care to those suffering from terminal illness. What started as a small venture influenced others to initiate their own local or regional hospices. The Irish Hospice Foundation now supports a range of palliative care and hospice facilities and services around the country.

Related Business Income

Related business income is a term used in non-profit economics and tax law, and refers to a specific **revenue** category attributed to the production of **non-preferred private goods** and services. If the non-preferred private good is related to the charitable purpose and supportive of the production of the **preferred private good**, then revenues achieved are classified as related business income, and usually remain untaxed. The revenues an art museum receives from its in-house cafeteria, bookstore or catalogue business would be an example. (See also **Unrelated business income**.)

Religion

The term religion is difficult to define, but generally refers to the human recognition of some superhuman power, and usually involves a specific system of beliefs about some form or kind of deity, rituals and worship, a **code of ethics** and moral teachings, and a philosophy of life. A narrower approach to defining religion would primarily refer to the major world religions, i.e. **Christianity**, **Islam**, Judaism, **Buddhism**, Confucianism and **Hinduism**.

There is a strong link between religion, **charity**, **philanthropy** and the **non-profit sector**, and religion is often the basis for the value orientation of many **non-profit organizations**. **Estelle James** and others have argued that religious entrepreneurs are among the most frequent founders of non-profit organizations, both sacramental and church-related, world-wide (See **entrepreneurship theories**). Religious leaders played an important role in the development of the **welfare state**, and missionary societies and religion-related **organizations** played equally central roles during colonial rule and the independence period and in developmental efforts in Africa, Asia and Latin America.

Religions differ not only in their theology and in the values and virtues they project, they also vary in the way they are organized and encourage proselytizing and missionary activities. Some religion systems actively seek new adherents, create vast networks of institutions outside the inner realm of religious devotion and sacramental service, and engage in, even embrace, the secular spheres of politics, economy and society. For example, Christian religions are typically highly institutionalized and organized in thousands of organizations such as dioceses, parishes, lay groups and numerous church-related organizations. Hinduism, by contrast, has been much less organizational, and has few, if any, over-arching institutions or centrally co-ordinated systems in place.

Religious Society of Friends (Quakers)

The Religious Society of Friends, also known as Quakers, originated in England in the 17th century under George Fox's leadership and evolved into a Christian

sect with members around the world, primarily in England and the USA. Quakers came to be known for their support for religious and political freedom, honesty in business, humane treatment of criminals, aid to war victims and others in distress, and staunch opposition to all forms of violence. The name Quaker, originally an insult, became a symbol of integrity. Their peacemaking and relief efforts were recognized in 1947 with the award of the Nobel Peace Prize, accepted by the British Friends Service Council and the American Friends Service Committee.

Website: www.quaker.org

Replacement Cost

In discussing the valuation of **volunteer** work, replacement cost refers to the costs that would arise if work done voluntarily were to be bought on the labour market, assuming that volunteers could be replaced by wage earners. Different types of wages could be used: that of the specialist, which assigns a wage rate equivalent to that of a professional performing the same kind of work, versus that of the generalist, which assumes volunteer work is multi-faceted and therefore uses a lower average wage rate. Because volunteer work is hetero-geneous, use of the former might overvalue total volunteer input, while use of the latter might undervalue it. In practice, the selection of valuation method depends on the information available about the work that volunteers in a particular **organization** or set of organizations do.

Resource-Dependency Theory

Resource-dependency theory argues that **organizations** face environmental constraints in the form of external control over resources needed to ensure operational efficiency and continued survival. Since few types of organizations are resource-independent, they necessarily become interdependent with their environments. At the same time, external actors in control over critical resources will attempt to influence the organization and threaten managerial autonomy. Organizations will, however, not simply comply with external demands, but attempt to employ various strategies to manage dependencies and regain managerial freedom and autonomy. In the process, the organization influences and changes its environment as well. Among the strategies organizations employ are various types of inter-organizational linkages, including **mergers**, joint ventures, interlocking directorates and movement of executives within industries. This may either help reduce dependence on given critical resources or help obtain other resources that are in turn critical to the external actors trying to exercise control.

In the non-profit context, the resource dependency perspective is particularly useful in understanding the perpetual quest for a balanced mix of **revenue** sources. In many countries, the overly heavy reliance of some types of **non-profit organizations** on government financing has given rise to concerns about governmentalization, bureaucratization, loss of autonomy, as well as goal deflection. All of this can be understood as a failure to manage and neutralize dependency on government resources. It may also partially explain the current revived interest in fostering **philanthropy** and civic engagement in many countries as an attempt to regain resources with no 'strings attached' that increase the managerial scope of action.

Revenue

The revenue structure of **non-profit organizations** is more complex than that of for-profit firms and public agencies, and non-profits typically have a mix of different revenue sources. Non-profit revenue is most commonly classified by origin: **public sector payments**, **private giving** and **private fees and charges** ('programme fees'). Other systems classify non-profit revenue by kind (monetary versus in-kind); intent (transfers such as **gifts** and **grants** versus exchanges of goods and services against money and other transactions); formality (contract-based exchanges, recording transfers and transactions, informal donation); source (donations; user fees; sale of ancillary goods and services); and restrictions (restricted versus unrestricted funds).

Rhodes Trust

The Rhodes Trust was established in 1902 by Cecil John Rhodes, British diamond magnate and statesman (for whom Rhodesia was named). Headquartered in the UK, the Trust is dedicated to providing future leaders with an education that will broaden their views and develop their abilities. Its main activity is the selection and financing of some 90 Rhodes Scholars annually. The scholarships enable students—mainly from the USA, parts of the British Empire and former British colonies—to study at Oxford University, which Rhodes himself attended.

Website: www.rhodeshouse.ox.ac.uk

Robinson, Mary (1944–)

The former UN Commissioner for Human Rights, Mary Robinson had a distinguished career as a progressive politician, lawyer and academic in Ireland prior to becoming the first woman President of Ireland. Closely associated with causes such as women's rights and contraception, Mary Robinson was Reid Professor of Law at Trinity College Dublin and served in the *Seanad* (Upper House of Parliament) from 1969 to 1989 as a Labour politician and an Independent. During her seven-year presidential term, she actively worked at changing the shape of the office of President from a retirement post for fading politicians to being accessible to community groups.

Rockefeller, Jr, John D. (1874–1960)

The only son of **John D. Rockefeller, Sr**, John D. Rockefeller, Jr (JDR Jr) devoted his efforts primarily to philanthropic and civic activities, believing that his inherited fortune should be used for the public good. JDR Jr also made his own mark in business, however, leading the movement against the twelve-hour work day and the seven-day work week. The largest portion of his charitable **gifts** (estimated lifetime total: US \$537m.) went to general and operating foundations, including the International Education Board and the **Rockefeller Brothers Fund**, which was created by his sons and daughter. Other major gifts included funds to purchase land in New York City for the site of the United Nations headquarters. In addition to contributing his own funds, JDR Jr lent his name and network to **leverage** additional resources for **organizations** such as the United Negro College Fund.

Rockefeller, Sr, John D. (1839–1937)

John D. Rockefeller, Sr was one of the first major philanthropists in the USA, establishing several important institutions and, over his lifetime, donating US \$540m. to charitable purposes. Born in New York state, Rockefeller relocated to Cleveland, Ohio, from where he created and built up the Standard Oil Company, which ultimately dominated the US oil industry. In 1896, Rockefeller gave up operating leadership of Standard Oil to focus on his philanthropic efforts guided by **Frederick T. Gates**. With the advice of Gates, Rockefeller contributed significantly to or established, among others, the University of Chicago; the Rockefeller Institute for Medical Research (1901, now Rockefeller University); the General Education Board (active 1902–1965); and the

Rockefeller Foundation (1913). Rockefeller sought to apply his managerial wisdom to the **charity** world, investing his resources to reduce waste and duplication in the charitable sphere and to overcome the lack of study behind much giving.

Rockefeller Brothers Fund

The Rockefeller Brothers Fund (RBF) was established in 1940 as a vehicle to enhance and combine the charitable activities of the five sons and daughter of **John D. Rockefeller, Jr,** who himself made significant gifts to the Fund's endowment. A grant-making foundation, the Fund works globally, nationally, and in its home town of New York City, providing support for **organizations** and activities promoting democratic practice, peace and security, human advancement and sustainable development. In addition to its geographical focus on North America and East Asia, RBF makes **grants** in 'pivotal places,' selected for their significance. In 1999, the Charles E. Culpeper Foundation merged with RBF.

Website: www.rbf.org

Rockefeller Foundation

Founded in 1913 by **John D. Rockefeller, Sr**, the Rockefeller Foundation is a private, **grant-making foundation** dedicated to poverty alleviation, disease eradication, employment, housing, education and cultural preservation. Headquartered in New York City (USA), the Foundation is active in Eastern and Southern Africa, South-East Asia and North America. Among its achievements are: the development of a vaccine to prevent yellow fever; the launch of the 'green revolution' that has modernized agriculture in the developing world; and the establishment of major cultural institutions, including the Lincoln Center in New York City. In 2002, the foundation reported **assets** of US $2,600m.

Website: www.rockfound.org

Rosenwald, Julius (1862–1932)

The son of German Jewish immigrants to the USA, Julius Rosenwald became one of the early 20th century's wealthiest retail merchants through his leadership of Sears, Roebuck and Company. Rosenwald is credited with donating more than US $65m. to various causes, mainly targeting Jewish and African-American populations. Through these **gifts** and the Julius Rosenwald Fund, created in 1917, Rosenwald established numerous YMCAs (see **Young Men's Christian Association**) to serve African-American communities throughout the USA and built thousands of schools for rural African-Americans in the country's south. Critical of perpetual **endowments**, Rosenwald wanted to end his Fund's activities as soon as practicable after his death, and so in 1948, per his wishes, the Fund was dissolved.

Rotary International

The first Rotary Club was established in Chicago, Illinois (USA) in 1905 as the world's first **service club**. Originally serving the professional and social interests of club members only, Rotary is now dedicated to serving communities in need throughout the world. There are approximately 1.2m. Rotarians in over 31,000 Rotary Clubs located in 166 countries. Among its many service projects and accomplishments, Rotary members served in delegations to the UN Charter conference in 1945, assisted in the creation of UNESCO, and, in 1985, launched a campaign to eradicate polio throughout the world.

Website: www.rotary.org

Rousseau, Jean-Jacques (1712–1778)

Jean-Jacques Rousseau was a Swiss-born writer, political theorist and philosopher whose ideas greatly influenced the French Revolution. Rousseau addressed the concept of individual liberty in society and forms of how power and authority are to be allocated to the state on the one hand and citizens and **civil society** institutions on the other. Dealing with the difficult questions of social inequality and authority, and anticipating some key arguments about **state–society relations** by **de Tocqueville** and others later, his most well known work is *The Social Contract* (1762), in which Rousseau explores the basis for social authority and legitimate political order.

Rowntree, Joseph (1836–1925)

Born to a family of Quakers (see **Religious Society of Friends**), Joseph Rowntree was a successful businessman and a noted British philanthropist. Rowntree began working in his father's grocery, but eventually acquired sole responsibility for his brother's cocoa business and gained notoriety for introducing improved working conditions for his staff including better wages, reasonable hours and one of the first occupational pension plans. In 1904, Rowntree established three trusts—the **Joseph Rowntree Foundation**, The Joseph Rowntree Reform Trust and the Joseph Rowntree Charitable Trust. Later in life, Rowntree worked to promote adult education and was an ardent supporter of the League of Nations.

Joseph Rowntree Foundation

Established in 1904 to administer the model village established by businessman **Joseph Rowntree**, the Joseph Rowntree Foundation now supports research and development activities throughout the United Kingdom that seek to better understand the causes of social difficulties and overcome them. The Foundation does not make **grants**, but rather initiates research activities, commissioning and managing most projects in **partnership** with a large variety of academic and other institutions. Topics include housing, social care and social policy, parenting, racial issues and neighbourhood renewal. The Foundation ultimately disseminates its research findings to appropriate audiences, e.g. policy-makers and practitioners, to influence change.

Website: www.jrf.org.uk

Rule of Law

The idea of the 'rule of law' (or *rechtsstaat, etat de droit, estado de derecho*) is found in many legal systems. Its core principle is that the law is supreme, so that every member of a society, including its ruler(s), is subject to the law. Beyond that, there is no single agreed definition.

For most scholars, legal and political systems must conform to a number of formal criteria to adhere to the rule of law. One of the most famous authors on the subject, Albert Venn Dicey (1885), laid down the following criteria: everyone is equal before the law; there can be no punishment without a prior law; everyone who believes his rights to have been infringed should have access to a judicial remedy. Further criteria in other scholarly definitions include independence and impartiality of the judiciary; public laws and a transparent legislative process; judicial review of government action; and a presumption of innocence and double jeopardy in criminal law.

One of the main elements stressed by the 'formal' authors is that there must be legal security through predictability. The rule of law is posited as the opposite of arbitrary rule. However, critics of the concept have pointed out that a legal system can meet all these formal criteria and none the less be repressive and unjust, for instance if its laws prohibit forms of freedom of expression or political opposition. Some recent definitions have tried to meet such objections by using a much wider definition of the rule of law. The Organisation for Security and Co-operation in Europe, for instance, includes free and democratic elections and respect for **human rights** in its definition.

There is also a more radical line of criticism of the concept, for instance in the work of critical theorists, who consider the law mainly as an instrument for the ruling classes to justify their rule and maintain their privileges. They will point out that equality in law does not guarantee equal circumstances in life. Some, such as the philosopher Dworkin, prefer a sense of substantive justice to a formal interpretation of the rule of law.

Politicians, activists and international **organizations** enjoy using the term 'rule of law', which has become associated with a whole spectrum of 'good things', including **democracy**, **transparency**, respect for human rights and space for **civil society**. They should, however, be aware that it is not a well-defined concept. As a recent author concludes, it belongs to the category of open-ended concepts that are subject to permanent debate.

S

Sage, Margaret Olivia Slocum (1828–1918)

Upon the death of her husband, financier Russell Sage, New York-born Margaret Olivia Slocum Sage used her inherited funds to become an active philanthropist and, during her lifetime, contributed over US $75m. to various causes. In 1907, she established the Russell Sage Foundation with an **endowment** of $10m. She also made substantial **gifts** to major institutions such as Harvard and Yale Universities and the **Young Women's Christian Association**. In 1910 she funded a new campus for Emma Willard School, and in 1916 she converted the old campus to the Russell Sage College, which provides vocational instruction for women.

Sasakawa Peace Foundation

The Sasakawa Peace Foundation was established in 1986 by the Sasakawa Foundation (now the **Nippon Foundation**) and the Japanese motorboat racing industry. Its **mission** is to promote world peace and foster international understanding through exchange and co-operation activities, either conducted directly by Foundation staff or supported through **grants** made to other **organizations**. The Foundation's current programme priorities include dialogue across cultures and civilizations, **capacity-building** and institutionalization of the **non-profit sector**, and East Asian renewal and transfer of experience. In addition to regular projects, the Foundation has created several special funds targeting work in specific regions, including Central Europe.

Website: www.spf.org

Schumpeter, Joseph A. (1883–1950)

An Austrian-born economist and one of the leading economic theorists of the early 20th century, Schumpeter pioneered economic theories on evolution and development, **entrepreneurship** and **innovation**. His major works include *The Nature and Essence of Theoretical Economics* (1908), *Capitalism, Socialism, and Democracy* (1942) and *History of Economic Analysis* (1954). Schumpeter's theories have made critical contributions not only to economics, but also to sociology and political science. Specifically, his theory of the role of entrepreneurs and the 'creative destructive process' of innovation continue to influence current work on **social entrepreneurship** and **social enterprise**.

Scientific Philanthropy

Scientific philanthropy was an approach to charitable work that emerged in the USA and England, in particular, in the second half of the 1800s to bring order to previously sporadic and largely unco-ordinated charitable efforts. Based on a growing understanding that truly helping the poor required more than impulsive generosity, the new approach called for investigating the causes of need, influencing the morals of the poor through personal involvement, and encouraging gainful employment at a time when jobs were readily available. In England, for example, 'friendly visiting' of the poor in their homes by **charity** workers was the core activity, reflecting the belief that the reform of the individual was the key to improvement. By the middle of the 20th century, such charity work had evolved into social work and become more **professionalized** and bureaucratized, and its connection to charitable efforts considerably attenuated. 'Scientific philanthropy', however, still relied heavily upon an individualistic model of social intervention.

Secours Catholique—Caritas de France

Catholic Assistance—Caritas France

Secours Catholique is the French organization of **Caritas International**, a confederation of 154 Catholic relief, development and social service **organizations** operating in 198 countries and territories. Secours Catholique was founded in 1946 and is dedicated to alleviating poverty. Its activities include programmes to promote education, **human rights**, health care and social welfare; financing **grants**, scholarships and fellowships; publishing annual statistical surveys of the extent of poverty in France; and providing aid to developing countries.

Website: www.secours-catholique.asso.fr

Sect

A sect is a subdivision of a larger religious group or religious denomination. For example, Catholicism and Lutheranism can be considered sects of **Christianity**; or Shi'ism and Sunnism as sects of **Islam**. The term sect often bears negative connotations, especially when it refers to extreme or heretical religious groupings. Sect can also mean more generally a smaller group or faction separated from a larger group because of values, beliefs, interests, race, or a specific doctrine. (See **Religion**).

Section 501(c)(3)

Section 501(c)(3) of the US Internal Revenue Code provides **tax exemption** for religious, educational, charitable, scientific and literary **organizations** as well as organizations that test for public safety, foster amateur sports competitions or prevent cruelty to children and animals. Nearly all **public-benefit non-profit organizations** in the USA are covered under this section, numbering at least 730,000 in 1998. Member-benefit as well as other exempt organizations are dealt with in more than 30 other sections of the Code (see **Section 501(c)(4)**). In contrast to most other types of non-profit designation, the principal benefit of a 501(c)(3) label is that '501(c)(3)s', as organizations receiving this designation are often called, not only are exempt from corporate income tax, but also offer **donors** deductibility for their **gifts** (see **charitable contribution deduction**). The 501(c)(3) designation corresponds to income tax exemptions in other countries, but is typically much broader and more flexible in terms of the range of purposes that qualify for exemption and deductibility of donations.

Section 501(c)(4)

Section 501(c)(4) of the US Internal Revenue Code provides for federal **tax exemption** of **civic leagues** and other **organizations** not organized for profit, but operated exclusively for the promotion of social welfare, and of local **associations** of employees, the income of which is devoted exclusively to charitable, educational or recreational purposes. Such organizations cannot primarily benefit a private group of citizens (e.g. a purchasing **co-operative**), but **membership** organizations are not necessarily excluded (e.g. certain homeowners' associations). They may undertake business activities to finance their social welfare programmes, but may not carry on a business with the general public in a manner similar to for-profit organizations. Unlike **Section 501(c)(3)** organizations, 501(c)(4) organizations may engage in germane **lobbying** activities (although other political activities may be limited or taxable) and in substantial non-exempt activities. Moreover, with few exceptions, contributions to 501(c)(4) organizations are not deductible. In 2002, more than 120,000 organizations were tax-exempt under this regulation.

Section 509

Section 509 of the US Internal Revenue Code defines a private foundation and, by doing so, lays out the difference between a private foundation and a public **non-profit organization**, each of which operates under different rules. According to this section, a private foundation is a domestic or foreign **organization** described in **Section 501(c)(3)** other than one of four different types of public organization that enjoy special privileges, e.g. exemption from excise tax on their investment income. These four types of public organization include: (1) Section 509(a)(1) organizations, i.e. those described in Section 170(b)(1)(A) such as churches, schools and health facilities; (2) Section 509(a)(2) organizations, i.e. organizations that normally receive more than one-third of their support from a combination of **gifts**, **grants**, **membership** fees, or related business income or from investment income and unrelated business; (3) Section 509(a)(3) organizations, i.e. **affiliates** or subsidiaries that are organized solely to support or aid one or several other public organizations; and (4) Section 509(a)(4) organizations, which are established to test public safety.

Hanns-Seidel-Stiftung

Hanns Seidel Foundation

Founded in 1967, the Hanns-Seidel-Stiftung is a German **political foundation**, linked by origin and purpose to the Christian Social Union (CSU). The Stiftung, named after one of the CSU's co-founders, engages in activities that promote **democracy**, freedom and development on a Christian basis in Germany, especially Bavaria, and abroad. Its main programmes include research and conferences examining current policy issues; adult civic education to increase citizens' interest in the political decision-making process on the local, federal and European levels; and international development projects throughout the world.

Website: www.hss.de

Self-Dealing

Self-dealing refers to an act in which a person is on both sides of a financial transaction. In a **non-profit organization**, this may occur when the organization does business with a board member. Although such activities may be perceived as a **conflict of interest**, self-dealing is not illegal for all non-profits. However, in the USA, Internal Revenue Code Section 4941 strictly forbids private foundations (as well as charitable lead trusts, charitable remainder trusts and pooled income funds) to engage in financial transactions with **disqualified persons**, i.e. substantial contributors, foundation managers, certain public officials, family members of disqualified persons, and corporations and partnerships in which disqualified persons hold significant interests. The few exceptions to the rule include paying reasonable compensation to a disqualified person for services that are necessary to fulfilling the foundation's charitable purposes. Violations will result in an initial penalty tax equal to 5% of the amount involved, payable by the self-dealer.

Self-Governance

Self-governance is one of the characteristics of **non-profit organizations** according to the **structural–operational definition**. It distinguishes autonomous non-profit organizations from those that are private and non-governmental, but are nevertheless so tightly controlled by either governmental agencies or private businesses that they essentially function as parts of these other institutions even though they are structurally separate. Self-governance requires that an organization be in a position to control its own activities to a significant extent, implying that it must have its own internal **governance** procedures. Under this definitional criterion, the presence of government or corporate representatives on the **board of directors** does not disqualify the organization from being non-profit. The question is the degree of authority they wield and the degree of autonomy the organization retains.

Self-Help Groups

Self-help groups (also referred to as support or mutual aid groups) provide a forum for enabling people who suffer from a similar predicament or experience or a common problem to help themselves while helping others. The groups build on the notion of healing through personal experience. This method of help challenges the professional model whereby people in distress receive guidance by a trained professional. Generally run by the members, these groups offer a sense of ownership and create a feeling of belonging. In cases where professionals are involved, they typically provide limited support roles.

An individual may choose a support group to address a wide range of issues, including addictions, bereavement, physical illness, mental health, abuse, disabilities, parenting, care-giver concerns and other life situations. The group setting offers a vehicle for individual **empowerment**, enabling people to address their issues in a supportive atmosphere. Support from the group and other group members offers an opportunity to share the isolation and individual suffering that can accompany such disorders. An effective group can assist participants in the course of addressing their shared issues, as well as provide relevant updated information to dispel myths and misconceptions.

Self-help groups are generally **voluntary non-profit organizations**. They are often found at the local or grassroots level and work independently within a given community. There are many successful groups that become national or international, with local chapters throughout the world. In the case of sexual and physical violence, for example, there may be local or national institutions that offer forums for survivors to share their experiences and work through the difficult issues related to abuse. In other cases, groups may be established to address health-related issues, including very specific physical and mental ailments (e.g. HIV, cancer or depression). One well-established example is groups that are based on the 12-step programme, which provide guiding principles for personal recovery and are tailored for specific ailments (e.g. Alcoholics Anonymous). Another model is Co-Counselling or Re-evaluation Counselling, which offers a process whereby people of all ages and of all backgrounds can learn how to exchange effective help with each other in order to free themselves from the effects of past, distressing, experiences.

Service Clubs

'Service club' is a generic term used to refer to **membership** organizations that are organized as federations of local chapters for individuals who seek to combine sociability and **public benefit**. Regular membership meetings, dinners and other social functions are combined with **fundraising** events and charitable work. Mostly American in origin, and in the past, local in orientation and membership, many service clubs have spread to other countries, and some are active internationally as well. Examples are **Kiwanis, Rotary International,** Lions or Zonta International.

Service Provider Organizations

Non-profit organizations that primarily provide professionalized services to client groups are usually referred to as service providers. Whether in health, education, social service, the arts or development, service providers tend to dominate the economic size and scope of the **non-profit sector** in most parts of the world. Although the delineation is not always clear-cut, the focus on professional services differentiates these organizations from expressive and **advocacy** groups, **grassroots associations** and **self-help groups**.

Simon, John G.

John G. Simon, presently Augustus E. Lines Professor Emeritus of Law and Professorial Lecturer in Law at Yale Law School, is regarded as one of the principal founders of the scholarly study of non-profit law, and mentor to many leading scholars in the field. Simon has held positions as Deputy Dean of the Yale School and trustee of the **Open Society Institute,** and served as the founding director of the Yale Program on Non-Profit Organizations, which became the world-wide intellectual centre of non-profit scholarship under his direction in the 1980s. His many publications include *The Ethical Investor* and an influential treatise on non-profit law.

Sliding-Scale Fees

Sliding-scale fees, or 'interpersonal price discrimination' in economic parlance, are used by **non-profit organizations** in determining their pricing policy. Sliding-scale fees charge consumers different fees based on characteristics such as age, income, ethnicity, or disability. Examples are day-care centre fees or tuition and school fees set according to parent income; dues levels for **professional associations** established according to seniority; and rent in social housing. Up to the marginal cost level, non-profit organizations and for-profit organizations may act similarly in establishing sliding-scale fees. However, non-profit firms are more likely to price-discriminate at prices just below marginal cost, and thereby offer some services for free, while businesses are more likely to price-discriminate at or above marginal cost and are unlikely to offer services free of charge.

Sloan, Alfred P., Jr (1875–1966)

Alfred P. Sloan, Jr, an American business leader and philanthropist, worked his way up through companies that were acquired ultimately by General Motors, for which he served as president (1923–37), chief executive officer (1923–46) and chairman of the board (1937–56). Sloan's philanthropic activities had a significant impact in a number of fields. An alumnus of the Massachusetts Institute of Technology (MIT), Sloan sponsored the creation in 1931 of the world's first university-based executive education programme, the MIT Sloan Fellows. In 1945, Sloan partnered with industrialist Charles Kettering to establish the Sloan-Kettering Institute for cancer research. The Alfred P. Sloan Foundation, which he created in 1934, continues to support science and technology, as well as economic development.

Smiles, Samuel (1812–1904)

Samuel Smiles was a Scottish author and social reformer actively involved in workmen's benefit societies and campaigns to extend the franchise. He spent over two decades involved with railway enterprises and simultaneously advocated self improvement for the working classes through hard work and education in a treatise entitled *Self-Help, with Illustrations of Conduct and Perseverance* (1859). *Self-Help* was one of the great success stories of Victorian publishing and had an immense influence in shaping the aspirations and careers of young working men. Smiles followed *Self-Help* with other titles, such as *Character* (1871), *Thrift* (1875) and *Duty* (1880), though none of these enjoyed the same success.

Social Audits

The term 'social audit' refers to both developing social accounts and having them verified. In the process of a social audit, an **organization** uses qualitative data and descriptive statistics to assess how it is meeting its **stakeholders**' expectations in executing its **mission** and to measure its positive and negative **externalities**. Social audits, which are most often coupled with environmental audits, are now being conducted by socially oriented businesses, **social enterprises**, **credit unions** and **non-profit organizations**, as well as by the International Finance Corporation in relation to projects or enterprises in which it invests. The set of six principles underpinning the concept and practice call for social audits to be multiperspective, comprehensive, regular, comparative, verified and disclosed.

Social Capital

Economic growth and democratic government depend critically on the presence of social capital, i.e. bonds of trust and norms of **reciprocity** that can facilitate social interaction. Without such norms, contracts cannot be enforced or compromises sustained. Hence markets and democratic institutions cannot easily develop or flourish.

Research has examined social capital as a resource from two perspectives: as an individual resource with aggregate effects at the group or community level, and as an emerging structural phenomenon. The individual perspective on social capital suggests that ties of trust and social cohesion are beneficial to members and groups alike. The argument made by Coleman is that 'connectivity and trust' among members of a given group or society more generally increases aspects associated with cohesive groups: lower delinquency, more collective action, and better enforcement of norms and values. Putnam applied this kind of thinking to economic development and social inclusion and linked it to the realm of **civil society**. This is related to what is called the neo-**Tocquevillian** perspective in which norms of reciprocity, **citizenship** and trust are embodied in networks of civic associations.

By contrast, others have argued that the absence rather than the presence of ties among individuals accounts for the true value of social capital at the individual level. The value of social capital is therefore in its unequal distribution, such that some people in a society have more than others. The uneven distribution of social capital, measured as the number and reach of social ties, creates gaps in social ties, which allow a third party to identify the 'structural hole' and to make the connection among otherwise disconnected individual actors. This 'gap-filling' social capital becomes the bridging material of modern society, and a key objective for **social entrepreneurs** and **voluntary associations** as they try to bridge different groups of society.

In this kind of structural analysis, social capital is a scarce and valued resource, and basically a **private good**, not the quasi-**public good** with many positive externalities as in Coleman's and Putnam's thinking. In a complementary alternative, Bourdieu links the unequal dispersion of social capital to other forms of inequalities in modern society. In other words, the distribution of social capital does not exist in isolation of the larger society: the network configurations that create structural holes and opportunities for social entrepreneurs endowed with scarce social capital exist in a broader economic and cultural context.

Indeed, Bourdieu operates with a much broader concept of capital. It is broader than the monetary notion of capital in economics, and also broader than the concept of social capital in Coleman's sense. In Bourdieu's thinking, capital becomes a generalized 'resource' that can assume monetary and non-monetary as well as tangible and intangible forms. He distinguishes between three major types of capital: economic, cultural and social, which differ in liquidity, convertibility and loss potential. These differences all entail different scenarios for actors in social fields. High volumes of economic capital, yet lower volumes of cultural and social capital, characterize some positions. *Nouveaux riches*, for example, are typically well-endowed with economic capital relative to a paucity of cultural capital. Others will rank high in terms of cultural capital, yet somewhat lower in other forms. International business consultants rely on high degrees of social capital, relative to cultural and economic capital, and intellectuals typically accumulate higher amounts of cultural and social capital than economic **assets**. A preliminary insight to be gained from looking at different perspectives on social capital suggests that Coleman/Putnam approaches see social capital closely related to a sense of community, whereas Bourdieu and others would argue that social capital is part of a wider system of social inequality and linked to stratification and status competition.

Putnam established a useful distinction between two types of social capital that differ in their structural implication for society. Bonding capital, also called exclusive social capital, is the sociological 'super-glue' for in-group cohesion and **solidarity**. Bridging capital or inclusive social capital refers to outward-looking networks across different groups, class and political cleavages.

Creating social capital seems more demanding today than in the past, and new institutions might be needed to integrate both the more marginal groups, that are suffering erosion in social capital, and the better-off segments of society that are replacing traditional forms of social capital with professional ways of organizing. This will certainly challenge the long-standing function of voluntary associations of providing cohesion for members with similar interests and serving as a mechanism of inclusion among different segments and groups of the community.

Social Economy

The concept of social economy (*économie sociale*) first emerged in France at the end of the 19th century, under the influence of the economist Charles Gide and the sociologist **Émile Durkheim**. It was disseminated one century later during the 1970s and the 1980s throughout France, Belgium, Spain, Portugal and Italy. Jacques Delors, in his capacity as first President of the European Commission, attempted to apply it to the whole European Union.

Organizations that might be considered part of the social economy include **co-operatives**, mutual organizations (see **mutual societies**), **associations** and **foundations**. As part of the social economy, these organizations share the following common principles and characteristics:

- Voluntary **membership** (the principle of the 'open door,' which means free entry and free exit)
- **Solidarity** among members, an historical principle rooted in the 19th century workers' movement. Solidarity is also invoked by many **NGOs** working in the Third World.
- Democratic **governance**, coveyed by the principle 'one person, one vote' in contrast to the rule 'one share, one vote,' which is symbolic of corporate governance.
- Board members are volunteers, as opposed to the practice of corporations.
- Independence from public authorities: central and local government representatives do not control the organization even if public funding is its major or only source of income.
- The profit, if any, can be shared among owners, members or managers, but profit-sharing has to be limited and not be the principal aim of the organization. Rather, the aim of the organization is the personal development and **empowerment** of members. The fact that profit-sharing is authorized is the main difference between the **non-profit sector** and the social economy. Associations, foundations and some mutuals are non-profit (i.e. not profit-sharing), while co-operatives and most mutuals are allowed to share profit within limits.
- However, the organization's registered capital and reserve funds cannot be shared among members and owners if the organization dissolves. In this case, the property of the organization has to be transferred to another social economy organization.

Of course, this set of principles is challenged by the dominant capitalist economy, and social economy organizations show a tendency to **isomorphism**. Despite the wish of Jacques Delors, the concept of social economy has had limited acceptance even in Europe, in part because it competes with other concepts such as the non-profit sector, **voluntary organizations**, **third sector** or **civil society** in the Anglo-Saxon world. Furthermore, in Germany and Austria, social economy means something quite different: *Marktsozialwirtschaft* refers to the joint management of companies by representatives of employers and employees.

Social Enterprises

Social enterprises are firms that blend social and commercial objectives as well as methods. They are part of a wider **social economy**. The term is used somewhat differently in the USA and in Europe. In the USA, social enterprises are non-profit and for-profit firms where the primary objective is to maintain and improve social conditions in a way that goes beyond the financial benefits created for the **organization**'s funders, managers, employees, or customers. Examples in the USA are such **non-profit organizations** as Habitat for Humanity, Goodwill Industries, and others like them that are different from traditional businesses. In Europe, social enterprises, unlike traditional non-profit organizations, are frequently constituted as **co-operatives** and **mutual societies** with the principal aim of serving the community or a specific group of people. Examples would be savings and loan associations such as Credit Agricole in France or farmers' unions like the Raiffeisen co-operative system in Germany. To some extent, a feature of social enterprises is their desire to promote a sense of **social justice** and **solidarity**.

Social Entrepreneurs

According to economist **Joseph Schumpeter**, entrepreneurs are the innovative force in capitalist economies. They are part of the 'creative destruction' that drives the capitalist system: they innovate by introducing new ways of seeing and doing things, and thereby displace old ones (see **Innovation**). In classical economic terms, the entrepreneur is understood as the one who assumes the risk of organizing and managing a new business venture or enterprise.

Social entrepreneurs are different from business entrepreneurs in that the focus of social entrepreneurs is the creation of social value, rather than the creation of monetary or economic value for the firm, although the latter may also be part of the resulting organizational model. They are innovative change agents, who see problems as opportunities and are skilled at doing more with less and attracting additional resources from others. Whether the entities through which social entrepreneurs work are non-profit or for-profit, the success of their activities is measured first and foremost by their social impact. (See also **Social entrepreneurship**, **Entrepreneurship theories**; **Social enterprise**.)

Social Entrepreneurship

Social entrepreneurship is a relatively young concept that first appeared in the 1980s in both academia and practice. Since the mid-1990s it has been increasingly taken up within the **non-profit sector** and by philanthropists.

Entrepreneurship is an established concept in economics and management studies, and is most strongly associated with **Joseph Schumpeter**, writing in the early 20th century. For Schumpeter, the essence of entrepreneurship is **innovation**, and this acts as a 'gale of creative destruction' driving capitalism and economic progress and resulting in the transformation or establishment of new industries and ways of life. It is often embodied in the motives, actions and force of personality of individual entrepreneurs. Such entrepreneurial individuals found new **organizations** and are rewarded for their efforts and the risks they take with financial profit, status and personal satisfaction.

Two trends have supported the emergence of social entrepreneurship. One is the impact of management gurus such as **Peter Drucker**, who applied **entrepreneurship theories** not only in business, but also within non-economic arenas, including the public, non-profit and community sectors. The other is the influence of neo-liberal political agendas that have sought to encourage individual enterprise and self-reliance throughout society and to develop an entrepreneurial spirit or culture in both business and public welfare.

Three definitions of social entrepreneurship are in common use:

1. the founding of new **non-profit organizations**. This definition is based on economic theory and is found in the academic literature on non-profits. It offers a supply-side account of the formation of **voluntary** organizations, and therefore of the whole sector, in terms of individual behaviours and motivations arising out of heterogeneous and particularistic social needs (see also **Supply-side theory**).
2. innovation and initiation of social change in all areas of need and in all parts of the world. Such entrepreneurial leaders, who are very much in a Schumpeterian mould, often set up new non-profit or community organizations, but can also be found within existing organizations and in the public and private sectors. They can operate at the local community level, across a country, or internationally.
3. income generation and commercial activities alongside social goals, especially within voluntary **organizations**, and most commonly referred to as **social enterprise**.

The contemporary relevance of social entrepreneurship is attributed to the acute need for social innovation and financially sustainable social services, given the decline of the **welfare state** and the failure of government and market to address a range of social problems. It is commonly linked with the emergence of interest in **social capital**, the **social economy**, **venture philanthropy**, **corporate social responsibility** and ethical business.

Social Investment

Social investment has been defined in a number of ways. In its most narrow sense, adopted by the Charity Commission for England and Wales, social investment is the equivalent of **programme-related investment**, i.e. providing financing through loans, loan guarantees and similar mechanisms in order to pursue a **donor** organization's **mission**. A somewhat broader concept among **grant-making foundations** describes social investment as the practice of aligning investment policies with the **organization**'s mission. This concept includes both making **programme-related investments** and refraining from investing in corporations with products or policies inconsistent with the foundation's values.

The most encompassing definition equates social investment with 'socially responsible investment,' which refers to the financial practices of individuals as well as a broader set of institutions, including universities, religious organizations, investment pools and pension plans, in addition to foundations. These practices attempt to integrate social responsibility and environmental **sustainability** with investment. They entail all the basic financial decision-making processes that are part of a prudent investment management approach, but also investment selection and management approaches that take into account issues of sustainability or social responsibility. Strategies include careful screening to determine the company's policies, direct investment in communities, generally through community loan funds or community-oriented enterprises, and shareholder **advocacy** to influence corporations on particular issues or actions.

Social Justice

Social justice refers to the concept of a fair and just society where all members are equally valued. Proponents of social justice argue that all members of society should (but generally do not) have equal access to opportunity so that they may enjoy later benefits. Social justice advocates also call for a more equal distribution of resources across the population. Social justice is a moral argument that is often invoked as the opposite of what activists identify as systematic or structural marginalization of people or groups, which can take place in the labour market, in educational opportunities or as a result of social stigma. Groups that are identified as suffering from this type of inequality are often those based upon race, class, **religion**, income, gender, age, sexual orientation or disability. On an international level, social justice takes on a broader meaning, focusing on reducing disparities among populations globally, particularly between countries in the North and the South.

Social Movements

Social movements can be defined as collectivities acting outside institutionalized channels to promote or resist change in an institution, society, or the world order. A social movement consists of a number of people organized and co-ordinated to achieve some task or a collection of goals; often the participants are interested in bringing about social change. Compared to other forms of collective behaviour, movements have a high degree of organization and are of longer duration.

Three main models have emerged to explain the genesis of social movements. First, the classical model of social movements argues that social change is the result of a systematic 'strain' on the social infrastructure of the political system. Hence, the commotion associated with the 'strain' is transformed into feelings of anxiety, frustration and hostility that lead to the emergence of a social movement. The second model, the resource mobilization model, argues that social movements are the result of the quantity of 'social resources' that are accessible to unorganized but aggrieved groups, thus making it possible to launch an organized demand for change. The third is the political process model, which defines social movements as a continuous phenomenon that thrives on the ability of the progressive community to capitalize on political opportunities and translate such opportunities into social change.

In the USA, social movements date back at least to the American Revolution when Philadelphia women proposed the creation of a national women's organizational movement to raise money for the troops and renounce the use of British tea and fabric. This became the Daughters of Liberty, a **non-profit organization** that still exists today. In addition, the settlement house movement of the late 19th century and early 20th century represented an aspect of a larger anti-poverty movement. The federal government has adopted some portions of the settlement house movement's agenda as public works, while many of the poverty-related issues that **Jane Addams** and her peers addressed still exist and are now battled by today's non-profit agencies. Prominent movements include the workers' movement in the early 20th century, the civil rights movement of the 1950s and 1960s, the anti-war movement of the 1970s and the women's movement and the environmental movement during the 1980s.

Europe has a long and rich history of social movements, e.g. farmers' movements and uprisings in the 15th and 16th centuries, a pronounced work-ing-class movement in the 19th century, nationalist social movements in the early 20th century, and a burgeoning of new social movements between 1960 and 1990. Specific examples include Sweden's *folkrörelse*, the green movement in Germany that led to the emergence of the Green Party, and the citizen movement in Central and Eastern Europe in the late 1980s that brought down state socialist regimes.

Philanthropy has long played a prominent role in the emergence and growth of social movements. During the 19th century, philanthropy became a factor in the American abolitionist movement and in the struggle for **social justice** in the broadest sense, in particular against the exclusion of women and minorities from effective political voice. Philanthropic acts of financial giving, **voluntary** action and association among individuals have been the basis for social movements throughout history.

Contemporary social movements differ from traditional movements in that they have ideological contexts that make them different, i.e. they are framed by concerns about individual/cultural rights rather than economic justice/human-political rights and are shaped by values about self-actualization, community and personal satisfaction. The more contemporary social movements favour small-scale and decentralized **organizations**, are anti-hierarchical, and advocate direct **democracy**. They are associated with the rise of a new middle class of educated professionals, especially those whose expertise is social/cultural rather than technocratic and who have achieved higher levels of education and a first-hand view of the cracks in contemporary society.

Many observers see a close link between social movements and non-profit organizations. Social movements create social movement organizations to become more effective and efficient in pressing their agenda. Over time, these organizations tend to become more formal and incorporate as non-profit organizations, which then lobby government, serve as watchdogs, or otherwise put forth and guard the interests of the movement and its constituency.

Social Origins Theory

This comparative–historical theory was developed by Salamon and Anheier (1998) in response to limitations of economic approaches on the one hand, and conventional **welfare state** literature on the other. The aim of the theory is to explain variations in the size and composition of the **non-profit sector** cross-nationally. To do so, the theory identifies those social factors that will lead to the development of a sizeable, economically important non-profit sector as opposed to a smaller, less important sector. Based largely on the notion of path-dependent development, Salamon and Anheier suggest that the non-profit sector across countries has different historical moorings and reveals different social and economic shapes.

Based on modifications of Esping-Andersen's analysis of the welfare state to incorporate the non-profit sector, Salamon and Anheier identify four more or less distinct models of non-profit development, four types of 'non-profit regimes'. Each of these types is characterized not only by a particular state role, but also by a particular position for the **third sector**; and, most importantly, each reflecting a particular constellation of social forces. They suggest that non-profit regime types as well as the policies and the policy-making style associated with them help account for cross-national differences in the non-profit sector scale and structure.

Thus, for example, where landed elites remain strong and forge working relationships with the dominant religious order, the most likely outcome is either a corporatist non-profit regime or a statist model—the former (e.g. Germany) characterized by sizeable state-sponsored social welfare protections delivered extensively through **non-profit organizations** and the latter (e.g. Japan) by limited state-sponsored social welfare protections and little non-profit growth. Which of these outcomes emerges depends on the strength of lower class (urban or rural) protest during the critical transition to modernity. By contrast, where the power of landed elements is broken by middle-class commercial and professional elements, liberal or social-democratic outcomes are more likely, depending again on the strength of lower-class protest. Where this protest is organized and robust, a social-democratic model (e.g. Sweden) is the likely outcome, in which state-sponsored and state-delivered social welfare protections are extensive and the room left for **service-providing** non-profit **organizations** quite constrained. Where it is more muted, commercial middle classes can produce a liberal pattern (e.g. USA, United Kingdom) characterized by very limited state social welfare protections and a more independent, relatively large non-profit sector.

Because of the complexity of the factors it identifies as important, the social origins theory is difficult to test empirically and lacks the parsimony of economic theories. However, it does bring into focus the limitations of those economic theories. Finally, the four patterns identified by this theory are ideal types, and many of the actual cases may be hybrids that encompass features from more than one pattern.

Social Return on Investment

Social return on investment (SROI) describes the social impact of an entity's operations in monetary terms relative to the investment required to make that impact and exclusive of its financial return to investors. Developed originally by the Roberts Enterprise Development Fund, the SROI tool is an extension of traditional **cost–benefit analysis** as a way of translating social objectives into financial measures. It is used by **donors**, **social enterprise** investors and **non-profit organizations** themselves for investment decision-making and performance measurement. SROI analysis differs from a **social audit**. Although both tend to quantify measures of social and other impacts, the former tends to be an investment tool, while the latter is more a tool for organizational development and **accountability** with a focus on the organization's **stakeholders**.

Social Trust

Social trust is a concept in sociology that emphasizes the ability to take for granted the relevant motivations and behaviours of others. It is a pre-rational, pre-existing trust that **Émile Durkheim** observed underlying all contracts: behind every contract is a host of 'tacit' agreements, and while they are not formally specified, they are nevertheless assumed to hold in contractual arrangements. The notion of social trust as presumed reliability is very different from the rationalistic conceptions of trust in rational choice approaches.

The sociological notion of trust has important implications for the relationship between trust and **non-profit organizations**. Trust is seen not as a matter of legally framed transactions between contracting parties, but as being generated by social structures not reducible to instrumental individual actions, and supported by a normative infrastructure. The notion of social trust as an assumption of reliability takes on an ethnomethodological perspective. Some types of **voluntary associations**, in particular religious ones, are particularly well positioned to draw upon pre-existing trust that is unlikely to be questioned in the course of transactions. In seeing members through extended periods of taste formation and socialization, non-profit organizations shape, develop and reinforce deep-seated convictions, values and beliefs. Thus, as socialization agents, they implicitly provide guidelines on whom to trust, whom not to trust, and in what circumstances. The relationship between trust and **associations** is a key part of the current **social capital** debates.

Social Welfare Organizations

In the USA, a social welfare organization is understood to be a type of tax-exempt **organization** under **Section 501(c)(4)** of the US Internal Revenue Code. Since the term 'social welfare' defies concrete definition, it and the corresponding section of the tax code tend to be a catch-all for organizations that are presumed to be beneficial but are not easily classified under one of the other sections. Such an organization must operate to further in some way the common good and general welfare of the people of the community, not a particular group of people. Examples range from volunteer fire departments and local airport operators to community associations that work to improve public spaces or preserve the community's traditions. The term 'social welfare organization', as used in the US context, has a different meaning in Europe where it is used in reference to social service and health-care providers.

Socialism

Socialism refers to a diverse set of political ideologies that developed out of Marxist schools of thought in the late 19th and early 20th centuries (see **Karl Marx**). What the various strands of socialism have in common is a belief that the collective—usually state—ownership or control of the means of production, distribution and exchange should replace the capitalist system to bring about a more equitable, egalitarian and just society. Socialism puts emphasis on **solidarity**, mutual interdependence and the possibility of achieving greater harmony in society to replace the conflicts and stability caused by capitalism.

In the 19th century, the socialist movement was organized in many working men's associations, leading to the development of an associational network that took on an international character and the emergence of socialist parties in many countries around the workplace.

After the Second World War, the socialist movement was split—and remained deeply divided until the end of the Cold War—between the social-democratic parties in pluralist democracies of the West and the Marxist socialist party in Eastern Europe and the Soviet sphere of influence. The latter suppressed **civil society** and its organizational forms, whereas the former increasingly embraced **non-profit organizations**, **social movements** and other civil society institutions, while remaining somewhat suspicious of independent, endowed **foundations**. The strong influence of Keynes on social-democratic parties meant that the emphasis on collective control of the means of production gave way to the notion of effective economic management of the economy for the greater public good, combined with a redistributive **welfare state**.

In addition to social democracy, other variants of socialism are guild socialism, which emerged in the early part of the 20th century and favoured a decentralized form of economic ownership and management by modernized versions of **guilds** and craft unions, in addition to workers' **co-operatives** and councils. Christian socialism, by contrast, seeks to relate the teachings of Christ, in particular the Sermon on the Mount, to socialism and calls for industrial reconciliation between workers and capitalists through joined councils and the development of co-operatives and public education systems, and stresses the moral obligation of the better-off by demanding a more egalitarian society through redistribution.

Solidarity

The concept of solidarity arose at the end of 19th century under the inspiration of the French sociologist **Durkheim** and philosopher Bourgeois. Solidarism is seen as a **third way** between capitalism and collectivism. According to this philosophy, everyone, including the newborn child, is indebted to society, which gives language, knowledge and know-how; rights counterbalance duties in a quasi-contract. The principle of solidarity among the members of a nation is the rationale of income redistribution, especially through progressive income tax; among the members of a professional group, it is the justification for mutual benefit societies and later for social security schemes. Durkheim brought renewed attention to intermediate bodies, especially professional **organizations** that could put the solidarity principle into effect to resolve minor issues better than the state could.

Secular solidarity is often contrasted with the Christian concept of **charity** in continental and southern Europe: solidarity is seen as a more egalitarian relation than charity, which is seen more as an act of condescension in those countries. Solidarity among members is still a basic principle of **social economy**, meaning interdependence, redistribution and joint responsibility. A recent revival of solidarism is the so-called 'solidarity economy,' a set of grassroots **non-profit organizations** involved in proximity services, in barter exchange, and more generally in the alleviation of economic and social vulnerability at a local level.

Solidarność

Solidarity

The independent and self-governing trade **union** Solidarność (Solidarity) was born out of the strikes in Poland in 1980. Originally established as a trade union, Solidarność became a huge **social** and political **movement** representing the Polish nation's aspirations for freedom and **democracy**. Its organizational structure adapted to the new, clandestine conditions after imposition of martial law in December 1981. Based on these clandestine structures and given unprecedented civil support, Solidarność was able to conduct protest actions on a wide scale. Its activity had far-reaching influence in Eastern and Central Europe, and thus contributed to the downfall of the state-socialist system.

Website: www.solidarnosc.org.pl

Soros, George (1930–)

Hungarian-born philanthropist, president and chairman of Soros Fund Management LLC, a successful private investment firm, George Soros is the chairman of the **Open Society Institute** and the founder of a network of philanthropic **organizations** that are active in more than 50 countries. Based primarily in Central and Eastern Europe and the former Soviet Union, these foundations are dedicated to building and maintaining the infrastructure and institutions of an open society. Soros is the author of several books, including *Underwriting Democracy, The Crisis of Global Capitalism: Open Society Endangered* and *Open Society: Reforming Global Capitalism.*

Southern African Grantmakers Association

Established in 1995, the Southern African Grantmakers Association (SAGA) is a Johannesburg-based service **organization** dedicated to support Southern African grant-makers. Its members include corporations with social responsibility programmes, international **donor** organizations, local private foundations, grant-making **NGOs**, **community foundations** and government funding agencies. Support for its members comes in the form of policy and strategy formulation, research and information, networking opportunities and customized professional development programmes.

Website: www.donors.org.za

Spanish Association of Foundations – *see* Asociación Española de Fundaciones

Sponsorship, Corporate

The understanding of corporate sponsorship varies from country to country and from business to business. It is, however, characterized as a concept between corporate **philanthropy** and advertising and refers to corporate support for other **organizations'** activities, including arts and sports events. According to US tax regulations, pure **corporate giving** to a **Section 501(c)(3) non-profit organization** is tax-deductible, and the recipient organization may exclude the donation from **unrelated business income** tax (UBIT). On the other hand, pure advertising is a cost of business, and the recipient non-profit organization must therefore pay UBIT. Sponsor logos and slogans that do not contain qualitative or comparative elements about the sponsor's product, services, or facilities are recognized not as advertisement, but as acknowledgment of the sponsorship. Because the **donor** enjoys only 'incidental' benefit, such acknowledgement is considered 'related income', which is not subject to UBIT. The French term *mécénat* is frequently translated into 'sponsorship', but this usage usually implies the exclusion of 'advertisement'.

Stakeholder Theories

The stakeholder theory, associated primarily with the work of Avner Ben-Ner, builds on **Hansmann**'s trust argument (see **trust-related theories**), in which a variety of problems might make it difficult for the consumers of a particular commodity to police the conduct of producers by normal contractual or market mechanisms, thus resulting in **contract** or **market failure**. According to this reasoning, **non-profit organizations** exist because some demand for trust goods in market situations are not met by private firms.

The theory also acknowledges the supply side and recognizes that non-profits are created by **social entrepreneurs**, religious leaders, and other actors who are not motivated by profit primarily. These and all other interested parties on both the demand side and the supply side are referred to as **stakeholders**. The stakeholder theory is built upon the interests and behaviours of stakeholders in the provision of trust-related goods.

The stakeholder theory begins with the assertion that the trade of trust-related goods typically entails a conflict of interest between seller and buyer. The buyer wants the lowest possible price at the best quality, while the seller wants the highest possible price at the lowest quality in order to maximize profits. In a perfect market with perfect information flows, the buyer knows how much it costs to produce the product and other relevant information, and firms know consumer preferences; therefore both parties maximize their utility and transactions occur at the most efficient price. Under conditions of **information asymmetry**, consumers are at a disadvantage and subject to profiteering by profit-seeking firms. Because of the **non-distribution constraint**, non-profit organizations can resolve this conflict because they are not motivated by profit and therefore are less likely to degrade their products to maximize profits.

The stakeholder theory argues that non-profits are created by consumers and other demand-side stakeholders in order to maximize control over output in the face of informational asymmetries. The key demand-side stakeholders are those who feel so strongly about the quality of the service provided and protection from moral hazard that they decide to exercise control over the delivery of service themselves. They thus become demand- and supply-side stakeholders at the same time. For example, parents may decide to start a day-care centre for their children to achieve greater control over day-care services.

The situation for stakeholder control applies primarily to non-rival goods, since providers cannot selectively downgrade the services provided. Ben-Ner suggests that the combination of information asymmetry, non-rivalry and stakeholder control sends much stronger signals of trustworthiness than the 'milder' formulation by Hansmann. In this sense, Ben-Ner's argument is a stricter theory than the trust-related theory and describes a narrower range of demand- and supply-side conditions under which non-profits emerge.

Stakeholders

Stakeholders are people or **organizations** that have a real, assumed or imagined stake in the organization, its performance and **sustainability** and can affect or are affected by the organization. Depending on the organization, stakeholders include members, trustees, employees, volunteers, clients or users, customers, funders, contractors, government oversight agencies, community groups and watchdog organizations. The existence of multiple constituencies lies at the core of **governance** and management dilemmas in **non-profit organizations**.

State–Society Relations

Beginning in the 15th and 16th centuries, a new sort of public power emerged. The state with large standing armies, huge bureaucracies and a codified law succeeded older forms of rule. By the mid-20th century, this European idea of a state was practically universal. Now, a few decades later, the very idea of the state has again become contentious. On the one hand, processes of economic globalization threaten state power through the empowering of private global actors. On the other hand, civil wars, international terrorism and the failure of developmental politics have made apparent the danger of too-strong societal actors and so-called 'failed states' that cannot develop effective means of social control.

The state can be defined as a set of **organizations** and institutions with the authority to make binding decisions upon those located in a specific territory and to implement these decisions, if necessary, by force (Rueschemeyer and Evans). State strength depends on the combination of state autonomy and state capacity. From the outside, states are confronted mainly by other states; from the inside, by a variety of collective actors such as classes, tribes, corporations and **social movements**. Following Weber, societies can be seen as networks of **associations** (*Vergesellschaftung*) and communities (*Vergemeinschaftung*).

If one distinguishes between strong and weak states and strong and weak societies, four relations are conceivable, with at least one relation—weak state and weak society—being rather unlikely to endure. At one end of the continuum, strong states, which destroy all local social forces, can be found in the form of a bureaucratic authoritarian or a totalitarian state. At the other end, strong societies prevail, which incorporate states by appropriating their organizations and symbols (Migdal).

Among the various trajectories to modernity, the European path was very specific—rooted in the transformations of the 11th and 12th centuries (Wittrock), namely: the papal revolution which led to a separation of ecclesiastical and worldly power; the feudal revolution with new rights and obligations; the urban revolution favourable for economic activities and municipal self-government; and the intellectual revolution based on self-governed universities.

At the end of the Middle Ages there were no real territorial units and the plurality of autonomous systems of rule prevented the constitution of 'societies'. The military and technological revolutions of the 16th century eventually enabled the process of centralizing power and forming societies (Mann). From the 16th to the late 18th century, the emergence of national, and often absolutist, monarchies served as vehicles for resource mobilization and the moulding of new collective identities. Civil societies, as the mediating arenas between state and society, were not constituted until the middle of the 18th century, and since the 19th century the middle and lower classes have been involved in the process of aligning with the state via tax policies. The consequence is that the state is confronted with collective actors like classes, associations and corporations that it co-produced but that now compete with the state for influence and power.

These processes developed concurrently with other projects such as the formation of liberal markets and the demands for a legally-protected private sphere. In Western Europe, the demands for active political participation were a constant feature of political life from the late 18th to the mid-20th century. The idea of active citizens was closely linked to newly emerging public spaces such as salons, academies and associations that enabled a public non-censored discourse.

The American state-building process shows a remarkable difference because the state is weak due to its earlier organization: suffrage (at least for white men) and participatory politics developed before the state administration could build up stronger capacities.

T. H. Marshall speaks of three levels of achieved **citizenship** in modern societies, i.e. institutionalized relations between citizens and the state: civil rights (created in the 18th century), political rights (19th century) and social rights (20th century). But the 20th century not only saw these liberal develop-ments but also witnessed authoritarian monarchist, fascistic and authoritarian socialistic forms of citizenship.

As to the social rights, many nations developed some kind of a **welfare state** during the 20th century. Esping-Andersen made the distinction between three types of regime: the conservative welfare state (e.g. Germany), the social-democratic (e.g. the Scandinavian countries) and the liberal welfare state (e.g. the USA).

Salomon and Anheier showed that different types of non-profit regimes can also be distinguished. In the liberal model (USA), low government social-welfare spending is associated with a large **non-profit sector**. In addition, they identified a social-democratic model (Sweden: strong welfare state and strong volunteer organizations), a corporatist model (Germany: **partnership** between state and non-profit sector) and a statist model (Japan: low social-welfare spending and small non-profit sector).

Statute of Charitable Uses, 1601

The turbulence of 16th-century England led to the disintegration of traditional social welfare institutions and a subsequent reorganization of the system of public and private responsibilities for the poor. While the Poor Law of 1601 (see **Poor Laws, Charity law**) placed administration of poor relief with local government, the 1601 Statute of Charitable Uses sought to address abuses in charitable **trusts** and to rationalize their operation and supervision. The Statute laid out the purposes for which **charities** could be established as well as the regulatory powers of government. Its preamble lists among charitable purposes: the relief of the aged, impotent and poor people; the maintenance of . . .schools of learning, free schools and scholars in universities; [and] . . . the education and preferment of orphans. Although the preamble does not define 'charitable' *per se*, it forms the basis of charity law in the UK and the Commonwealth.

Statutory Transfers

Statutory transfers are contributions by the government to support **non-profit organizations** in carrying out public programmes and meeting entitlements. Such transfers are mandated by law, although the definition of what constitutes such transfers differs cross-nationally and according to the welfare system in place. In general, statutory transfers are for the general support of organizations.

Stiftelsen Riksbankens Jubileumsfond

Bank of Sweden Tercentenary Foundation

The Stiftelsen Riksbankens Jubileumsfond was established in 1962 with an **endowment** from the Bank of Sweden to mark its 300th anniversary. Subsequently, the Swedish Parliament gave the Riksbankens Jubileumsfond another endowment earmarked to promote research in the humanities. These endowments have allowed the Riksbankens Jubileumsfond to become the largest private financier of research in the social sciences and humanities in Scandinavia as well as Europe.

Website: www.rj.se

Stifterverband für die Deutsche Wissenschaft
Donors' Association for the Promotion of Sciences and Humanities

The Stifterverband für die Deutsche Wissenschaft is an international **association** established in 1949 representing approximately 4,000 companies, associations and individuals to advance and improve scientific and technical research in higher education. The Stifterverband promotes dialogue between the research sector, industry and the general public. Its activities include self-conducted programmes, research, **grants**, fellowships, scholarships, conferences, publications and lectures. In addition, the association administers more than 300 **trusts** and **foundations** and operates a foundation centre. In 1998, in conjunction with the **Bundesverband Deutscher Stiftungen** (Federal Association of German Foundations), the Stifterverband established the *StiftungsAkademie* to provide training for foundation staff and others.

Website: www.stifterverband.de

Stockholm International Peace Research Institute (SIPRI)

Established by act of Parliament in 1966 to commemorate over 150 years of peace in Sweden, the primary task of the Stockholm International Peace Research Institute (SIPRI) is to conduct and disseminate research on questions of conflict and co-operation with the aim of contributing to an understanding of the conditions for peaceful solution of international conflicts and for a stable peace. An independent institute that receives the majority of its funding from the Swedish government, SIPRI has published an annual yearbook since 1969, detailing information on world arms expenditures, nuclear weapons stockpiles, chemical and biological warfare, etc.

Website: www.sipri.se

Strategic Philanthropy

Strategic philanthropy is a multi-faceted concept that refers to both the working philosophy and the programme strategies of foundations and other philanthropic institutions. It is grounded in an entrepreneurial view of **foundation functions**, objectives and activities, and emphasizes the capacity of **philanthropy** to bring about social and policy change. In this sense, strategic philanthropy refers to longer-term, **vision**-driven philanthropy, in contrast with the more conventional approach of short- to medium-term project funding.

The term 'strategic philanthropy' applies to all phases and facets of philanthropic activity, from first ideas to final **evaluations**. Its beginnings are based on some **theory of change**, either explicitly or implicitly, filtered through something like a needs assessment or a feasibility study to determine the real needs of the target group, the possibility of meeting those needs given available resources, and similar issues. The strategic approach to philanthropy also carries over into organizational management and evaluation, seeking ways to enhance philanthropic impact and make it sustainable.

Strategic philanthropy has drawn criticism of being 'top-down', technocratic and managerialist. Submitting philanthropy to strategic management regimes and thinking would take away the spontaneity and creativity that is frequently expressed in and through philanthropy. In response, others have argued that strategic philanthropy is simply the evolution of, and adaptation to, a more managerialist world.

Strategic philanthropy also emerges in the context of debates about corporate **citizenship** and **corporate social responsibility**. The argument is that the best way for corporations to invest in the future of the communities and markets in which they operate can only be found in activities linked to the corporation's key interests and capacities. The term strategic philanthropy is used then to differentiate the more traditional corporate philanthropy that may lack a clear policy objective from the newer, more strategic forms of corporate social responsibility.

Strategic Planning

Strategic planning is a management tool designed to produce fundamental decisions and actions that guide what an **organization** is, what it does, and why it does it. In essence, it provides non-profits with greater clarity of direction and a clearer sense of purpose. Because it is concerned with a longer term **vision** of the entire organization, strategic planning is more appropriate for established, growing organizations than for start-ups, for which a **business plan** with a focus on the immediate future is more suitable. A variety of strategic planning models exist, the most common being goals-based planning, which starts with a focus on the organization's **mission**, goals to work toward the mission, strategies to achieve the goals, and action planning. More important than the strategic plan document is the planning process itself, which helps ensure that key leaders and, in the optimal case, **stakeholders**, are all 'on the same page'.

Structural–Operational Definition

The structural–operational definition of **non-profit organizations** was developed by Salamon, Anheier and associates in the Johns Hopkins Comparative Non-profit Sector Project for the specific purpose of comparative cross-national analysis, and in response to deficiencies in functional, legal and economic definitions of this set of institutions. According to this definition, non-profit organizations are entities that are organized (see **organization**), private (see **private organization**), self-governing (see **self-governance**), **non-profit-distributing** and **voluntary**. The definition was developed against the empirical background of definitions and organizational realities in a broad cross-section of countries.

Subsidiarity Principle

Subsidiarity is a policy principle stipulating that decisions should always be taken at the lowest possible level or closest to where they will have their effect, for example in a local area rather than nationally, and through private rather than public action. In government, subsidiarity has been generally understood as a principle for determining how powers should be divided or shared between different levels of government. In essence, it justifies non-intervention by the state in individual affairs. In social policy, it states that government should only become active if citizens, **private organizations** and local communities are unable to tackle social problems.

The exact history of the subsidiarity principle is still an object of some debate among historians, but its lineage ranges back to Aristotle, Thomas Aquinas and **John Stuart Mill**, to the Catholic social philosophers of the 19th and 20th centuries, and perhaps most importantly, to Pope Pius XI's Encyclical *Quadragesimo Anno* (1931). This Encyclical influenced social policy in a number of countries, most clearly in Germany, where subsidiarity fitted well with a tradition of decentralization and local **self-governance**. More recently, subsidiarity has become an important part of policy-making in the European Union and figures prominently in policy initiatives of the **World Bank** and other international organizations seeking to devolve government to smaller units.

In the German case, the free welfare associations, i.e. large networks of **non-profit organizations** linked to religious or political associations, became the embodiment of the principle of subsidiarity, particularly the Protestant (**Diakonisches Werk**) and Catholic (**Caritas**) associations that form the largest of the six networks. In essence, many public welfare programmes were implemented through the free welfare associations, whose role became deeply imprinted in the relevant social welfare legislation. Until the mid-1990s, this translated into a situation whereby the six welfare associations, and not just any **voluntary** or non-profit organizations in general, found themselves in a relatively privileged position such that government was required to respect the autonomy and presence of the free welfare associations and support them in achieving their objectives.

The principle of subsidiarity provides the political and economic bedrock for the German **non-profit sector**. It spells out a specific form of **partnership** between the state and parts of the non-profit sector, which is, at some level, related to the principle of **third-party government** in the USA. Where this partnership developed, as it did in the field of social services, the non-profit sector grew substantially, and where it did not develop, as in education, the growth of the sector was less pronounced.

Subsidies

Subsidies are forms of direct or indirect financial assistance granted by government or philanthropic foundations to a person or association for the purpose of promoting an enterprise or activity considered to be of **public benefit**. Subsidies may be granted to keep prices low, to maintain incomes or to preserve employment. They are most important as **grants** either to private corporations for performing some public service, such as to shipping companies and airlines for carrying the post and to railways for maintaining passenger service, or to **non-profit organizations** for providing services to users unable to pay the cost of production. For example, social service providers may receive a direct subsidy for operating expenditures or an indirect subsidy (tax reduction or utility rate concessions) for serving the poor.

Sunk Costs

Sunk costs are costs that have been incurred and cannot be recovered. Their occurrence is often used to justify the continuation of a course of action (e.g. purchase decisions, project designs, organizational strategies) even if it has no future economic or programmatic merit, just because of the resources that were already invested. This behaviour results from loss aversion, i.e. the pronounced tendency of individuals and **organizations** to prefer avoiding losses to acquiring gains. Economists argue that rational decision-making should not consider sunk costs since they have no bearing on future merits and possible courses of action. Sunk costs are a problem for **non-profit organizations** facing the discontinuation of projects or funding sources, e.g. the withdrawal of foundation grants that can impact the **sustainability** of the entire organization.

Supply-Side Theory

Supply-side theory is an economic theory, also known as **entrepreneurship theory**, that argues that **non-profit organizations** are a reflection of demand heterogeneity served and created by entrepreneurs seeking to maximize non-monetary returns.

Supporting Organizations

Supporting organizations are a specific type of American charitable **organization** that are regulated under Section 509(a)(3) of the US Internal Revenue Code. Supporting organizations include privately funded organizations that make **grants** to pre-specified **public charities**, which also control the organization. The US tax code introduces the 509(a)(3) option so that single-**donor**-funded organizations can escape the more heavily regulated independent, private foundation tax classification, since control over the organization is effectively yielded to an otherwise publicly-controlled charity. Supporting organizations are frequently used as the **fundraising** arms of other institutions, but also include 'true' single-donor endowed foundations, which lack the characteristic of independence. Many 'Friends of ...' organizations are supporting organizations. When such 'Friends of ...' groups are set up to support non-US institutions, they facilitate the tax-deductibility of donations by US donors.

Surdna Foundation

The Surdna Foundation was established in 1917 by John Emory Andrus, an American businessman and investor who made his fortune through the Arlington Chemical Company, which produced and distributed medicines of the late 1800s, and through savvy purchases of undervalued **assets**, particularly real estate. With family members on its **board of directors** helping apply Mr. Andrus's values, Surdna makes **grants** in the areas of the environment, community revitalization, civic participation, the arts, youth development and **non-profit sector capacity-building**. Headquartered in New York, the foundation focuses its grant-making primarily in the USA, and provided over US $33m. in grant support in 2002.

Website: www.surdna.org

Sustainability

According to the World Commission on Environment and Development, sustainable development means meeting the needs of the present without sacrificing the ability of future generations to meet their own needs. Economics and ecology must be completely integrated in decision-making and law-making processes not just to protect the environment, but also to protect and promote development. In the field of **philanthropy** and the **non-profit sector**, sustainability also refers to the long-term survival, performance and impact of projects initiated and supported by short- to medium-term **grant** programmes. Designing and implementing sustainable projects is seen as a key challenge of grant-making.

SWOT Analysis

SWOT analysis is a planning tool that allows **organizations** to isolate key issues and manage risk. Using the SWOT (strengths, weaknesses, opportunities and threats) framework helps an organization direct its attention and focus its activities into areas with greater opportunities while being aware of its limitations and external threats. Strengths and weaknesses are largely internal factors over which the organization's board and management have some influence, whereas opportunities and threats are external factors over which the organization has less influence, and sometimes none. The process involves a series of direct questions developed in the context of the planning issue or problem at hand. These questions are answered either individually or as part of a group process.

T

Tax Exemption

Tax exemption refers to immunity from the requirement of paying taxes. Depending on the tax system in place, tax exemption may refer to national or local taxes. The taxes may include excise, income, sales, use, personal property and real property taxes. Tax laws provide exemption from taxation for a wide variety of **organizations**—again depending on the jurisdiction—usually non-profit, such as churches, colleges, universities, health-care providers, various charities, **civic leagues**, labour unions, trade associations, social clubs and political organizations. In the USA, tax-exempt status under federal law can mean comparable status under state and local law. In the UK, such policies date back to 1894, and for most common law jurisdictions, the 1601 **Poor Law** and subsequent legislation provide the foundation for tax exemption based on the notion of **charity** (see also **Charity law**). In civil-law countries, the concept of **public benefit** serves a similar purpose, and was introduced in the wake of civil law reforms in the late 19th–early 20th century.

The principal advantage of tax exemption is obviously that the organization is free of certain if not most tax liabilities on **revenue** and **assets** relating to activities in pursuance of its charitable purpose, including related activities. **Unrelated business income**, however, is usually taxed, although wide differences in the treatment of related and unrelated business income exist across jurisdictions. The disadvantages of tax exemption are that tax-exempt organizations may be precluded from engaging in certain income-generating activities. Moreover, **accountability** requirements and annual reporting obligations may be greater than if the entity were taxable.

There are several rationales for the tax exemption for various categories of **non-profit organizations**. First, tax exemption is a way of providing a subsidy to private actors for offering services that the government would be required to provide itself otherwise, such as care for the elderly and educational or health services. Second, non-profit organizations are tax-exempt because they contribute or add to **public sector** programmes, thereby strengthening and enhancing government programmes in synergetic ways. Third, non-profit organizations are tax-exempt because of their indirect contributions to **civil society** and a functioning community. By engaging people in activities that benefit the common good, non-profit organizations contribute to the health of society, an activity legislatures find worthy of support and, hence, tax exemption. Fourth, some non-profit activities are tax-exempt less on grounds of public choice and more for reasons of political expediency and influence, having succeeded in convincing the appropriate authority that tax exemption is necessary if they are to function.

In recent years, and with increased competition between for-profit business and non-profit organizations for contracts and clients in similar fields of activity, the tax-exempt status of non-profit organizations has been challenged by the business community as unfair competition. According to this view, non-profit organizations are granted unfair **subsidies** that distort market relations to the disadvantage of tax-paying businesses.

Theories X, Y and Z

In management literature, three basic approaches or **visions** of **organizations** in relation to the motivations of staff and volunteers and the resulting management style have been proposed. Theory X states that most people dislike work and will try to avoid it; most people need to be coerced, controlled, directed to work toward organizational goals; most people want to be directed, shun responsibility, have little ambition, and seek security above all. Theory Y suggests that people do not inherently dislike work; rewards are more important than punishment; people will exercise self-direction if given the chance and favour self-control over external control; people accept responsibility; people value creativity and seek ways to express it. Theory Z states that people seek long-term employment, consensual decision-making and individual responsibility; a combination of informal control with explicit and formalized **evaluation** criteria; moderately specialized job descriptions that allow for personal advancement; and a holistic concern for the organizational culture, including the well-being of employees and their families. It is assumed that the management style and the motivations of the staff and volunteers of **non-profit organizations** would typically come closer to Theories Y and Z than to Theory X.

Theory of Change

A theory of change articulates the underlying assumptions upon which a programme or strategy is based. It establishes a context for considering the connection between an **organization** or programme's **mission**, strategies and actual outcomes, while creating links between who is being served, the strategies or activities that are being implemented, and the desired outcomes. A theory of change is an essential tool for orienting and motivating staff and volunteers and a critical input to **evaluation** efforts.

Theory of the Commons

The theory of the **commons** seeks to describe non-profit and **voluntary** action in a way that breaks away from the dichotomy of comparing the **non-profit sector** to the public and private sectors and describing what the **third sector** is not, and from the theories that explain the non-profit sector's emergence as the result of government or **market failures**. Instead, the theory of the commons, introduced by Roger Lohmann, attempts to explain the sector in terms of its common values, functions and goals. In the context of this approach, the commons are real, physical places such as land and forest areas, as well as intangible items such as art, language, human capital and **social capital**, all considered '**endowments**'. A basic value of the non-profit sector, then, is that there is no individual ownership of these endowments nor are these endowments used for individual gain. The non-profit sector's overarching goal is to preserve these endowments and pass them on to future generations. While called a theory, the theory of the commons is not a theory in the conventional sense, rather it is more like a functional approach around a rich conceptual image.

Think Tanks

Think tanks are private, non-profit institutions engaged primarily in research, policy analysis, convening, and the production of reports that address particular issues (e.g. national security, welfare, tax reform, etc.) and often directly influence public policy. Think tanks influence public policy in many ways, including writing articles for 'op-ed' pages, providing sound bites for politicians, supplying expert commentators for television and radio programmes, and testifying before the legislature, although they do not typically undertake direct **lobbying**. Critics of think tanks argue that, since the **organizations** or research programmes are primarily privately funded and their results are not necessarily submitted to peer review, research reports are often biased in favour of whatever group established them.

Third Sector

The term 'third sector' was initially suggested by **Amitai Etzioni** but came to prominence when the **Filer Commission** picked it up in the 1970s. At the time, the term was used as a convenient shorthand and pragmatic convention to draw public and scholarly interest to **organizations** located between the market (the first sector) and the state (the second sector). The term initially gained currency in Europe, where it has been applied to all organizations that for one reason or another do not fit into the dichotomy of for-profit versus **public sector**, but is now being replaced by the term **third system**. It also appears in Latin America more frequently than other terms such as '**non-profit sector**'. The **International Society for Third-Sector Research (ISTR)** selected the term as a unifying label.

Third System

The Third System refers to a diverse array of **organizations** that are neither governmental agencies nor for-profit firms, and includes **co-operatives, mutual societies, associations, self-help groups, foundations** and charities as well as **voluntary** and **non-profit organizations**. It differs from the term '**non-profit sector**' in that it includes co-operatives and mutuals, and from the term '**third sector**' in that it includes parts of the informal economy. It is broader than the term '**social economy**' as it also emphasizes informal networks and communities. It is an imprecise term, used primarily in the context of the European Union for labour market purposes.

Third Way

The Third Way is a broad policy framework that, in contrast to both neo-liberal policy approaches and traditional socialdemocratic policies, pays systematic attention to the **voluntary** or **third sector**. The Third Way rose to prominence in the mid- to late 1990s, with a succession of influential speeches, pamphlets and books by Tony Blair, Bill Clinton and Gerhard Schroeder, and supported by political successes in the USA, the United Kingdom, Germany, France, Italy and the Netherlands. While some of these successes were cut short when conservative politicians later came to power (USA, France, Italy, the Netherlands), the influence of the Third Way continues, despite much criticism, in large measure because it is the only major ideological challenger of neo-liberal policies.

At the same time, it is difficult to identify what the Third Way is, in particular its ideological core. In many ways, it is still an emerging political **vision** to modernize 'old style social democracy' that rested on **solidarity** and state-led welfare, and seeks to develop a comprehensive framework for a renewal of both state and society to counteract neo-liberal policies that are regarded as socially blind, simplistic and unsustainable. The Third Way calls for decentralized forms of government based on **transparency**, efficient administration, more opportunities for direct **democracy**, and an environmentally-friendly economy. The role of the state changes from welfare provider to risk manager and enabler—a fundamental redefinition from the social democratic **welfare state**, and one that is complemented by a change in the notion of **citizenship** that stresses individual rights and responsibilities alike.

The Third Way foresees a reorganization of the state that requires a renewal and activation of **civil society**, social participation, the encouragement of **social entrepreneurship**, and new approaches to public–private partnerships in the provision of **public goods** and services. Specifically, the framework involves a renewal of political institutions to encourage greater citizen participation; a new relationship between government and civil society that involves an engaged government as well as a vibrant set of **voluntary associations** of many kinds; a wider role for business as socially and environmentally responsible institutions; and a structural reform of the welfare state away from 'entitlement' towards risk management.

More generally, Third Way principles state that a good society is founded on a balance between the interests of business, government and the **voluntary sector**; institutions of the third sector are insulated from the immediate pressures of the market and electoral democracy and are, therefore, not only able to identify and anticipate needs, but also to act as guardians of much longer-term value; and institutions of the third sector can play a crucial role in fostering habits of responsibility and cultures of co-operation, self-control and self-expression.

Third-Party Government

The theory that **non-profit organizations** are complements to government was proposed by Salamon, and finds its expression in the third-party government thesis, the notion that governments implement programmes through third parties such as non-profit organizations. Non-profits are typically the first line of defence in addressing emerging social problems of many kinds, but face resource insufficiencies over time that, in turn, can be compensated for by government funding (see **voluntary failure**). The theory implies that (i) non-profit weaknesses correspond to government strengths, i.e. **public sector** revenue to guarantee non-profit funding and regulatory frameworks to ensure equity; and (ii) the financing (government) and providing (**non-profit sector**) roles are split. Transaction cost theory, which also supports the complementary role, suggests that contracting out non-core functions to non-profit organizations brings a number of advantages to the public sector, such as avoiding start-up costs, generating more accurate cost determinants, avoiding civil service staff regulations, and easing the process of altering and stopping programmes. Even though there are also disadvantages involved (e.g. difficulty to maintain equal standards, loss of public control and **accountability**, monitoring costs), both government and non-profits have incentives to co-operate. Third-party government is related to the concept of **subsidiarity**.

Third-Party Payments

Third-party payments are payments received by **non-profit organizations** from a 'third party' for contract work. Non-profits are contracted by third parties such as governments or businesses to provide services, which are not paid for directly by the **beneficiary**, but rather by the contracting agency. Third-party payment also refers to funds, **subsidies**, or **grants** given to non-profits to offset the cost of providing services to needy populations. The beneficiaries can either receive the service for free or pay a lower user fee for services when non-profits receive third-party payments.

Thomas, Franklin (1934–)

Born in Brooklyn, New York and trained as a lawyer, Franklin Thomas has been one of the most influential African–American leaders in the USA of the latter 20th century. From 1967 to 1977, Thomas was president and chief executive officer of Bedford Stuyvesant Restoration Corporation, a non-profit community development corporation. Under his leadership as president of the **Ford Foundation** from 1979 to 1996, the foundation's **assets** increased from US $2,200m. to $7,700m., and its programmes extended to providing support for economic and democratic transitions, including peaceful change in South

Africa. He is currently consultant to the TFF Study Group, board member of several corporations and **non-profit organizations**, and chairman of the September 11 Fund.

Fritz–Thyssen-Stiftung
Fritz Thyssen Foundation

One of the largest German foundations, the Fritz Thyssen Foundation, established in 1959, was the first major private foundation established in Germany after the Second World War. Along with the Volkswagen Foundation and the Robert Bosch Foundation (see **Robert-Bosch-Stiftung**), it helped pave the way for the subsequent expansion and greater relevance of the foundation sector in the country. It focuses on support for science and research at higher education institutions, with special consideration for new and emerging scientists. The Foundation also promotes international scientific dialogue by organizing international symposia and lectures. Its other fields of interest include history, languages, cultural images and representations, and international relations.

Website: www.fritz-thyssen-stiftung.de

Tithing

A tithe is described as a tenth part of one's income or **assets** contributed voluntarily, especially for the support of the clergy or church. Therefore, tithing is defined as the practice or paying of tithes. Christian churches expound a Law of Tithing, which encourages parishioners to give as a moral duty. In most countries and in most **religions**, tithing remained legally **voluntary** and was enforced through moral and peer pressure such as during Sunday Mass collections. Only in a few countries did tithing find its way into tax law; for example, members of the Catholic and Protestant churches in Germany are levied a **church tax** of about 10% of their personal income tax. Versions of tithing are also practiced in other religions, such as **Zakat** in **Islam**.

Tobin Tax

The Tobin tax, named after the Nobel prize-winning economist James Tobin who first proposed it in the 1970s, would impose a tax on foreign exchange transactions with the purpose of calming currency speculation and avoiding the damaging currency crises of the 1990s. Many current proposals suggest dedicating the revenue generated by the tax to financing international development and relief. The Tobin tax has been taken up as an issue by a number of prominent international **NGOs**, including **ATTAC**, **Oxfam** and **Friends of the Earth**, and has found support among various national governmental bodies, including the Canadian and French Parliaments and the German Bundestag Commission on Globalization.

Total Quality Management (TQM)

Total Quality Management (TQM) is a set of management principles and practices evident throughout an **organization**, geared to ensure that the organization consistently meets or exceeds client or **stakeholder** requirements. The approach originated in Japanese industry in the 1950s, but became increasingly popular in the West and in **non-profit organizations**—especially health-care organizations—since the 1980s. TQM's basic principles are a focus on customers and, in the case of non-profit organizations, also funders and other stakeholders; error prevention rather than repair; the conviction that quality goods and services cost less to produce than inferior ones; and the belief that quality management is essential for organizational survival. In applying TQM, the emphasis is on shared decision-making and responsibility, with a focus on employee commitment and dedication rather than numerical performance criteria.

Toyota Foundation

The Toyota Foundation, based in Tokyo, Japan, is a private, non-profit, **grant-making foundation** endowed in 1974 by the Toyota Motor Corporation to commemorate its 40th anniversary of automobile production. The foundation relies for its operations on income from its **endowment**—approximately 29,500m. yen (roughly US $250m.), is governed by its own **board of directors**, and is therefore able to maintain independence from the policies of the corporation that created it. The Toyota Foundation supports primarily research, conferences or public seminars, and publications in a diverse range of fields, among them human and natural environments, social welfare, education and culture, and strengthening **civil society**.

Website: www.toyotafound.or.jp

Trade Unions

Trade unions are a category of labour **organization**. As associations representing the interests of workers or employees, their purpose is the betterment of working conditions (wages, work hours, benefits, etc.) for their members. The principal activity of a union is to bargain with one or more employers on behalf of their employees. In most countries, trade unions can qualify for **tax exemptions**.

Unions tend to be controversial organizations, and their role can be analysed from three broad standpoints. Conservative pluralists maintain that unions are economic organizations whose role is to follow a narrow agenda concerned with the terms and conditions of employment. In this view, although their agenda may legitimately encompass welfare and training issues, trade unions are denied an immediate, political role in society. Writers in the social-democratic tradition argue that the purpose of trade unionism is democratic participation in job regulation. The primary focus of union activity remains the workplace, but, as democratic, representative organizations, trade unions should play a broader role in social reconstruction. Marxist approaches to trade unionism centre on the extent to which unions both facilitate collective action and consciousness and simultaneously constrain and divide the working class.

Membership in trade unions has dropped in most developed market economies, and many unions find themselves on the political defensive despite major successes in the 1960s and 1970s in improving the working conditions of millions of their members, as well as society at large.

Tragedy of the Commons

The tragedy of the commons, a concept introduced by Garrett Hardin in the 1960s, helps illustrate the processes of free-riding (see **free-rider problem**), depletion, markets, and collective action. Hardin's parable involves open pastures, with herds of animals grazing on a common ground, i.e. the **commons**. As rational beings, farmers have an incentive to increase their herd as this would also increase their profit; yet if all act that way, the commons will ultimately be destroyed. The notion of a tragedy of the commons goes back to Aristotle, Hobbes and others, but Hardin's concept casts it in economic terms (**public goods**) and links it to aspects of environmental policies (over-fishing, pollution). Furthermore, the tragedy allows for multiple solutions with each pointing to different institutional mechanisms: government and the power to control, enforce and sanction; market forces to establish clear cost and profit relations to avoid free-riding; and collective action through self-organized co-operative **organizations**, which would most likely be non-profit in nature.

Transaction Costs

Transaction costs are the cost of exchange, doing business and contracting. If possible, markets seek to minimize such costs, as they take away from the efficiency of market exchange by adding to the cost of transactions. If transaction costs rise, they can ultimately lead to **market failure**. As non-profit economists have argued, consumer trust in the assumed quality of the good or service being provided can reduce transaction costs under conditions of **information asymmetry** (see **trust-related theories**).

Transparency

Transparency refers to the clarity with which an activity, **organization**, or part of an organization can be understood and anticipated. It depends in part on the openness with which the activity is conducted or the organization operated and the accessibility of information. In essence, transparency allows **stakeholders**—among them, board members, employees, volunteers, clients, funders and the general public—to gather information that may be critical to uncovering abuses and defending their interests.

Transparency International

Transparency International (TI) is an **NGO** dedicated to combating corruption by raising awareness about its damaging effects, advocating policy reform and monitoring performance of key institutions. Formally launched in 1993, TI, through its International Secretariat in Berlin, today supports over 85 national chapters in both the North and the South. Rather than exposing individual cases, TI diagnoses and analyses corruption more broadly, using tools such as its Corruption Perceptions Index, its Bribe Payers Index and its annual *Global Corruption Report*. TI also seeks to address the roots and symptoms of corruption through active engagement of and building coalitions among business, government and **civil society**.

Website: www.transparency.org

Triple Bottom Line

The triple bottom line is a term from the field of **corporate social responsibility**, advocating a business approach that integrates financial, environmental and social considerations. At its narrowest, the term 'triple bottom line' is used as a framework for measuring and reporting corporate performance against economic, social and environmental parameters. In a broader sense, the term is used to capture the whole set of values, issues and processes that companies must address in order to minimize any harm resulting from their activities and to create economic, social and environmental value. This involves being clear about the company's purpose and taking into consideration the needs of all the company's **stakeholders**—shareholders, customers, employees, business partners, governments, local communities and the general public. In its broadest sense, the three lines represent the balance between society, the economy and the environment. Society depends on the economy - and the economy depends on the global ecosystem, whose health represents the ultimate **bottom line**.

Trust

A trust is a legal arrangement, typically written in a **deed**, in which an individual (the trustor) gives fiduciary control of property to a **trustee** for the benefit of another or for a particular purpose. In most common-law countries, a trust is also a legal form often used by **non-profit organizations** (although not all trusts are non-profit). Many foundations, e.g. **Pew Charitable Trusts** and **Rhodes Trust**, are established as trusts, as are most employee benefit funds and **political action committees**. Unlike the corporate form, the trust form does not provide trustees with a shield against personal liability. (See **trust-related theories** for discussion of the term in the sense of reliance on someone's or something's character, ability or strength.)

Trust Company

A trust company is an **organization**, typically linked to a commercial bank or other financial institution, that acts as a fiduciary or **trustee** for individuals and businesses in the administration of **trusts** and other custodial arrangements. Trust companies may offer a broad range of complementary services, including portfolio management, estate planning and other related products.

Trustee

In a strict sense, a trustee is an individual or **organization** (see **trust company**) that holds or manages **assets** for the benefit of another. The trustee is legally obliged to make all **trust**-related decisions with the **beneficiary**'s interest in mind and may be liable for damages in the event of not doing so. Trustees may be entitled to remuneration if specified in the trust **deed**. More generally, trustees are those entrusted with the **governance** of a **non-profit organization** (see **board of trustees, board of directors**).

Trust-Related Theories

Trust-related theories take as their starting point information problems inherent in the good or service provided and the trust dilemmas associated with them. For example, for parents, the quality of services actually provided by a day-care centre can be difficult to judge and very costly to monitor on an ongoing basis. Likewise, the donation made to a charity to help child soldiers in war-torn countries involves trust on behalf of the **donor** in the charity to 'deliver' on its promise.

Building on **market failure** thinking, **Hansmann** (1980) suggested that non-profits typically arise in situations in which consumers feel unable to evaluate accurately the quantity and quality of the service a firm produces for them. The advantage **non-profit organizations** have over for-profit firms is the signal of trustworthiness that arises from the **non-distribution constraint**, i.e. the prohibition of distributing profits to owners and equivalents. Constrained in their ability to benefit from **information asymmetries**, non-profits have less incentive to profit at the expense of consumers than do for-profit organizations.

The advantage of non-profit organizations is however only a relative one, as lower incentives to profiteer from information asymmetries may be part of a larger incentive structure that tends to reduce both cost and **revenue**-related efficiencies. In other words, non-profit organizations have a comparative advantage over for-profit organizations where the value of consumer protection signalled by the non-distribution constraint outweighs inefficiencies associated with the non-profit form, in particular limited access to capital markets (because of disincentives for profit-seeking investors) and lower incentives for managers to impose strict cost minimization.

One shortcoming pointed out by critics is the failure of trust-related theories to take account of government and the possibility that information asymmetries may find a response through **public sector** rather than **non-profit sector** action.

In this sense, by helping explain why private non-market rather than market solutions arise, trust-related theories complement the **heterogeneity theory** or the **public goods theory**, which explained why some organizations are private rather than government-run.

Another criticism argues that the centrality of the non-distribution constraint finds no corresponding weight in the legal and tax systems of most countries. In fact, the non-distribution constraint may be overstated, as **organizations** use **cross-subsidization** or engage in indirect profit-taking by increasing costs, e.g. luxurious offices, generous travel budgets and personal accounts. Moreover, many legal systems have fairly light oversight regimes in place to monitor adherence to non-distribution, and penalties for violations tend to be relatively mild.

Despite these and other criticisms, the trust-related theories have influenced many subsequent developments in the field. The basic tenet is that the non-profit form emerges when it is more efficient to monitor financial behaviour, in particular the treatment of potential profits, than it is to assess the true quality of output. The non-distribution constraint serves as a proxy-insurance signalling protection from profiteering.

TÜSEV

Third Sector Foundation of Turkey

The Third Sector Foundation of Turkey was established to promote the development of **philanthropy** and **civil society** in Turkey and to promote the **third sector** internationally. Its domestic activities include creating a national centre for information exchange and co-operation between foundations and associations; awarding **grants** for research projects; promoting the creation of foundations; and advocating for and fostering a regulatory and policy environment conducive to the development and operation of foundations. Its international activities include organizing international and regional meetings and representing the Turkish third sector within **international NGOs** and **organizations**.

Website: www.tusev.org.tr

U

Uncivil Society

'Uncivil society' is the conceptual twin of **civil society**, and these days no scholarly analysis of one is ever complete without at least an analytic nod in the direction of the other. This has not made its meaning clearer, for 'uncivil society' is as difficult to apprehend as 'civil society'. Part of the problem lies in the clear cultural connotations that 'uncivil' society undoubtedly carries, having been used historically by generations of Western social theorists to characterise non-Western societies and formations. The earliest scholarship on civil society in Africa and Asia was thus understandably reactive, anchored on the imperative to reject this normative attribution of 'incivility'. In recent times, 'uncivil society' has been used, controversially, to describe terrorist, fundamentalist and other groups sworn to the use of violence to achieve their objectives.

Union of International Associations

Based in Belgium, the Union of International Associations was founded in 1907 to assist the activities of non-profit, non-governmental and voluntary **organizations** throughout the world in both developed and developing countries. It is a **clearing-house** of information for over 40,000 international organizations and promotes research to improve the operations, effectiveness and efficiency of constituent organizations. Numerous publications and references are generated from the Union's extensive database. Publications include: *Transnational Associations*, *Yearbook of International Organizations* and *Encyclopedia of World Problems and Human Potential*. The Union has consultative status with the United Nations (ECOSOC), UNESCO and the International Labour Organization (ILO).

Website: www.uia.org

UNIOPSS

Union of Health and Welfare Non-Profit Organizations

Created in 1947, UNIOPSS is the principal umbrella **organization** in France. It embraces 120,000 associations employing 630,000 salaried workers and 195,000 full-time equivalent volunteers. Of US \$30,000m. in **revenue**, **public sector** funding accounts for two-thirds, which means a significant **partnership** with the State and social security. This partnership has two components: first, **non-profit organizations** provide health and social services, financed by the government according to the **subsidiarity principle**; and second, non-profits are also involved in the formulation and implementation of public policies against poverty or in favour of the disabled, the elderly or the socially vulnerable.

Website: www.uniopss.asso.fr

United Nations: Partners in Civil Society

The United Nations Partners in Civil Society programme, as part of its reform process, is an effort to build stronger relationships with **NGOs** and other **civil society** organizations on issues of global **governance** and multiculturalism. It is a recognition by the UN that in order to build lasting peace and prosperity, it must engage not only governments but also civil society. The **partnership** works in many ways, and UN offices and agencies have formal and informal associations with NGOs including the Department of Public Information (UN/DPI), the Non-Governmental Liaison Service, and consultative status with various UN agencies. In June 2004, the Secretary-General's Panel of Eminent Persons on Civil Society and UN Relationships released its final report detailing recommendations on further improving the UN's relationship with civil society.

Website: www.un.org/partners/civil_society/home.htm

United Way

United Way is a movement of **community chests** and similar **organizations** that mobilize and allocate financial and volunteer resources in their communities. Though the community chest concept had its most significant growth in the USA in the 1940s, the name United Way was first adopted only in 1963 in Los Angeles. Today some 1,400 independent United Way organizations throughout the USA are served by United Way of America, while United Way International, founded in 1974, provides support to and encourages the development of United Ways around the world. Local United Way organizations raise a significant portion of their funds through annual campaigns conducted at workplaces, through which employees agree to designate a portion of their compensation to the United Way. United Way in turn provides assurance that the recipient organizations meet certain standards of performance and **account-ability**. (See also **Federated fundraising campaigns**.)

Website: www.unitedway.org

Unrelated Business Income (UBI)

The tax laws in many countries include provisions on income unrelated to the charitable or tax-exempt purpose of **non-profit organizations**. The US Internal Revenue Service defines UBI as income generated from a trade or business, regularly carried on, that is not substantially related to the furtherance of the organization's exempt purpose or function. In the USA, activities must meet all three criteria to be treated as UBI, whereas other countries have either stricter or more lenient requirements. In most cases, however, engaging in UBI activities will not jeopardize the tax-exempt status of non-profit organizations, although some tax regimes establish guidelines on the overall extent of UBI relative to total revenue (see **for-profits in disguise**). Tax authorities impose unrelated business income tax (UBIT) on non-profit organizations engaged in UBI activities. UBIT rates tend to be similar to tax on the net income of for-profit corporations.

V

Value-Added Tax (VAT)

Value-added tax (VAT) is an indirect tax, first applied in France in 1954 and subsequently introduced in the European Community (1967–73) and elsewhere around the world. According to the origin principle, the tax is applied on value added at each stage of exchange of goods and services, proportional to the extra value added to the product or service at that stage. VAT is increasingly popular because of its potential for higher **revenue** yields and its effect on controlling the underground or informal economy. In many countries, **non-profit organizations** that are exempt from other types of taxes are also exempt—entirely or partially—from VAT, although the policy rationale of VAT exemptions continues to be debated in others, in particular the United Kingdom.

Value–Return Matrix

The value–return matrix is a managerial planning tool that takes an approach similar to the **product portfolio map**. It is based on two dimensions: the social value the board attaches to the programme, and the financial return and resource effectiveness management can achieve with the activities the programme entails. It suggests that programmes with high financial return and high social values for the **organization**'s **mission** should be built upon and benefit from **cross-subsidization** and **economies of scope**; and that programmes with high financial returns and low mission values should be judged by their net contribution to other preferred activities only. Programmes with low financial returns and low mission values should be cut back, if not discontinued. Finally, for programmes that rank high in terms of value but low when it comes to financial contribution, the organization may decide to lobby government for **subsidies**, apply to foundations for **grants** to increase **revenue**, approach corporations to underwrite some of the costs, or seek co-operation with other non-profits in an effort to reduce costs.

Venture Philanthropy

Venture philanthropy applies venture capital strategies, skills and resources to charitable giving. It typically seeks new or expanding **organizations**—sometimes also programmes or projects—with high potential for social impact. As with venture capital, venture philanthropy adds value to whatever financing might be offered through the provision of **capacity-building** support. In fact, the focus tends to be more on building greater organizational capacity and infrastructure, rather than or in addition to covering programme costs. Venture philanthropists, also called **donor**-investors, support such capacity-building by providing management and other expertise and through the **leverage** of a wide network of outside contacts, resources and professional advisers.

Vereniging van Fondsen in Nederland

Association of Foundations in the Netherlands

Established in 1988, the Vereniging van Fondsen in Nederland (the FIN) seeks to promote the interests and improve the operations of its 200 private **foundation** members. The FIN works with public authorities, social **organizations** and the media; advises its members in daily operational matters; and fosters communication and co-operation among its members. It also establishes guidelines and standards for operations and grant-making policy among its members. The FIN publishes a directory which provides information on approximately 600 Dutch foundations every two years.

Website: www.verenigingvanfondsen.nl

Verzuiling

Verzuiling (literally 'pillarization') is a Dutch word first used in the 1950s to refer to the vertical segregation of Dutch society along religious or political lines beginning in the second half of the 19th century. The bottom-up and top-down building of associations and linking existing **organizations** into blocks had resulted in a Catholic, (several) Protestant, and smaller, more loosely organized socialist, liberal, Jewish and humanist *zuilen*, or pillars. The confessional pillars, in particular, cross-cut socioeconomic layers. They covered all spheres of social life, with denominational political parties, labour unions and employer organizations, housing associations, newspapers and broadcasting associations, schools, hospitals, burial funds and sport clubs. Preceded by the full recognition and equal financial rights for private schools in the constitution of 1920, pillarized organizations became an integrated part of the growing **welfare state** after the Second World War, leading to a large **non-profit sector**. Since the 1970s most non-profits have been 'depillarized', but the tradition of publicly-paid private initiatives is still strong. The idea of *verzuiling* is also used in Belgium and could be applied to phenomena in other countries, such as the *Lager* in Austria, but the Dutch *zuilen* were probably the most vertically integrative and encompassing.

Vision

A vision conveys the ideal future of an **organization**, its aspirations and hopes of what it will become, achieve or contribute. Often an organization's vision is stated explicitly in a vision statement, whose purpose is to inspire and help frame the wider context in which the organization's **mission** is formulated. In some cases, the organization's vision is implicit in its mission statement.

Voluntary

Voluntary status is a criterion of the **structural–operational definition** of **non-profit organizations** developed by Salamon, Anheier and associates. To be included under this definition of the **non-profit sector**, **organizations** must embody the concept of **voluntarism** to a meaningful extent. This involves two different, but related, considerations. First, the organization must engage volunteers in its operations and management, either on its board or through the use of volunteer staff and voluntary contributions. This does not mean that all or most of the income of an organization must come from voluntary contributions, or that most of its staff must be volunteers. The presence of some meaningful voluntary input, even if only a voluntary **board of directors**, suffices to qualify an organization as in some sense 'voluntary'. Second, 'voluntary' also carries the meaning of 'non-compulsory'. Organizations in which **membership** is required or otherwise stipulated by law would be excluded from the non-profit sector. For example, some professions (medical, legal) may require compulsory membership in a particular **professional association**; owners of small-scale industries may be required to join the local chamber of commerce; or employees may be required to join a **trade union**. In such cases, the criterion of 'voluntary' would not be met, and the associations consequently not considered to be part of the non-profit sector. Similarly, 'voluntary' implies that contributions of time (**volunteering**) and money (donations) as well as contributions in-kind may not be required or enforced by law, or otherwise be openly coerced.

Voluntary Associations

The term 'voluntary association' figures differently in the social sciences, with definitions varying somewhat by theory and field. Specific examples are organizational studies, where voluntary associations are seen as one of the three basic forms next to the business firm and the government agency; urban and community studies, where voluntary associations have been identified as vehicles of local integration and sources of community power; political sociology, where voluntary associations are related to **social movements**, interest groups and status politics; or development studies, where voluntary associations play an important role in building a social infrastructure for economic growth by generating networks of mutual trust.

The various definitions share a common core in the sense that voluntary associations are seen as private, membership-based **organizations** in which membership is non-compulsory. In addition, the organization should have identifiable boundaries to distinguish members from non-members, be self-governing, and non-commercial in objective and behaviour. Definitions differ mostly in emphasis and 'at the margins,' i.e. along the demarcation lines to related forms such as business (partnerships, **co-operatives**, **mutual organizations, business** and **professional associations**), compulsory organizations (**guilds**, bar associations, and, in some countries, chambers of commerce), political organizations (parties, **political action committees**, interest groups) and quasi-governmental institutions (mass membership organizations in the autocratic societies, state churches).

Some of the definitional complexities arise from significant overlaps with related terms such as **non-profit organization, non-governmental organization** or **third sector** organization. In contrast to these forms, **voluntary** organizations have a **membership** focus, whereas many non-profit organizations like hospitals, social service agencies or art museums may have a governing board but no broad membership base.

In traditional, pre-modern societies, voluntary organizations fulfilled a number of functions. They served as integrative mechanisms cross-cutting family and clan structures as well as age groups, thereby avoiding potential divisions within the community; they operated as alternative mobility strata in societies with rigid, often hereditary status systems; they were part of the division of labour and provided mutual assistance and economic benefit to members (farmers, craftsmen, traders); or they were in fact precursors of social classes grouping similar economic statuses, occupations and property owners around some joint interest.

Researchers emphasize the contributions voluntary associations make to the integration of migrants and minorities. African village associations in urban areas facilitate the acculturation of rural-urban migrants from the same area by providing a buffer zone between village life and the more diverse city culture. Other examples include ethnic associations among Italian, Greek or German immigrants to the USA in the 19th century, or Turkish clubs in Germany in the late 20th century. More generally, voluntary associations are said to 'give voice' to interests and concerns that otherwise might not be heard. As a form of collective action, they group people and organizations sharing similar interests in sport, hobbies, culture or politics. Furthermore, voluntary associations serve a complementary economic function as well, providing a mechanism for mutual **self-help** among marginal population groups. Savings and credit associations among the poor and co-operative-type organizations among small-scale producers are examples of how excluded members of society pool resources to improve their economic well-being.

The modern voluntary association emerged in most European countries in the 19th century during the industrialization period, with the rise of urban elites, a growing middle class, and a rapidly expanding working class. Examples are the **Law of 1901** in France and the civil law legislation in other European countries that established **freedom of association**. Associations occupied a prominent place throughout US history: as service providers in the absence of a **welfare state**, as an important source of political mobilization (e.g. civil rights), and as a platform for status competition in a formally egalitarian society. Analysts suggest that multiple memberships in voluntary associations created overlapping social circles and criss-crossing social conflicts, thereby avoiding the emergence of significant class cleavages and other fault lines that could potentially divide US society into antagonistic groups.

Despite some progress, the study of voluntary associations continues to face considerable methodological and theoretical challenges. In terms of methodology, the measurement of central variables, such as membership, voluntary activities and formality/informality remains a problem because of significant cross-cultural variations in meaning. In terms of theory, research on voluntary associations will gain by addressing the notions of **civil society** and **social capital**.

Voluntary Failure

The concept of **voluntary** or philanthropic failure arises in **non-profit sector** theories focusing on the relationship between government and the **third sector**. The voluntary failure theory argues that voluntary action exists because of people's natural tendencies for collective action and sense of social obligation. Because of relatively lower costs, at least initially, **non-profit organizations** tend to pioneer in addressing various social problems, including HIV/AIDS, domestic violence, etc. At a certain point, however, non-profits cannot adequately provide a service or address a social problem at a scale necessary for its alleviation. Voluntary failure, therefore, results from the inability of non-profits to mobilize the resources needed in a substantial and sustainable way; since they cannot tax nor raise funds on capital markets, non-profits rely on voluntary contributions that in the end may be insufficient for the task at hand. Thus, government steps in to assist the **voluntary sector** in areas of weakness.

Voluntary Price Discrimination

A term in the economics of non-profit pricing, voluntary price discrimination refers to situations of **information asymmetry** between provider and user. When the provider is unable to determine eligibility for particular prices (fees, donations) for services or **membership**, users or consumers are asked to assess their own eligibility and select a price they find fair and affordable to them. Examples are supporting member dues, entry fees to museums, or contributions to public radio or television stations. **Non-profit organizations** make extensive use of this price mechanism since tendencies to free-riding can, in part, be avoided due to value commitments on the part of users, or can also be off-set by **fundraising** campaigns. By contrast, for-profit **organizations** rarely use voluntary price discrimination as it invites free-riding. (See also **Free-rider problem**.)

Voluntary Sector

The term 'voluntary sector' is used in the UK, Ireland and many Commonwealth countries, often interchangeably with the terms **non-profit**

sector, **third sector** and non-statutory sector. The five characteristic features of **organizations** comprising the voluntary sector are a degree of organizational formality, relative autonomy from government, a degree of self-government, **non-profit distribution**, and a commitment to service to **public benefit**. The voluntary sector has always played an important role in social policy in the UK, in particular in social service provision and community development. Over the last decade, developments like **new public management**, the **Compact**, **active citizenship**, and other initiatives have placed the sector even closer to policy-making, and have led to the development of a **partnership** with the state in many areas of welfare reform.

Volunteering, Voluntarism

The notion of what is volunteering and what is a volunteer varies across countries and is closely related to aspects of culture and history. The British and American concept of volunteering, the French *voluntariat*, the Italian *voluntariato*, the Swedish *frivillig verksamhet* or the German *Ehrenamt* have different histories and carry different cultural and political connotations.

The notion of voluntarism has its roots in Lockeian concepts of a self-organizing society outside the confines of the state. **Voluntary** action also resonates in the thinking of Scottish Enlightenment philosophy, yet finds its most eloquent expression in **Alexis de Tocqueville**'s *Democracy in America*. For de Tocqueville, voluntary action and voluntary association become corner-stones of a functioning democratic polity, in which voluntary action shields society from the tyranny of the majority. The link between voluntarism and **democracy** became deeply imprinted in American culture and the country's political self-understanding.

In other countries, however, the notion of volunteering is different and puts emphasis on communal service to the public good. The German term Ehrenamt or 'honorary office' comes closest to this tradition. In the middle and late 19th century, a vast network of associations and foundations emerged, frequently involving paid staff, but run and managed by volunteers. But unlike in the USA, the German notion of voluntarism as a system of 'honorary officers' took place in a—still basically autocratic—society where local and national democratic institutions remained underdeveloped. This trusteeship aspect of voluntarism began to be seen separately from other voluntary service activities such as caring for the poor, visiting the sick or assisting at school. These latter volunteer activities remained the domain of **religion** and increasingly became also part of the emerging workers' movement during the industrialisation period.

In addition to different national traditions, voluntarism is also closely linked to the self-understanding of larger **non-profit organizations** like the Red Cross: voluntary service is one of the seven fundamental principles of the **International Red Cross and Red Crescent Movement**. The Movement defines volunteers as individuals who reach out beyond the confines of paid employment and normal responsibilities to contribute in different ways without expectation of profit or reward, in the belief that their activities are beneficial to the community as well as satisfying to themselves. The United Nations offers a broader definition of volunteering as 'contributions that individuals make as non-profit, non-wage, and non-career action for the well-being of their neighbours, and society at large' —a definition that is rather broad and includes mutual self-help (see **self-help groups**) and many forms of collective action.

The way in which 'volunteering' is defined has massive implications for measuring the scope and scale of this work form. The United Nations System of National Accounts (SNA), for example, treats volunteer work as a non-market activity just like housework or leisure activities such as gardening. However, volunteering work is work in the sense that it different from leisure; and it is voluntary and therefore distinct from paid work.

Voluntary work is most commonly understood to be work without monetary pay or legal obligation provided for persons living outside the volunteer's own household. It is therefore distinct from:

- paid work, although volunteers often receive some kind of (also monetary) remuneration and the borderline between paid work and voluntary work therefore contains a certain grey area;
- household work;
- hobbies and other purely consumptive activities, since others have to benefit from the result of voluntary work;
- obligatory service, such as that performed by persons who are legally obliged to provide 'voluntary' services like civil servants as part of their job description.

Volunteering takes place in different forms across many fields. To calculate the imputed value of volunteer work, economists typically rely on data from population surveys. The two key items are the number of volunteers in the sample and the number of hours volunteered per volunteer. The proportionate share of volunteers is extrapolated to the whole adult population to obtain the total number of volunteers, which, in turn, is multiplied by the average number of hours volunteered. Finally, the total number of hours volunteered is then multiplied by a monetary value or shadow wage, which yields the imputed value of total volunteer time. Typically, the **replacement cost** of volunteer time is used as the shadow wage, but other approaches are also possible.

Vouchers

Vouchers are a form of government **third-party payment** and are favoured as a way to bring market mechanisms into the delivery of services such as day-care, substance abuse treatment and primary education. In these programmes, an individual is given a voucher, entitling him or her to services, the cost of which is reimbursed by a government agency. The individual can then take that voucher to a variety of different providers, which are generally required to be accredited by the paying agency in some way. Ideally, this enables the client to select more personalized services and introduces competition among providers, which will improve service delivery overall. Critics of voucher systems, however, argue that they allow **cream-skimming** by prestigious **organizations**, leaving clients with more substantial or expensive needs to rely on increasingly underfunded public providers or organizations providing lower quality services.

W

Waiting Lists

Waiting lists are a form of rationing under situations of excess demand, when the provider is either unable or unwilling to increase supply by expanding capacity. Waiting lists are either on a first-come, first-served basis, or use some form of priority criteria. Examples in the non-profit field are nursing homes and hospices, day-care centres, schools, universities and certain kinds of hospitals. Research has shown that **non-profit organizations** are more likely to use waiting lists than expand capacity, as such lists are seen as a sign of reputation and quality. Businesses, however, are more likely to regard waiting lists as inefficient, and will seek to expand capacity to meet demand.

Al Wakf

Al Wakf, also *Waqf*, is the Muslim system of donations or bequests of properties that generate income for charitable purposes, similar to the concept of charitable **trusts** or **endowment**s. The income generated by the property is earmarked by the **donor** for a variety of purposes including schools, hospitals and mosques. The administration of *Wakfs* has historically been the province of Islamic **non-profit organizations**. In Egypt, however, government took over *Wakf* administration in the 1950s, leading to a steep drop in activity and a subsequent reversal of the government's policy. More recently, efforts are under way in several countries, including Kuwait and Morocco, to partially deregulate the system of *Wakfs* to protect their **assets** from government bodies while still holding them accountable to the legal system.

Knut och Alice Wallenbergs Stiftelse

Knut and Alice Wallenberg Foundation

The Knut and Alice Wallenberg Foundation was established in 1917 to promote scientific research and educational activities which benefit Sweden. The Foundation began as a **family foundation**, and funds primarily domestic programmes in the fields of education, medicine, arts, the natural sciences, and expensive scientific equipment and major scientific programmes. It is among the largest foundations in Europe, with a highly diversified portfolio in different branches of Swedish industry.

Website: www.wallenberg.org/kaw

Warm Glow

In the economic theory of 'pure **altruism**', **donors** are agnostic as to whether the provision of a given, desired **public good** is funded publicly or privately, given certain conditions. In essence, this would lead to a perfect (dollar for dollar) **crowding out** of private donations by increases of government support for the public good. Empirical studies, however, have consistently shown that the crowding out effect is below the one-to-one ratio. Accordingly, donors are assumed to be motivated to give by more than just the desire to see a public good provided. The theory of 'impure **altruism**' therefore suggests that the act of giving conveys for the donor other benefits, such as control of the provision of the good, social prestige and recognition, or simply a 'warm glow', or a good feeling from doing good.

Webb, Beatrice Potter (1858–1943)

Beatrice Potter Webb, daughter of an English industrialist, benefited from little formal education, but ultimately her research and writings had a significant impact on social thinking and policy. Her first major publication, *The Co-operative Movement in Great Britain* (1891), emerged from her early work with London's poor. With husband Sydney James Webb, she played an instrumental role in the formation of the British Labour Party and in the creation of the London School of Economics. In their Minority Report to the Commission on the **Poor Laws** (1909), the Webbs outlined a charter for a comprehensive social security scheme and a wider **welfare state** that was to emerge later in Europe and North America.

Weisbrod, Burton A. (1931–)

Burton Weisbrod is a leading economist and **non-profit sector** theorist. Currently serving as John Evans Professor of Economics at Northwestern University, he has worked on the economics and public policy analysis of **non-profit organizations**, education, health and other topics. He served on the Council of Economic Advisors to Presidents John F. Kennedy and Lyndon B. Johnson, is one of the founders of non-profit economics, and is credited with the development of demand-side theories that emphasize demand heterogeneity and **public goods** provision. His research examines the comparative economic behaviour of for-profit, government and private non-profit organizations and the causes and consequences of the growing commercialism of non-profits. He is author of *The Nonprofit Economy* (1988) and of *To Profit or Not to Profit? The Commercial Transformation of the Nonprofit Sector* (1998).

Welfare Mix

The term 'welfare mix' is used in European debates about the reform of the **welfare state**, and is a general descriptor for the increasing number of ways and combinations in which social services, health-care and welfare entitlements are financed, provided and monitored. Involved in the welfare mix are the **public sector**, the **non-profit sector**, and increasingly also for-profit providers. Moreover, the welfare mix recognizes the importance of informal care offered by local communities, **self-help groups** and family. The term is used synonymously with the term 'mixed economy of care'.

Welfare State

A welfare state is a system in which the government assumes the main responsibility for providing for the social and economic security of the population by means of pensions, social security, unemployment benefits, health care, and so forth. Once the **beneficiaries** meet selected criteria, such services are provided at little to no cost and are paid for primarily through tax **revenue**. Proponents of an activist welfare state emphasize policies that secure a minimum standard of living for all citizens, control of the business cycle, manipulation of total output to allow for social costs and revenues, and the production of social goods and services.

The historical roots of the welfare state vary from country to country. The 1942 **Beveridge** Report proposed for the UK a system of benefits, financed by contributions from workers, employers and the state, together with a public assistance safety-net, as part of a wider social and economic reconstruction that was to take place following the close of the Second World War. New Deal legislation of the 1930s, the impact of the Second World War, and the Great Society programmes in the 1960s introduced welfare state elements to the USA. In Germany the Bismarck reforms of the 1880s, which introduced old age and unemployment insurance, became the cornerstone for more comprehensive welfare state legislation from the 1950s onwards under the concept of a social market economy—a system perfected in the social-democratic countries of Scandinavia.

Since the 1970s, a 'crisis' of the welfare state has emerged, with growing disagreement about the effects of the welfare state and its future direction. This disagreement is thought to have stemmed from both changed economic and social circumstances and a disintegration of post-Second World War consensus. Critics from the right argue that policies of the welfare state lead to dependence and stifle individual initiative. Critics from the left argue that the current welfare state may indeed be 'oppressive', but identifies the cause as a failure to attack the root causes of class, gender and race inequalities. This latter approach was a radical departure from the socialist analysis of the welfare state during the 1940s and 1950s, likely due to the influence of **social movements** that had emerged in the 1960s.

'Welfare state regimes', as introduced by Esping-Andersen in *The Three Worlds of Welfare Capitalism*, can be labelled as one of three main types within market societies: 'conservative', 'social-democratic', or 'liberal', depending on the extent to which they seek to work with, or to counter the effects of the market on social inequalities. Germany, characterized by high welfare service provision within a hierarchical and ordered society, is therefore considered 'conservative', while Sweden comes closest to an egalitarian 'social-democratic' regime. The British welfare state most closely illustrates the 'liberal' model, with only limited attempts to use government programmes to mitigate social inequalities.

The literature on the welfare state itself has been rather state-oriented and ignores the critical role **non-profit organizations** have played—and continue to play—even though government has assumed a greater role in non-profit financing. Examples are the US system of **third-party government**, the Dutch *verzuiling*, or the German **subsidiarity principle** in social policy, and the approaches of **new public management** and competitive contracting. The **social origins theory** introduced by Salamon and Anheier tries to link welfare state development with non-profit roles and introduces four non-profit regime types (liberal, corporatist, social-democratic and statist); it is in the former two that state–non-profit partnerships are most pronounced in welfare services. Even though the **non-profit sector** has been part of the welfare state delivery system in many countries, its increased recognition today is closely linked to welfare state reforms.

The Wellcome Trust

Established in 1936 with a bequest from Sir Henry Wellcome, American co-founder of the Burroughs Wellcome pharmaceutical company, the Wellcome Trust is dedicated to funding research to improve human and animal health. With an **endowment** of approximately £10,000 million, it is the United Kingdom's largest non-governmental resource for biomedical research. The Trust makes **grants** to universities and academic centres in the UK and overseas and conducts its own research, projects and initiatives, including policy-oriented work in education and health-care delivery. Trust funds have contributed to such medical advances as sequencing of the human genome and development of the anti-malarial drug artemisinin.

Website: www.wellcome.ac.uk

WINGS (Worldwide Initiatives for Grantmaker Support)

WINGS, established in 2000, is a global network of some 100 **membership** associations and support **organizations** serving grant-makers. With its secretar-iat currently hosted by the **European Foundation Centre**, WINGS is dedicated to fostering communication and co-operation among its members; developing new modes of communication and collaboration; and contributing to the strengthening of **philanthropy** world-wide. WINGS organizes meetings and conferences, offers internships and provides technical assistance. In addition, WINGS has established a sister-network WINGS-CF (Community Foundations) to support the development and work of **community foundations** world-wide.

Website: www.wingsweb.org

Worker's Welfare – *see* Arbeiterwohlfahrt (AWO)

Workhouses

Workhouses arose in Britain after the **Poor Law** of 1601, and were also common in the USA throughout the 1800s, where they were often known as poorhouses or **alms**houses. Workhouses were run by parishes or counties to provide minimum care for the poor while attempting to instil better work habits, which the residents were believed to be lacking. Workhouses were also intended to serve as a deterrent to accepting aid as it was thought they were so unpleasant, anyone who could possibly support themselves in another way would do so. Men and women were generally housed separately, and children were often removed from their parents. Social welfare legislation, such as unemployment insurance and old-age pensions, combined with growing negative public sentiment, brought about the end of the workhouses in their traditional form, and many were converted to hospitals in the 1940s.

World Bank

The World Bank is a specialized agency of the United Nations initially conceived during the Second World War at Bretton Woods, New Hampshire, to help rebuild Europe. Since its inception in 1944, the World Bank has refocused its goals from reconstruction to world-wide poverty reduction and has expanded from a single institution to a group of five development institutions, including the International Bank for Reconstruction and Development and the International Development Association, which provide low-interest loans, interest-free credit and **grants** to developing countries. The World Bank is owned by 184 member countries acting as shareholders. In 2003, the World Bank provided over US $18,000m. to more than 100 developing countries. Since the 1980s, the World Bank has been a target of **NGO advocacy** efforts, especially on environmental policy and on social and other related policies.

Website: www.worldbank.org

World Bank—The Civil Society Team

The Civil Society Team is a cross-cutting unit of the Bank's External Affairs and Social Development Departments and has replaced the Bank's former **NGO** Unit, which was initially established in the early 1990s to co-ordinate relations with NGOs. The Team serves as the institutional and global focal point for the Bank's engagement with **civil society**, and works closely with over 120 country and regional co-ordinators across different projects world-wide. In addition, the Team is responsible for formulating institutional strategy, providing advice, guidance and technical assistance to programme staff on how to consult and involve civil society in Bank operations, undertaking ongoing outreach efforts to **global civil society** networks and providing civil society groups with access to Bank information, personnel and other resources.

Website: www.worldbank.org

World Council of Churches

Rooted in the modern ecumenical movement of the late 19th and early 20th centuries, the World Council of Churches (WCC) was established formally in 1948 as a fellowship that now brings together more than 340 Orthodox, Anglican, Lutheran, Methodist, independent and other churches in over 120 countries around the world. In pursuing its goal of Christian unity, the WCC develops activities and networks among clergy and lay people, especially women and youth. With its administrative centre in Geneva, the WCC is financed by member contributions and **grants** from foundations and individuals, as well as fees for services and publications.

Website: www.wcc-coe.org

World Economic Forum

Founded by **Klaus Schwab** in 1970 as a gathering of Europe's corporate executives in the Swiss town of Davos, the World Economic Forum has become an influential and controversial international **non-profit organization**. Incorporated as a Swiss non-profit **foundation**, but with a **membership** base that provides a significant part of its funding, the Forum offers a platform for world leaders to address policy issues of global public interest. In the first decade of the 21st century, its high profile annual meetings and other events have drawn significant protest, largely because the Forum itself has been seen as the corporate architect behind economic globalization and therefore responsible for its impact. Like other influential **international NGOs**, the Forum enjoys consultative status with the United Nations Economic and Social Council.

Website: www.weforum.org

The World of NGOs

The World of NGOs was established in 1975 and works to promote and support Austria's **non-profit sector**. A **non-profit organization** itself, the World of NGOs serves as an information resource for Austria's **civil society** organizations and as a promoter of co-ordination among initiatives and **organizations** within Austria and Europe more generally. Its activities include conducting research, organizing conferences and training courses, and issuing publications, including an *Annual Report* on Austria's non-profit sector.

Website: www.ngo.at

World Social Forum

Started in 2001 from the inspiration of Brazilian philanthropist Oded Grajev and the support of **ATTAC**, among others, as an alternative to the **World Economic Forum**, the World Social Forum is a meeting place for democratic debate, common strategizing and networking for effective action. Established to discuss the concerns of **global civil society** regarding the effects of globalization, the WSF debates alternatives for building a society based on **solidarity** and respect for **human rights**. The first three WSF took place in Brazil and in 2004 in India. After returning to Brazil in 2005, the WSF will move to Africa to realize its goal of becoming a fully global process.

Website: www.forumsocialmundial.org.br

World Vision

World Vision is an independent Christian relief and development **organization**, founded in 1950 to assist orphans of the Korean War. Since then, it has evolved into a global **partnership** conducting child-focused projects on six continents, with **fundraising** offices in North America, Europe and Asia. **Christianity** is not a prerequisite for assistance and, although Christian education is often included in project activities, World Vision respects local laws and values regarding evangelism. Nearly 80% of World Vision's funds come from private sources, and about half of its programmes are funded through child sponsorship, by which a **donor** pledges a monthly contribution in support of a child or project benefiting the child.

Website: www.wvi.org/wvi/home.htm

World Wide Fund for Nature (WWF)

Inspired by British biologist Sir Julian Huxley, the World Wide Fund for Nature (WWF) began in the 1960s as the World Wildlife Fund with a focus on endangered species. Although the panda remains its trademark, WWF has extended its scope to cover climate change, pollution, forest preservation, and river and water conservation. WWF is active at the national level mainly through independent offices conducting local conservation, **advocacy** and environmental education activities, and at the international level through its Swtizerland-based secretariat and offices in Brussels and Washington, DC engaging in advocacy. Contributions from individuals remain WWF's most important **revenue** source, accounting for more than half of its annual income.

Website: www.panda.org

Y

Young, Michael (1915–2002)

Michael Young, Lord Young of Dartington, was a prolific British social reformer. His abilities matched his extraordinary range of interests: he was a qualified barrister, he wrote the Labour party manifesto of 1945, gained a Ph.D. in social policy at the London School of Economics, but found his place when he set up the Institute of Community Studies in Bethnal Green, London. From there he launched more than 50 new **organizations**, including the Consumers' Association, the Open University and the School for **Social Entrepreneurs**. He was also an influential social researcher and author, and coined the term 'meritocracy'.

Young Men's Christian Association (YMCA)

The first Young Men's Christian Association (YMCA) was founded in London in 1844 as a response to unhealthy social conditions in big cities at the end of the Industrial Revolution. YMCAs are now found in more than 120 countries, joined together through the Geneva-based World Alliance of YMCAs, the oldest **voluntary** international **organization** in the world today. Originally intended for Bible study and prayer for young men of all Christian faiths, YMCAs have extended their programmes to include development of youth of both genders; recreation, sports and educational activities; services to refugees and displaced persons; and building safer, stronger communities.

Website: www.ymca.int

Young Women's Christian Association (YWCA)

The Young Women's Christian Association (YWCA) was formed in London by Emma Roberts and Mrs Arthur Kinnaird in 1855 as a way to combine religious practice with social action. The YWCA movement has since evolved not only to provide services to young women but also as a key player in most of the major **social movements** throughout the 19th and 20th centuries, particularly in the USA. Today, the YWCA is a world-wide **organization** with affiliates in over 100 countries. Each local YWCA is an autonomous community-based **non-governmental organization**. As a non-profit **membership** association, each YWCA is run by and for women of the community and their families. Local YWCAs provide services and programmes specific to the needs of the community including leadership training, hostels, shelters and job training.

Website: www.worldywca.org

Z

Al-Zakat

Also known as *Zakaat*, *Al-Zakat* refers to charitable **tithing** required by Muslims who possess a minimum wealth or earn a minimum income. Derived from the word *Zakaa*, which means to increase, purify and bless, *Al-Zakat* is one of the five pillars of **Islam**, the others being prayer, fasting, pilgrimage and belief in one God. Institutional arrangements for administering *Zakat* vary from place to place. In Egypt, for example, the Nasser Bank of Social Work was founded by the government in 1971 to administer *Zakat* deposits made through a network of thousands of mosques. Still, rather than working through an organized structure, many Muslims give *Zakat* directly to the poor and other eligible recipients, including new converts to Islam, people in debt and those making an effort to raise the banner of Islam. In all cases, *Zakat* should be practised in secret, without bringing the **donor** publicity (see **Charity**).

Zedaka

Zedaka (or Tzedakah) is the Jewish equivalent for '**charity**'. It is derived from the Hebrew term *Tzedek* that means fairness or justice. It includes the provision of aid, assistance and money to the poor or needy and can take the form of financial, material or emotional support. In Jewish tradition, it is important that the Zedaka be appropriate to the need. The act of giving charity is equated with the performance of a duty or precept, not a generous or benevolent act. In fact, the spiritual benefit of giving to the poor is so great that the needy person does a favour to the **donor** by providing an opportunity to make the contribution. In Judaism, Zedaka is seen as a vehicle for creating justice or correcting the wrongs in the world (*tikun olam*), or in other words, the person who performs Zedaka is contributing to justice.

ZEIT-Stiftung Ebelin und Gerd Bucerius

Ebelin and Gerd Bucerius ZEIT Foundation

Established in 1971 by Gerd Bucerius, founder of the German weekly newspaper DIE ZEIT, the ZEIT-Stiftung Ebelin und Gerd Bucerius is dedicated to promoting science and scholarship, education and training, and the arts and culture. The ZEIT-Stiftung is an **operating foundation**, but also makes **grants**, offers scholarships and awards prizes. Among its activities are support for journalists, especially in the developing press in Eastern Europe; sponsorship of several professorship chairs, particularly in the new German federal states; preservation of important archives and cultural monuments; and internationally, promotion of intercultural dialogue.

Website: www.zeit-stiftung.de

SELECT BIBLIOGRAPHY

Anheier, H. K. *Nonprofit Organizations: Approaches, Management, Policy.* London, Routledge, 2005.

Anheier, H. K. and Ben-Ner, A. (eds.) *The Study of the Nonprofit Enterprise: Theories and Approaches*, New York, Kluwer Academic/Plenum Publishers, 2003.

Anheier, H. K. and Kendall, J. (eds.) *Third Sector Policy at the Crossroads: An International Nonprofit Analysis.* London, Routledge, 2001.

Anheier, H. K. and Toepler, S. (eds.) *Private Funds and Public Purpose, Philanthropic Foundations in International Perspectives*, New York, Kluwer Academic/Plenum Publishers, 1999.

Anheier, H. K., Glasius, M. and Kaldor, M. (eds.) *Global Civil Society 2004/5*, London, Sage, 2004.

Ascoli, U. and Ranci, C. (eds.) *Dilemmas of the Welfare Mix: The New Structure of Welfare in an Era of Privatization.* New York, Kluwer Academic/Plenum Publishers, 2002.

Boris, E. and Steuerle, C. E. (eds.) *Nonprofits and Government: Collaboration and Conflict.* Washington, DC, Urban Institute Press, 1999.

Borzaga, C. and Defourney, J. (eds.) *The Emergence of Social Enterprise.* London, Routledge, 2001.

Bryce, H. J. *Financial and Strategic Management for Nonprofit Organizations*, San Francisco, Jossey-Bass, 2000.

Clark, J. *Worlds Apart: Civil Society and the Battle for Ethical Globalization*, London, Earthscan and Bloomfield, CT, Kumarian Press, 2003.

Clotfelter, C.T. and Ehrlich, T. (eds.) . *Philanthropy and the Nonprofit Sector in a Changing America.* Bloomington and Indianapolis, Indiana University Press, 1999.

Dasgupta, P. and Serageldin, I. (eds.) *Social Capital: A Multifaceted Approach.* Washington, DC, The World Bank, 2000.

Deakin, N. *In Search of Civil Society.* London, Palgrave, 2001.

Edwards, M. *Civil Society*, Cambridge, Polity Press, 2004.

Florini, A., Senta, K. and Kokusai, N. *The Third Force: The Rise of Transnational Civil Society.* New York, Carnegie Endowment For International Peace and Tokyo, Japan Center for International Exchange, 2000.

Flynn, P. and Hodgkinson, V. (eds.) *Measuring the Impact of the Nonprofit Sector.* New York, Plenum/Kluwer, 2002.

Fowler, A. *The Virtuous Spiral: a Guide to Sustainability of NGOs in International Development.* London, Earthscan, 2000.

Frumkin, P. *On Being Nonprofit: A Conceptual and Policy Primer.* Cambridge, MA, Harvard University Press, 2002.

Hammack, D. C. (ed.) *Making the Nonprofit Sector in the United States.* Bloomington and Indianapolis, Indiana University Press, 1998.

Hansmann, H. *The Ownership of Enterprise.* Cambridge, MA, Harvard University Press, 1996.

Herman, R. (ed.) *The Jossey-Bass Handbook of Nonprofit Management and Leadership.* San Francisco, Jossey-Bass, 2005.

Hodgkinson, V. A. and Foley, M. (eds.) *The Civil Society Reader*, Hanover, NH and London, University Press of New England, 2003.

Hudson, M. *Managing at the Leading Edge: New Challenges in Managing Nonprofit Organisations*, London, Directory of Social Change, 2003.

Keane, J. *Civil Society: Old Images, New Visions.* Cambridge, Polity Press, 1998.

Keck, M. E., and Sikkink, K. *Activists beyond Borders: Advocacy Networks in International Politics*, Ithaca, NY, Cornell University Press, 1998.

Kendall, J. *The Voluntary Sector: Comparative Perspectives in the UK*. London and New York, Routledge, 2003.

Letts, C. W., Ryan, W. P. and Grossman, A. *High Performance Nonprofit Organizations: Managing Upstream for Greater Impact*, New York, John Wiley & Sons, 1999.

Lewis, D. J. *The Management of Non-Governmental Development Organisations: An Introduction*. London, Routledge, 2001.

Light, P. *Making Nonprofits Work: A Report on the Tides of Nonprofit Management Reform*. Washington, DC, Brookings Institution Press, 2000.

Lindenberg, M. and Bryant, C. *Going Global: Transforming Relief and Development NGOs*. Bloomfield, CT, Kumarian Press, 2001.

McCarthy, K. *American Creed: Philanthropy and the Rise of Civil Society 1700–1865*, Chicago, The University of Chicago Press, 2003.

Oster, S. *Strategic Management for Nonprofit Organizations*. New York and Oxford, Oxford University Press, 1995.

Ott, J. S. (ed.) *The Nature of the Nonprofit Sector*, Boulder, CO, Westview Press, 2001.

Powell, W. W. and Clemens, E. S. (eds.) *Private Action and the Public Good*. New Haven, CT, Yale University Press, 1998.

Powell, W. W. and Steinberg, R. S. (eds.) *The Nonprofit Sector: A Research Handbook (2nd edition)*. New Haven, CT and London, Yale University Press, 2005.

Putnam, R. (ed.) *Democracies in Flux*. New York and Oxford, Oxford University Press, 2002.

Salamon, L. M. *The Resilient Sector: The State of Nonprofit America*, Washington, DC, Brookings Institution Press, 2003.

Salamon, L. M. (ed.) *The State of Nonprofit America*. Washington, DC, Brookings Institution Press in collaboration with the Aspen Institute, 2002.

Salamon, L. M., List, R., and Sokolowski, S. W. and associates. *Global Civil Society: Dimensions of the Non-profit Sector*. Bloomfield, CT, Kumarian Press, 2004.

Schlueter, A., Then, V. and Walkenhorst, P. (eds.) *Foundations in Europe: Society, Management and Law.* London, Directory of Social Change, 2001.

Skocpol, T. and Fiorina, M. P. (eds.) *Civic Engagement in American Democracy.* Washington, DC, Brookings Institution Press and New York, Russell Sage Foundation, 1999.

Weisbrod, B. (ed.) . *To Profit or Not to Profit: the Commercial Transformation of the Nonprofit Sector.* Cambridge and New York, Cambridge University Press, 1998.

Young, D. R. and Steinberg, R. S. *Economics for Nonprofit Managers*, New York, The Foundation Center, 1995.